Cutie and the BEAST

3

story & art by
YUHI AZUMI

Contents

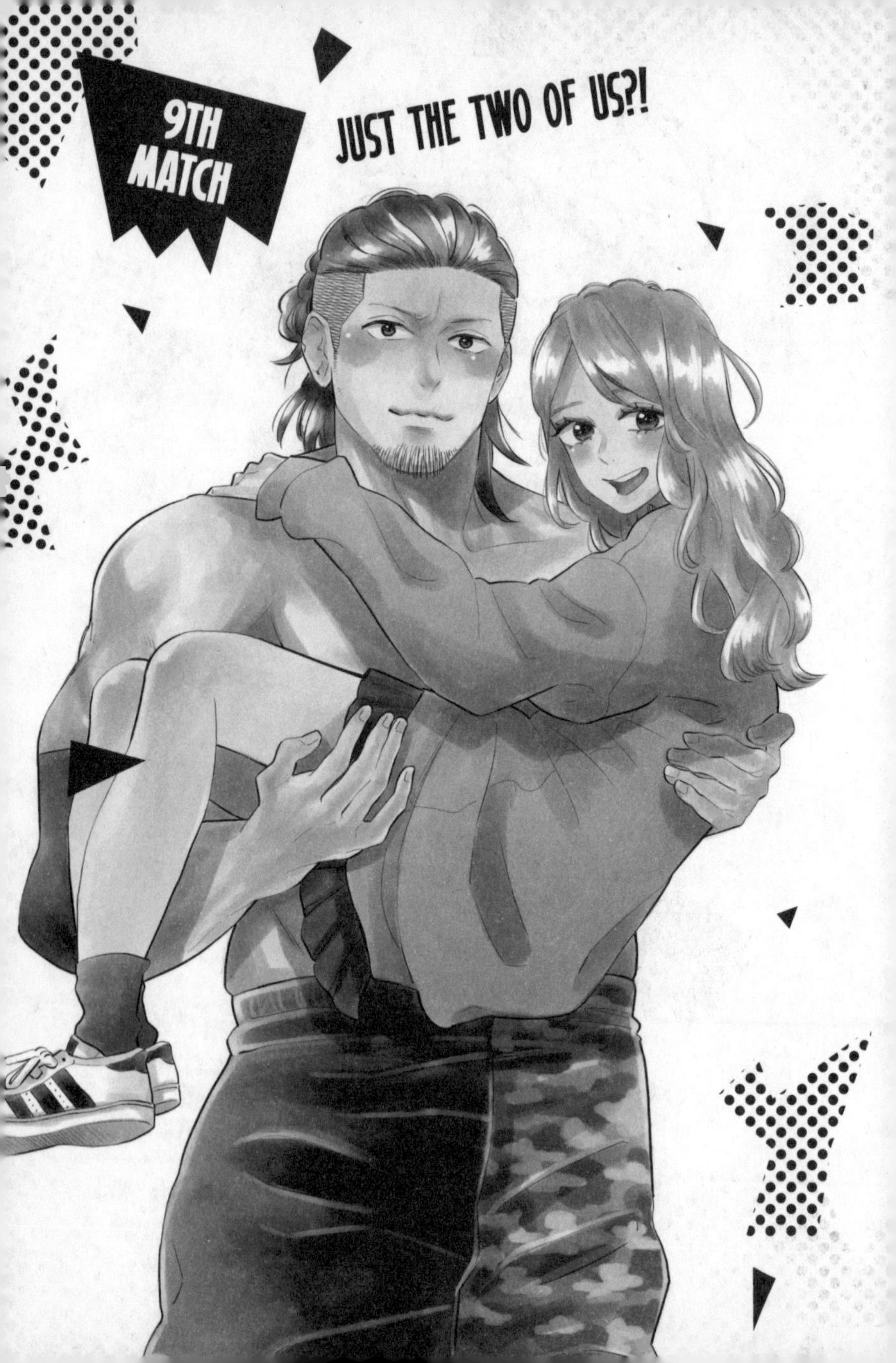
9TH MATCH
JUST THE TWO OF US?!

Story

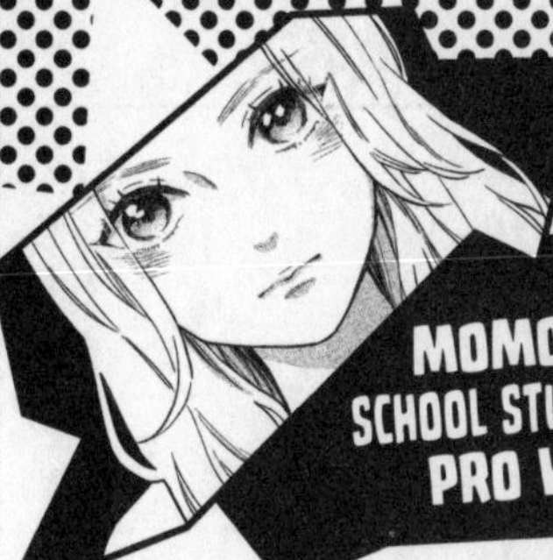

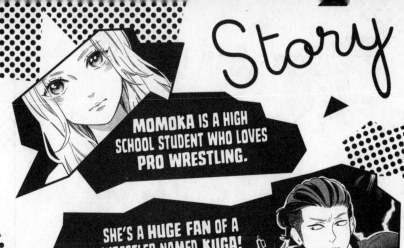

MOMOKA IS A HIGH SCHOOL STUDENT WHO LOVES PRO WRESTLING.

SHE'S A HUGE FAN OF A WRESTLER NAMED KUGA!

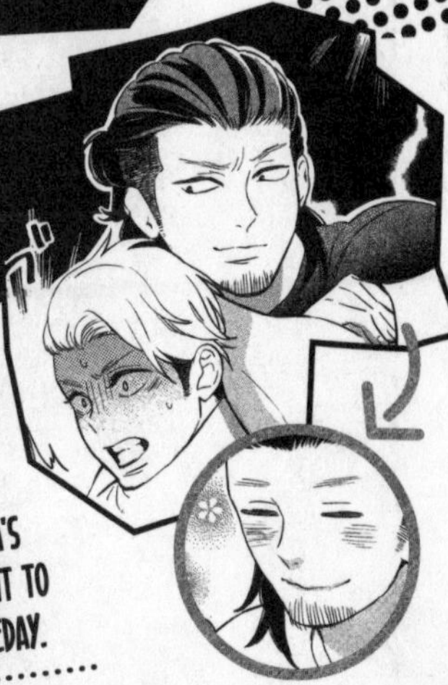

MOMOKA'S A HIGH SCHOOL STUDENT, BUT AFTER SHE SENDS A FAN LETTER TO KUGA, A WHOLE SERIES OF EVENTS LEADS TO THE TWO OF THEM DATING. WHILE HE INITIALLY HAS SECOND THOUGHTS, KUGA EVENTUALLY RECOGNIZES MOMOKA'S DETERMINATION AND FEELINGS. HE REALIZES HE DOESN'T WANT TO LET HER GO--AND PROPOSES THAT THEY GET MARRIED SOMEDAY.

MOMOKA'S FATHER DOESN'T APPROVE OF THIS ONE BIT, BUT KUGA DOES EVERYTHING IN HIS POWER TO SHOW HIM HOW SERIOUS HE IS ABOUT BEING WITH HIS DAUGHTER. AFTER SEEING THE WAY KUGA CONDUCTS HIMSELF IN THE RING, MOMOKA'S DAD FINALLY GIVES THEIR RELATIONSHIP HIS GRUDGING APPROVAL.

KUGA TAKES MOMOKA TO THE ZOO FOR THEIR FIRST DATE, BUT EVEN THOUGH HE'S IN DISGUISE, HE GETS TOTALLY MOBBED BY FANS. THE DATE NEVER EVEN GETS OFF THE GROUND. MOMOKA DECIDES IT'S TIME TO LEAVE. SHE FIGURES IF THEIR RELATIONSHIP DREW TOO MUCH ATTENTION, IT'D MAKE KUGA'S LIFE COMPLICATED.

LATER, KUGA TEXTS MOMOKA HIS ADDRESS, SO THEY CAN MEET UP AND HAVE A PROPER CONVERSATION. WHEN SHE SHOWS UP, SHE FINDS OUT HE LIVES ALONE...!

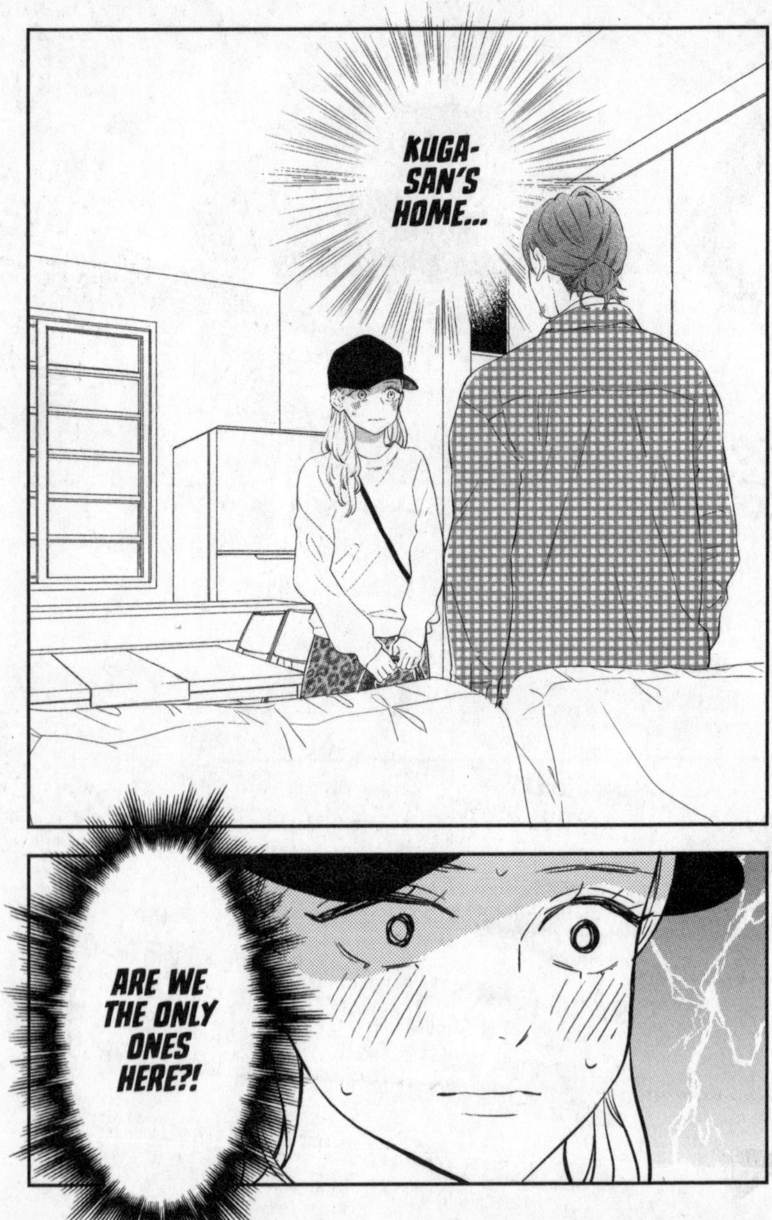
KUGA-SAN'S HOME...
ARE WE THE ONLY ONES HERE?!

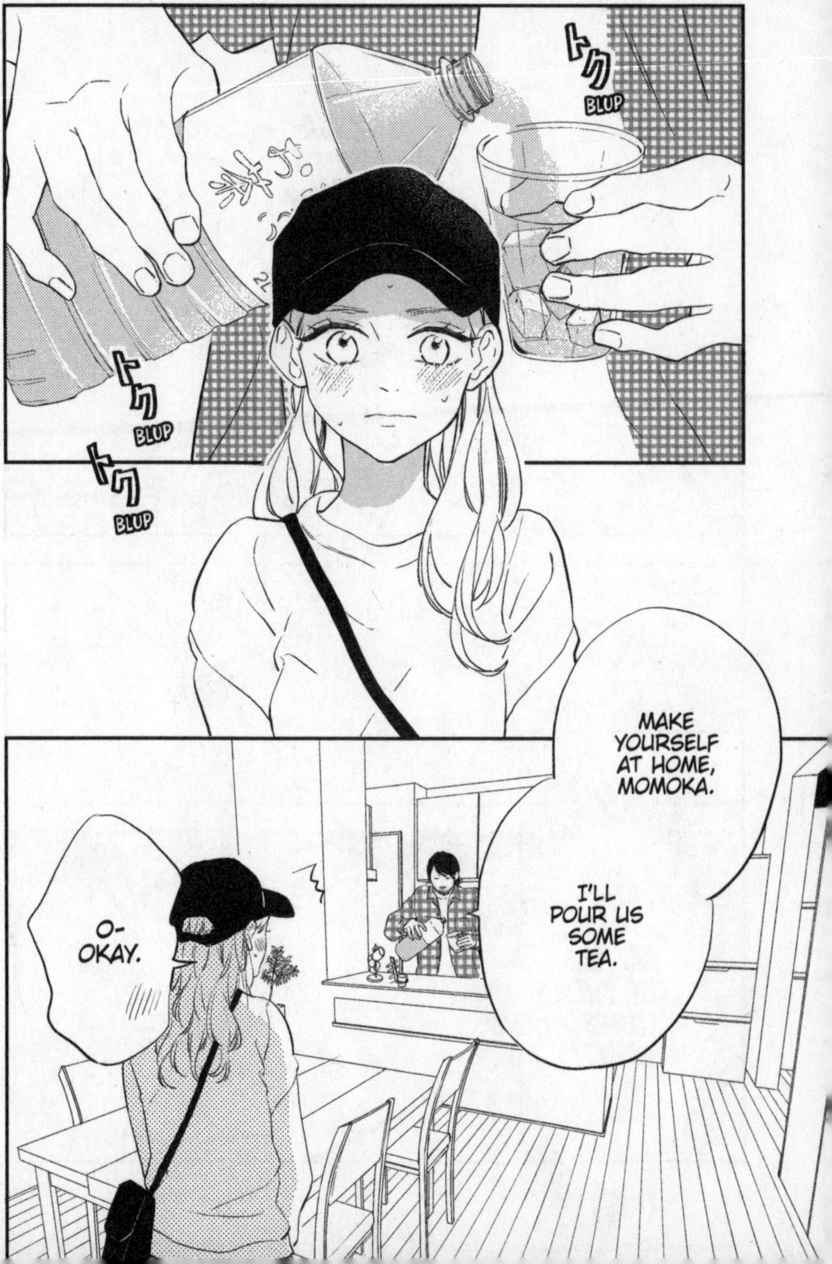
トク
BLUP
トク
BLUP
トク
BLUP
MAKE YOURSELF AT HOME, MOMOKA.
I'LL POUR US SOME TEA.
O-OKAY.

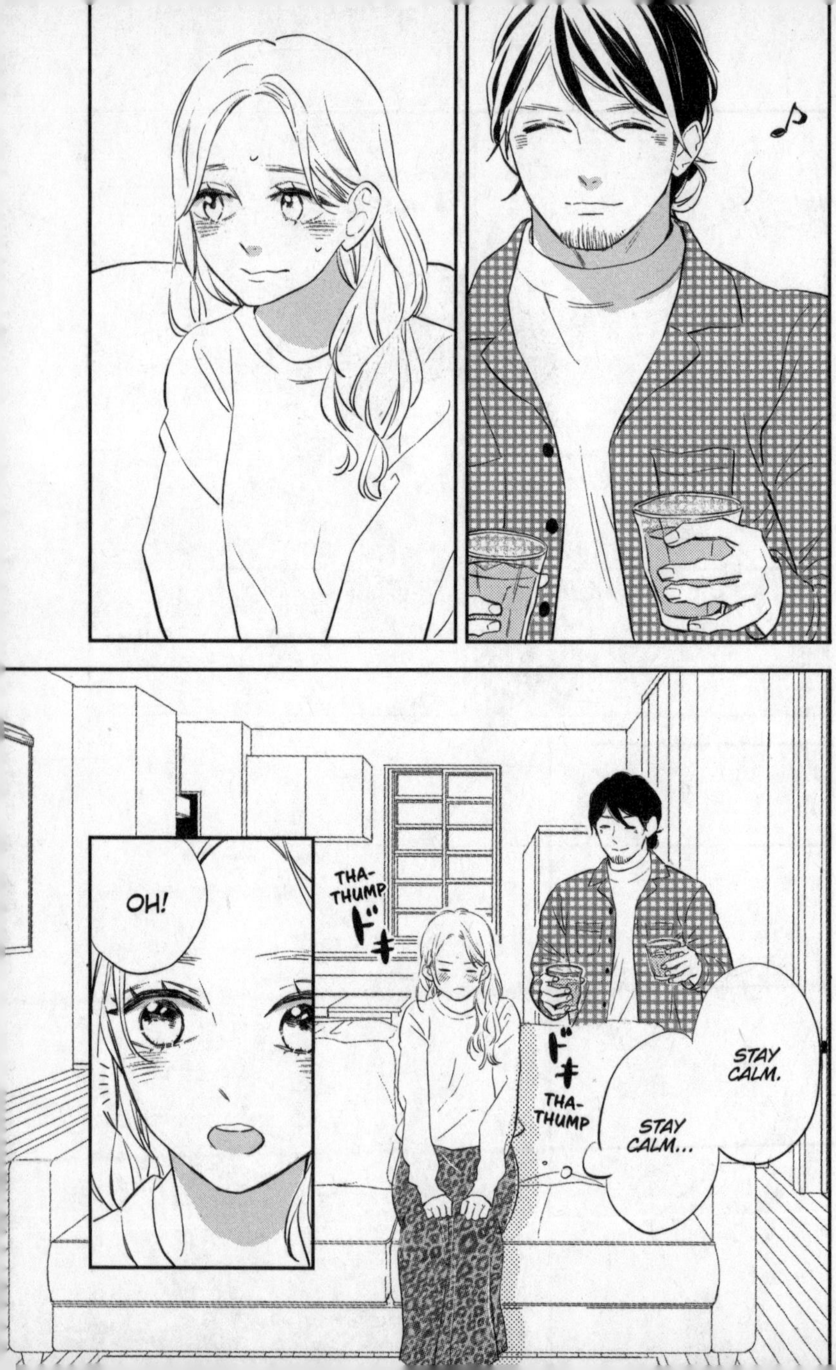
STAY CALM.
STAY CALM...
ドキ
THA-THUMP
THA-THUMP
ドキ
OH!

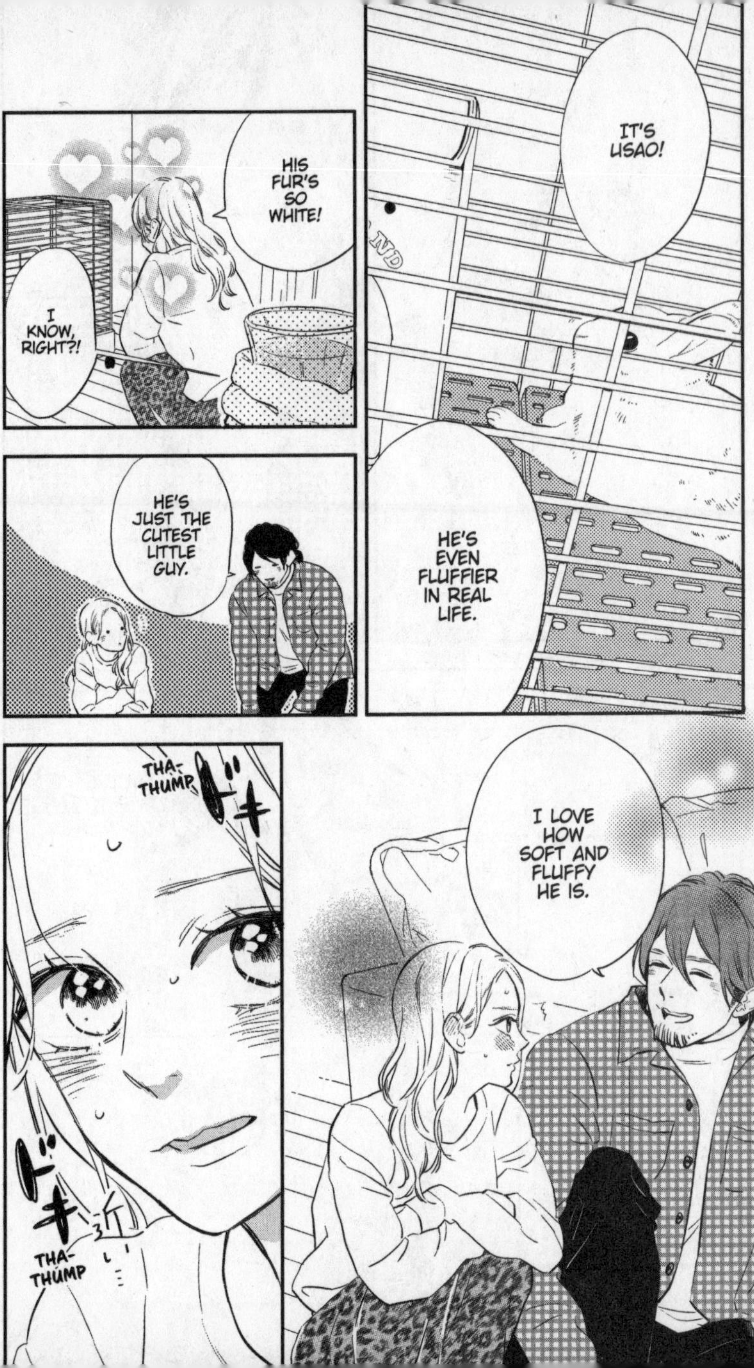
IT'S USAO!
HE'S EVEN FLUFFIER IN REAL LIFE.
HIS FUR'S SO WHITE!
I KNOW, RIGHT?!
HE'S JUST THE CUTEST LITTLE GUY.
I LOVE HOW SOFT AND FLUFFY HE IS.
THA-THUMP
THA-THUMP

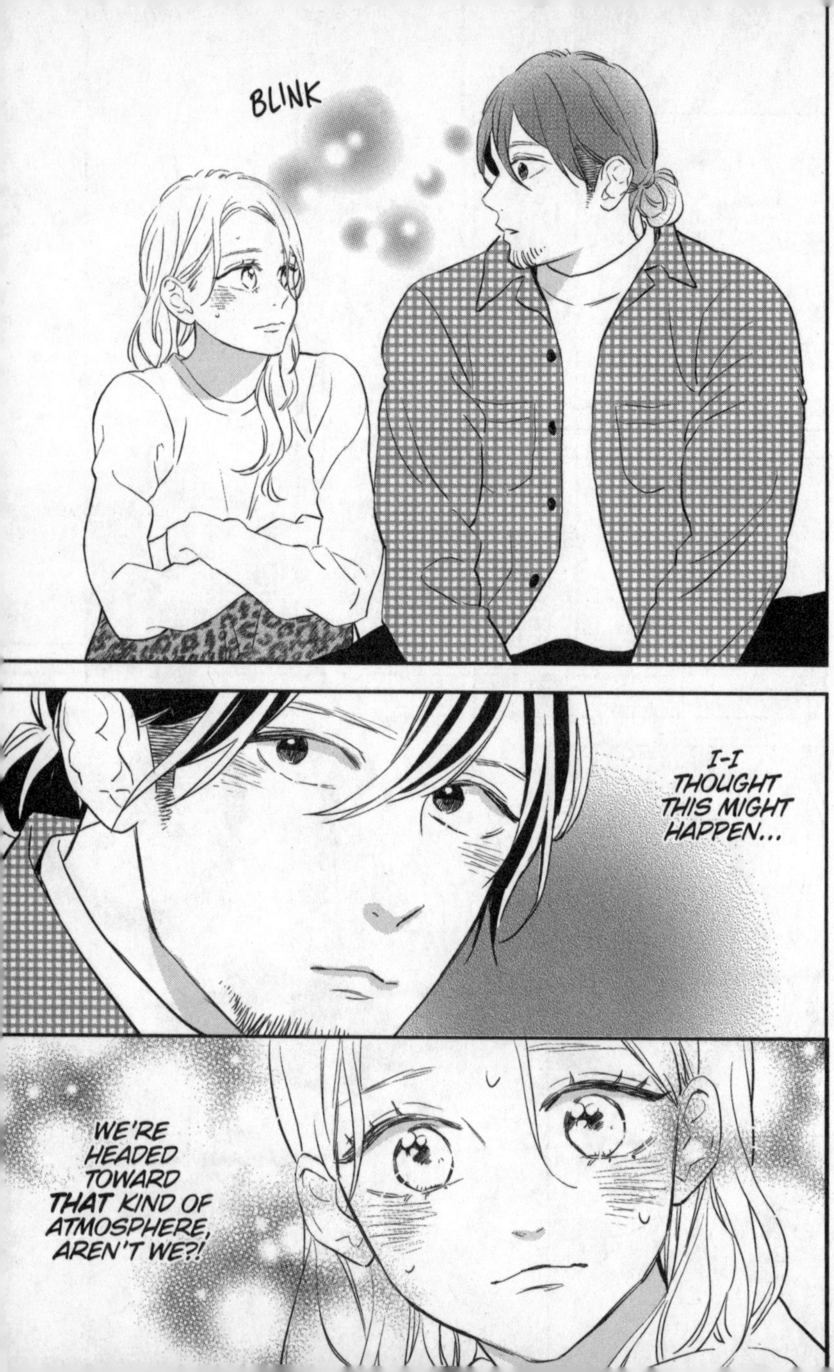
BLINK
I-I THOUGHT THIS MIGHT HAPPEN...
WE'RE HEADED TOWARD THAT KIND OF ATMOSPHERE, AREN'T WE?!

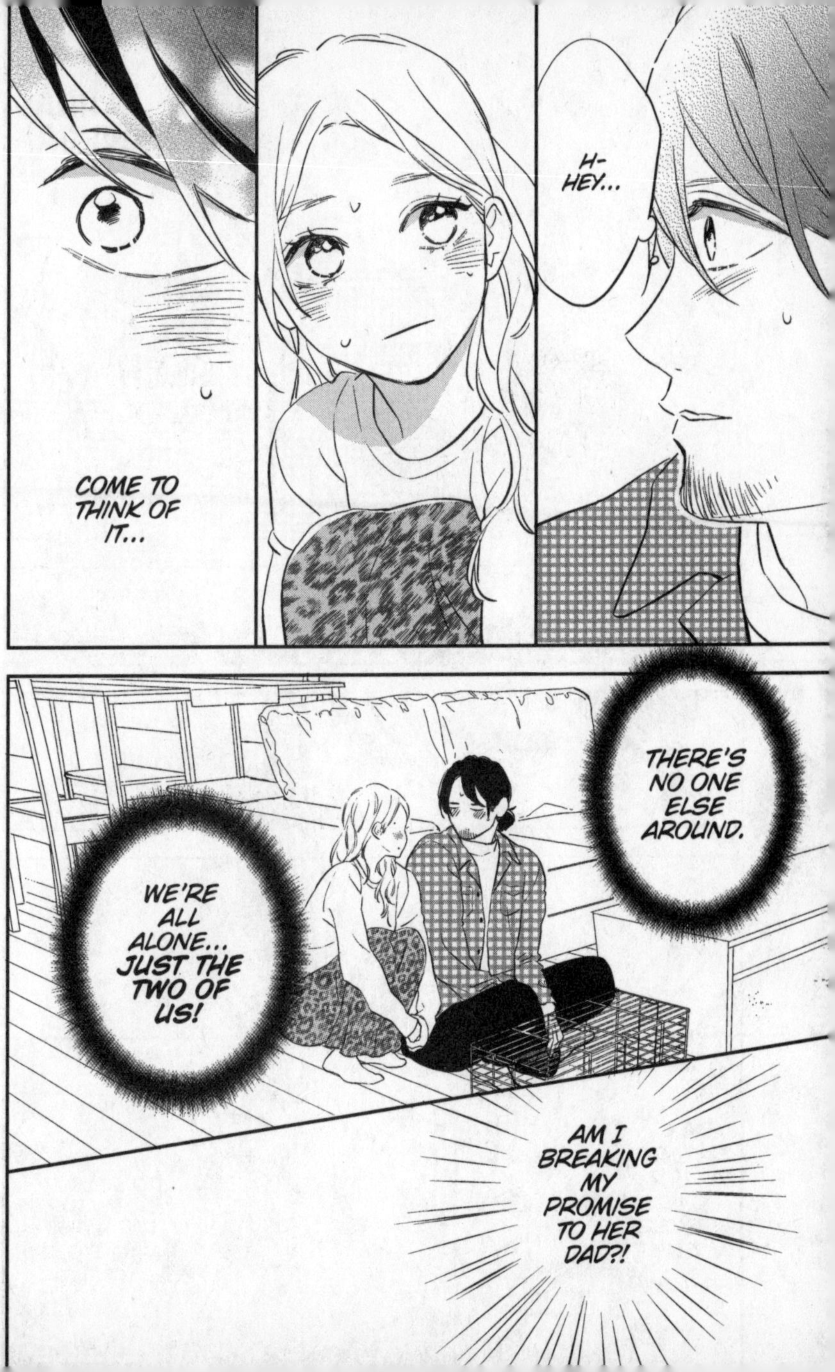
H-HEY...
COME TO THINK OF IT...
THERE'S NO ONE ELSE AROUND.
WE'RE ALL ALONE... JUST THE TWO OF US!
AM I BREAKING MY PROMISE TO HER DAD?!

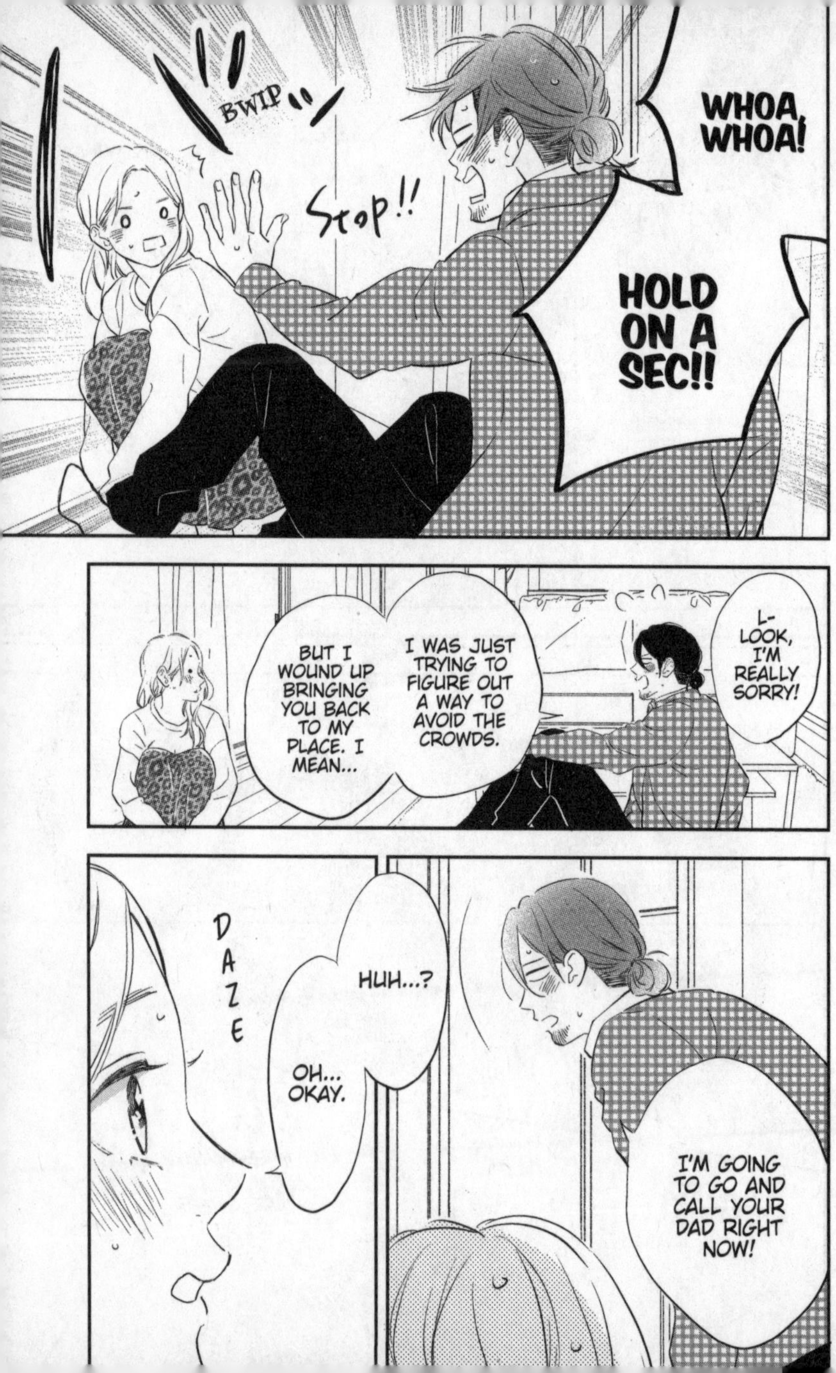
WHOA WHOA!
HOLD ON A SEC!!
Stop!!
BWIP
L-LOOK, I'M REALLY SORRY!
I WAS JUST TRYING TO FIGURE OUT A WAY TO AVOID THE CROWDS.
BUT I WOUND UP BRINGING YOU BACK TO MY PLACE. I MEAN...
I'M GOING TO GO AND CALL YOUR DAD RIGHT NOW!
HUH...?
OH... OKAY.
DAZE

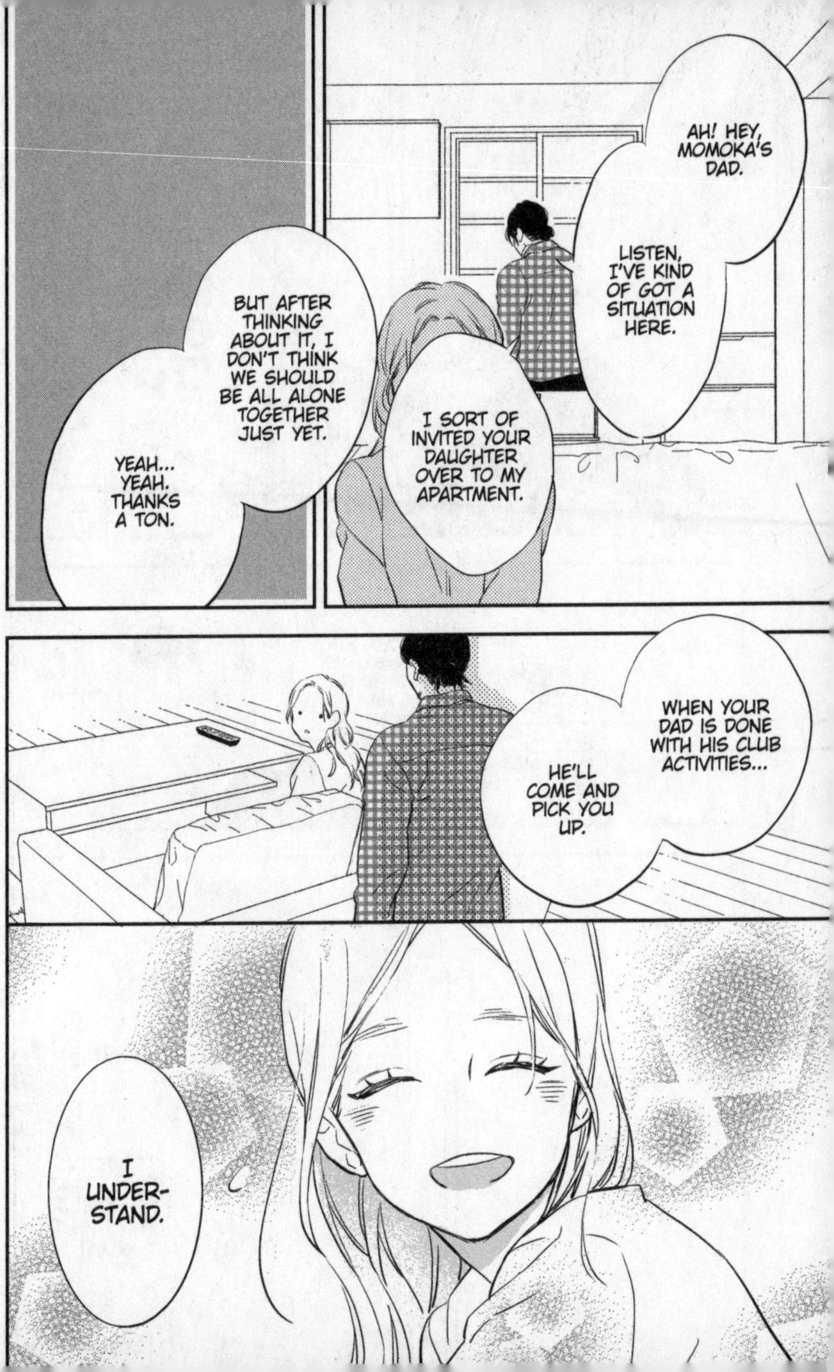
AH! HEY, MOMOKA'S DAD.
LISTEN, I'VE KIND OF GOT A SITUATION HERE.
I SORT OF INVITED YOUR DAUGHTER OVER TO MY APARTMENT.
BUT AFTER THINKING ABOUT IT, I DON'T THINK WE SHOULD BE ALL ALONE TOGETHER JUST YET.
YEAH... YEAH. THANKS A TON.
WHEN YOUR DAD IS DONE WITH HIS CLUB ACTIVITIES...
HE'LL COME AND PICK YOU UP.
I UNDER-STAND.

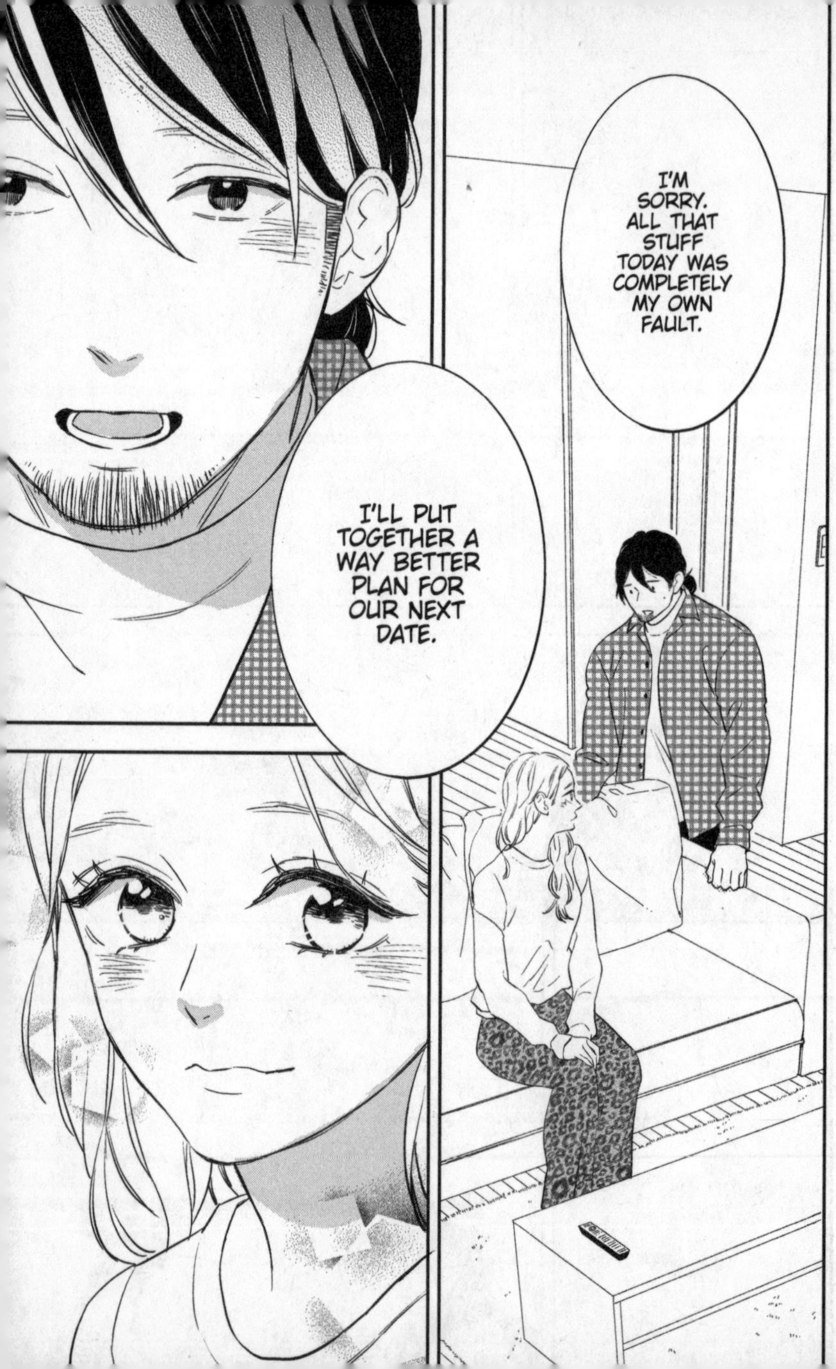
I'M SORRY. ALL THAT STUFF TODAY WAS COMPLETELY MY OWN FAULT.
I'LL PUT TOGETHER A WAY BETTER PLAN FOR OUR NEXT DATE.

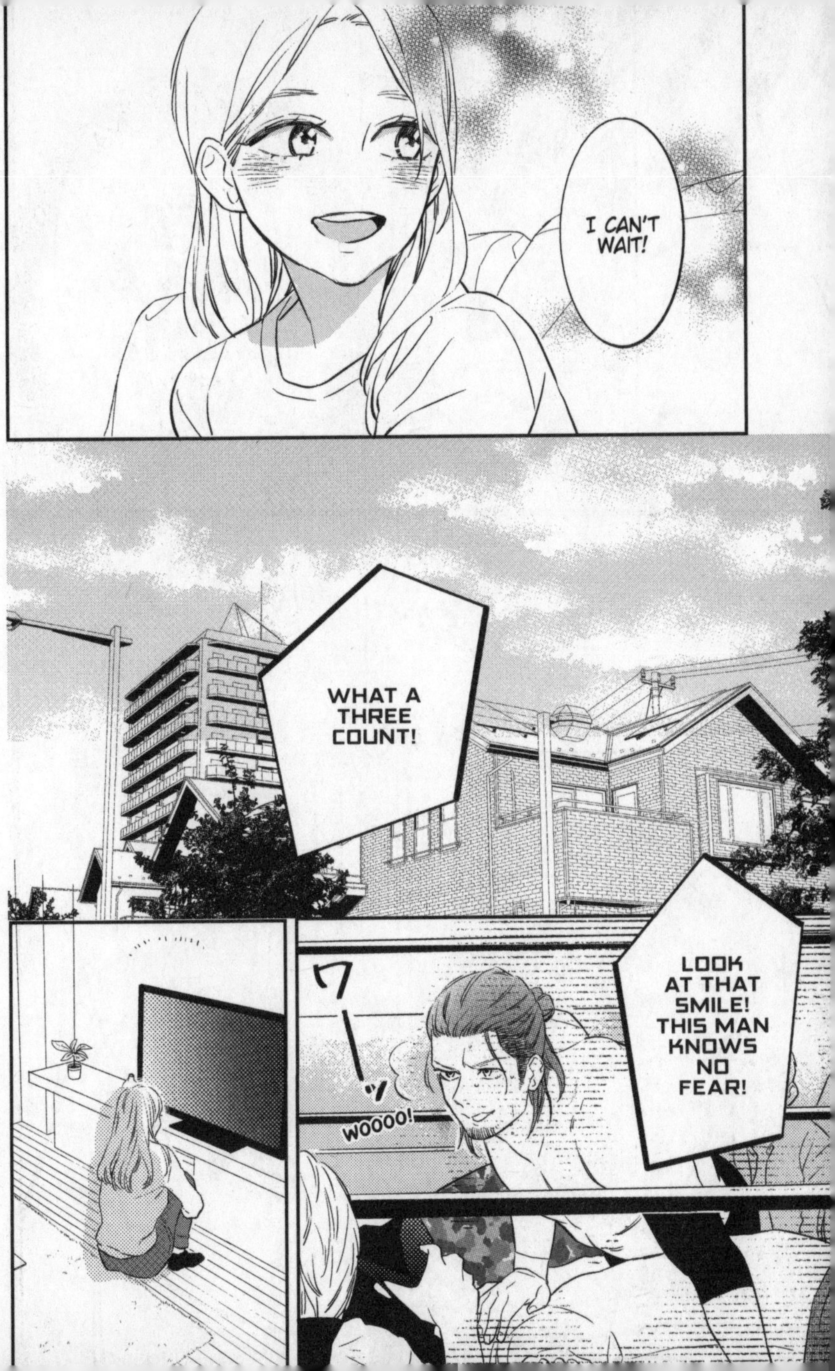
I CAN'T WAIT!
WHAT A THREE COUNT!
LOOK AT THAT SMILE! THIS MAN KNOWS NO FEAR!
ワーッ
WOOOO!

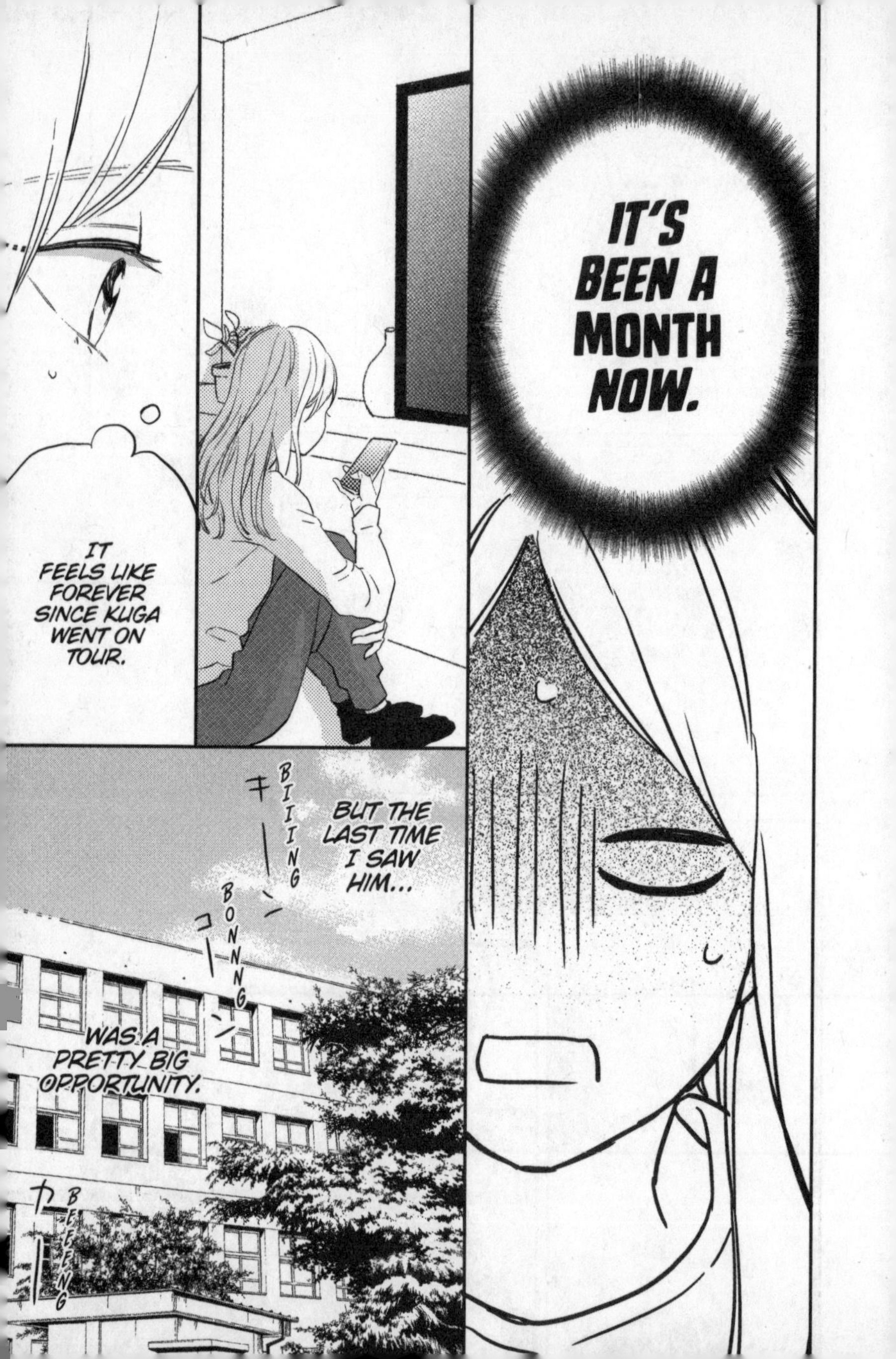
IT'S BEEN A MONTH NOW.
IT FEELS LIKE FOREVER SINCE KUGA WENT ON TOUR.
BUT THE LAST TIME I SAW HIM...
BIIING
BONNNG
WAS A PRETTY BIG OPPORTUNITY.
BEEEENG

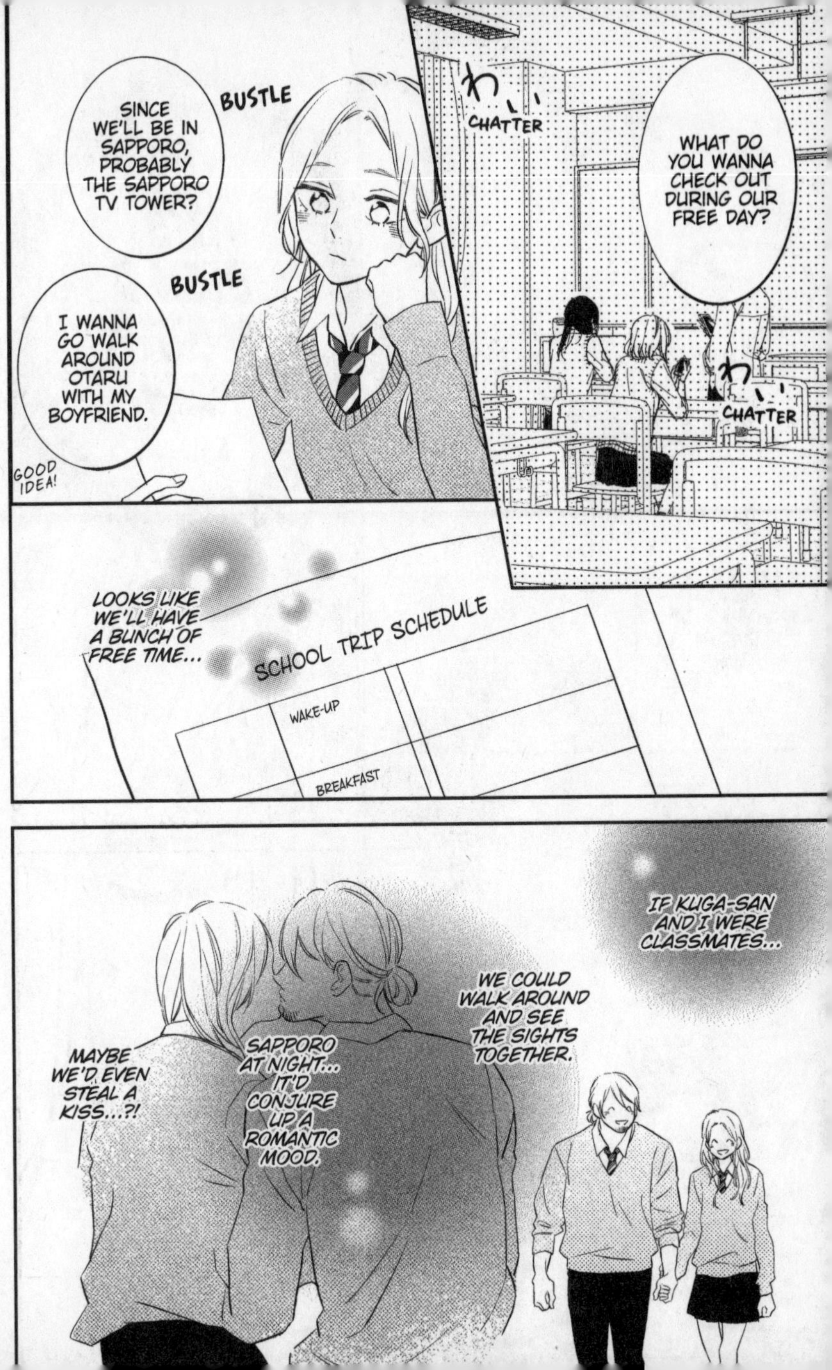
CHATTER
WHAT DO YOU WANNA CHECK OUT DURING OUR FREE DAY?
CHATTER
BUSTLE
SINCE WE'LL BE IN SAPPORO, PROBABLY THE SAPPORO TV TOWER?
BUSTLE
I WANNA GO WALK AROUND OTARU WITH MY BOYFRIEND.
GOOD IDEA!
LOOKS LIKE WE'LL HAVE A BUNCH OF FREE TIME...
SCHOOL TRIP SCHEDULE
WAKE-UP
BREAKFAST
IF KUGA-SAN AND I WERE CLASSMATES...
WE COULD WALK AROUND AND SEE THE SIGHTS TOGETHER.
SAPPORO AT NIGHT... IT'D CONJURE UP A ROMANTIC MOOD.
MAYBE WE'D EVEN STEAL A KISS...?!

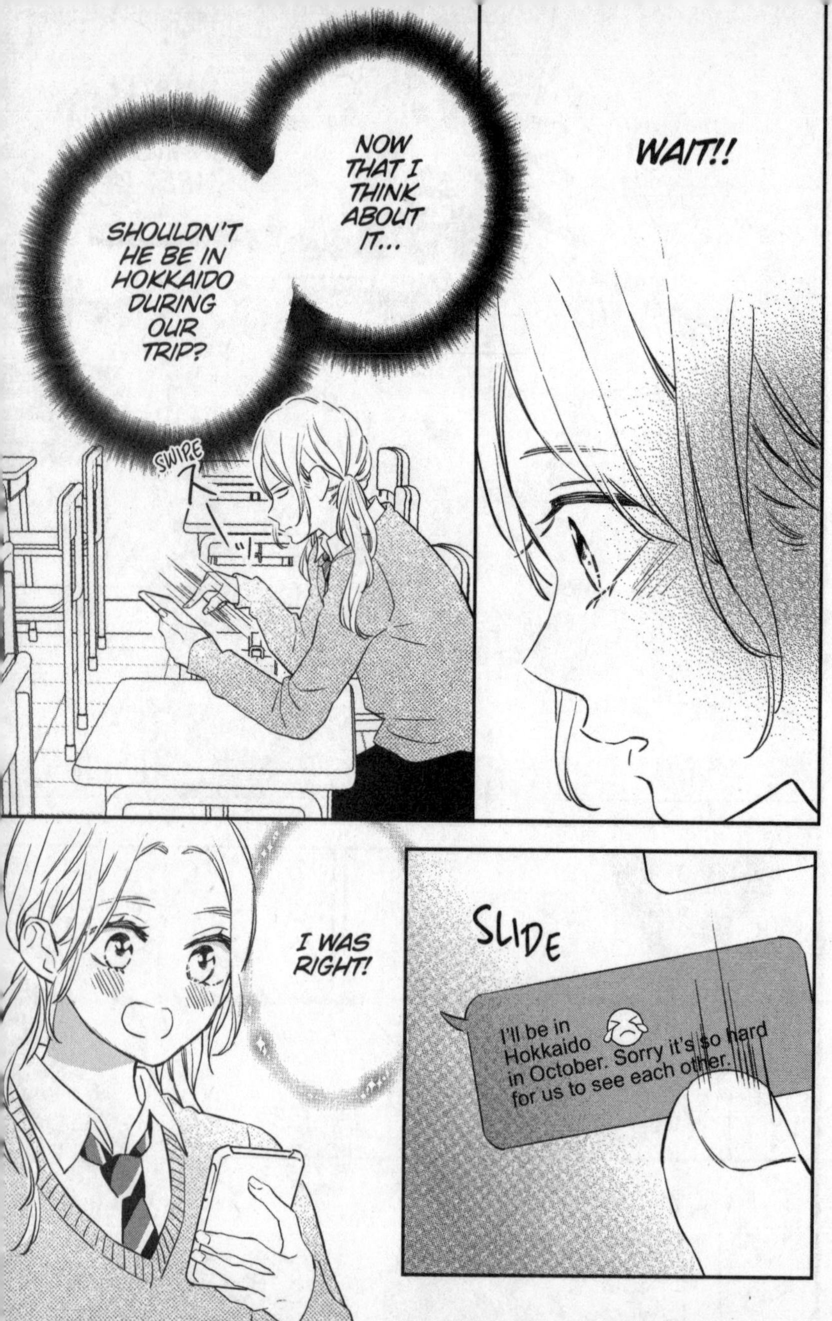
WAIT!!
NOW THAT I THINK ABOUT IT...
SHOULDN'T HE BE IN HOKKAIDO DURING OUR TRIP?
SWIPE
SLIDE
I'll be in Hokkaido in October. Sorry it's so hard for us to see each other.
I WAS RIGHT!

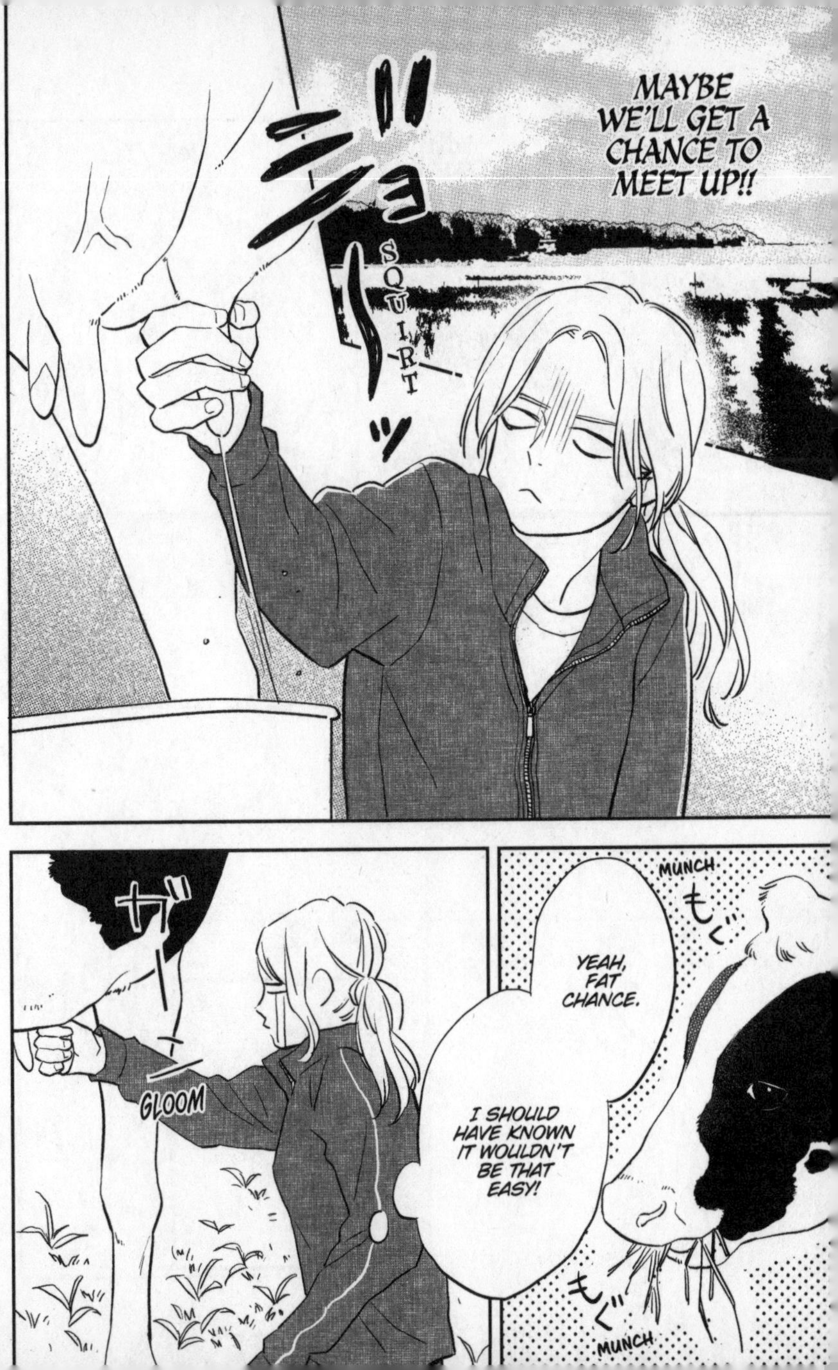
MAYBE WE'LL GET A CHANCE TO MEET UP!!
SQUIRT
MUNCH
もぐ
YEAH, FAT CHANCE.
I SHOULD HAVE KNOWN IT WOULDN'T BE THAT EASY!
もぐ
MUNCH
GLOOM

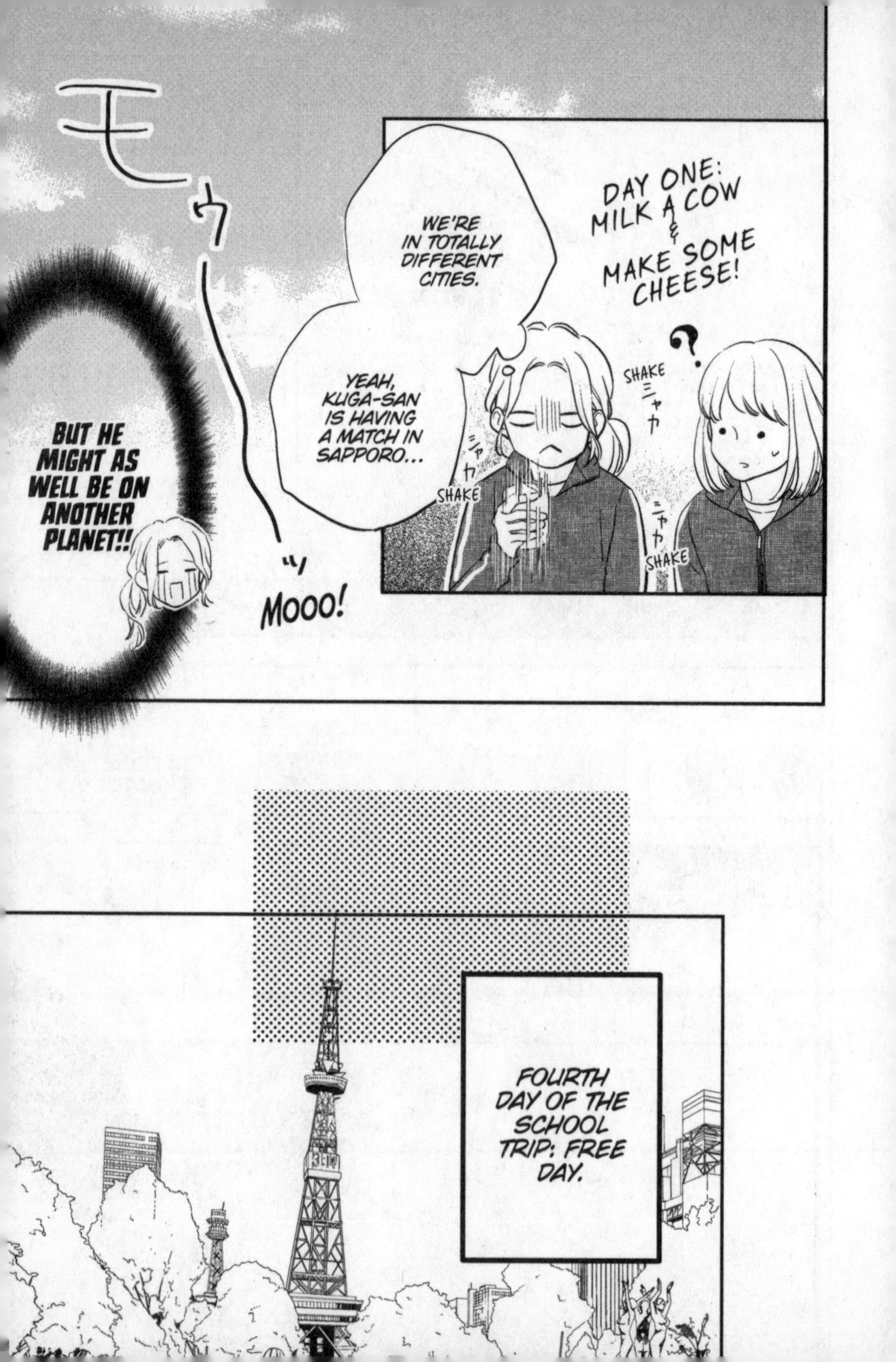

DAY ONE: MILK A COW & MAKE SOME CHEESE!
WE'RE IN TOTALLY DIFFERENT CITIES.
YEAH, KUGA-SAN IS HAVING A MATCH IN SAPPORO...
?
SHAKE
SHAKE
SHAKE
MOOO!
BUT HE MIGHT AS WELL BE ON ANOTHER PLANET!!
FOURTH DAY OF THE SCHOOL TRIP: FREE DAY.

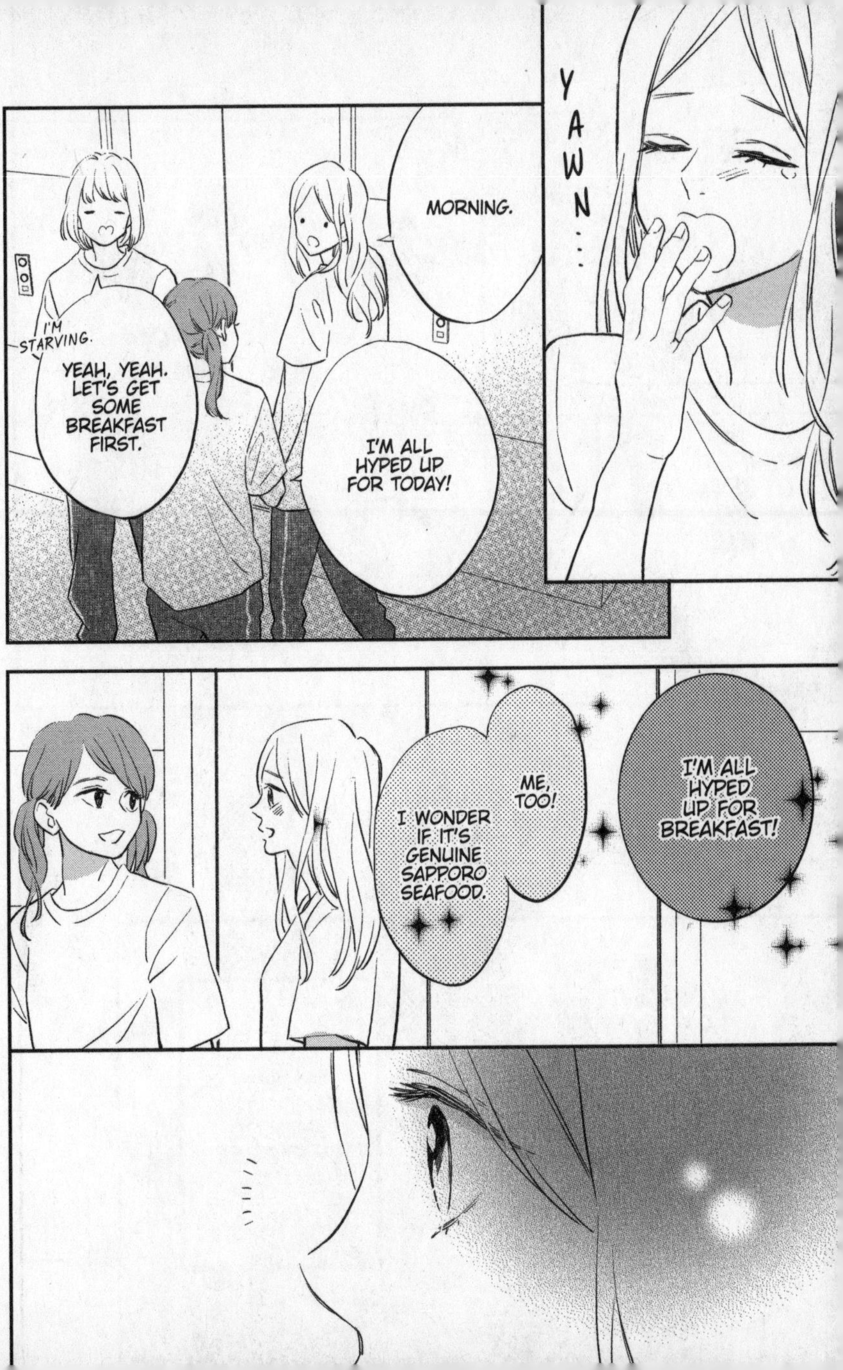
YAWN...
MORNING.
I'M ALL HYPED UP FOR TODAY!
I'M STARVING.
YEAH, YEAH. LET'S GET SOME BREAKFAST FIRST.
I'M ALL HYPED UP FOR BREAKFAST!
ME, TOO!
I WONDER IF IT'S GENUINE SAPPORO SEAFOOD.

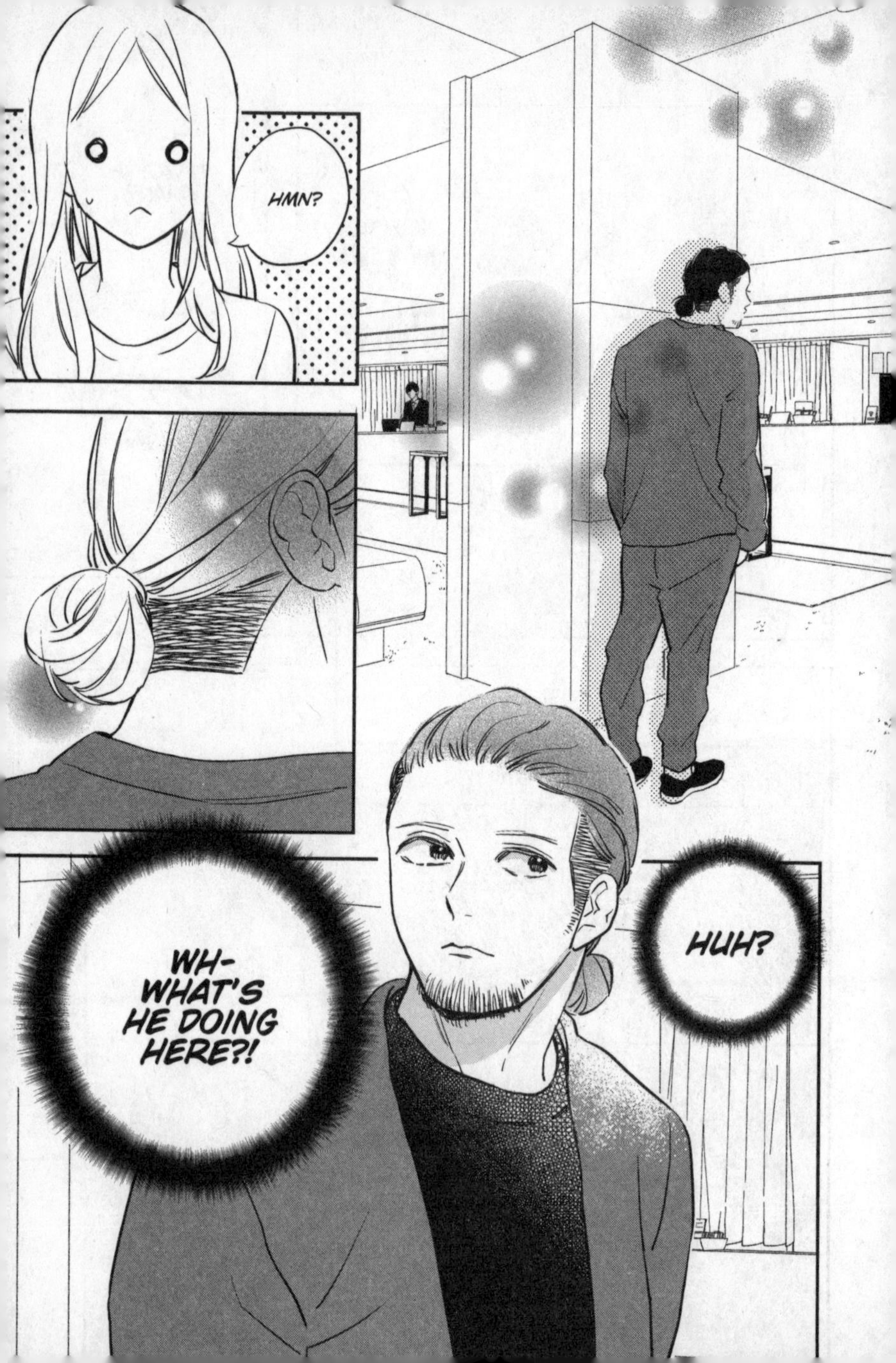
HMN?
HUH?
WH- WHAT'S HE DOING HERE?!

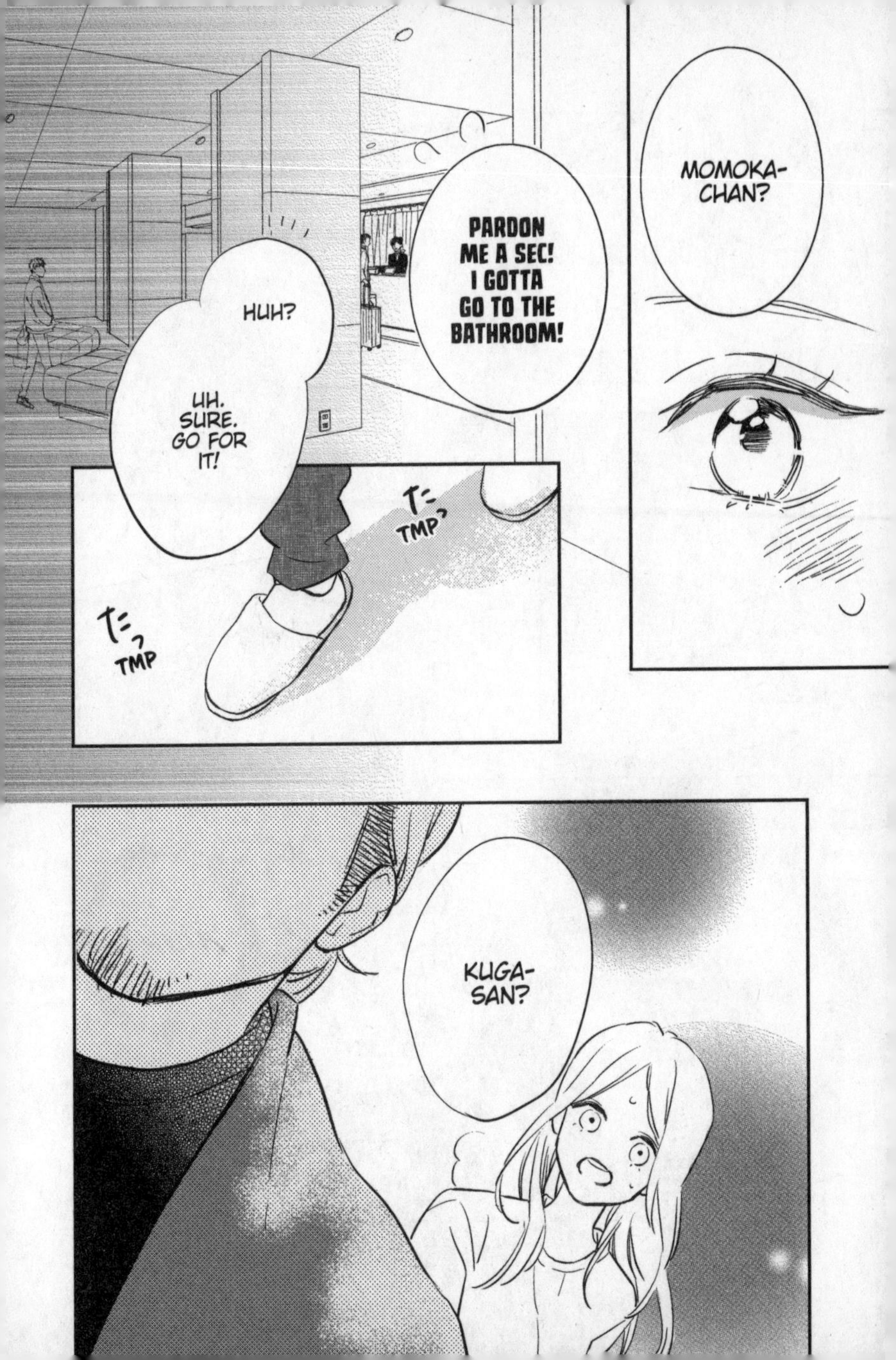

MOMOKA-CHAN?
PARDON ME A SEC! I GOTTA GO TO THE BATHROOM!
HUH?
UH. SURE. GO FOR IT!
TMP
TMP
KUGA-SAN?

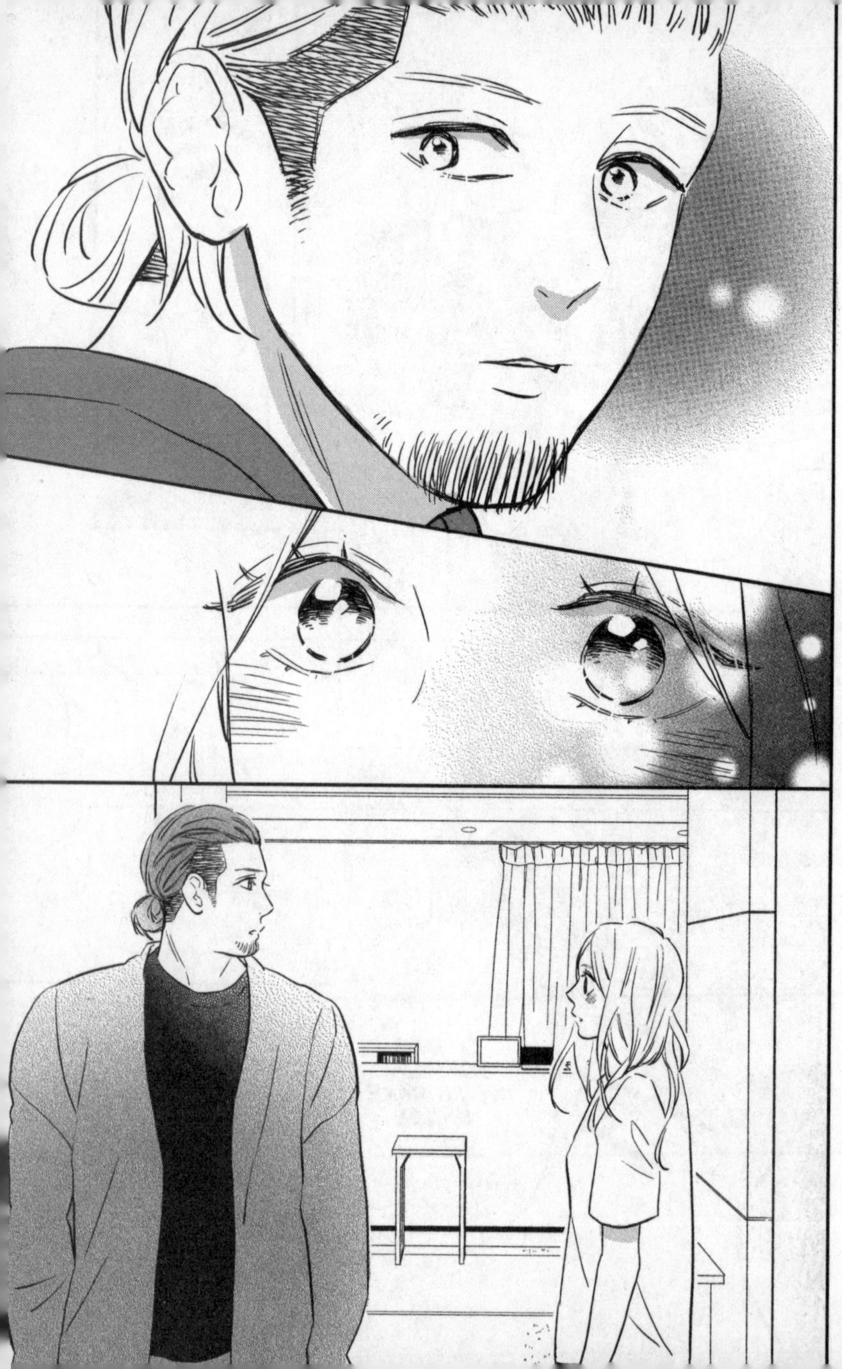

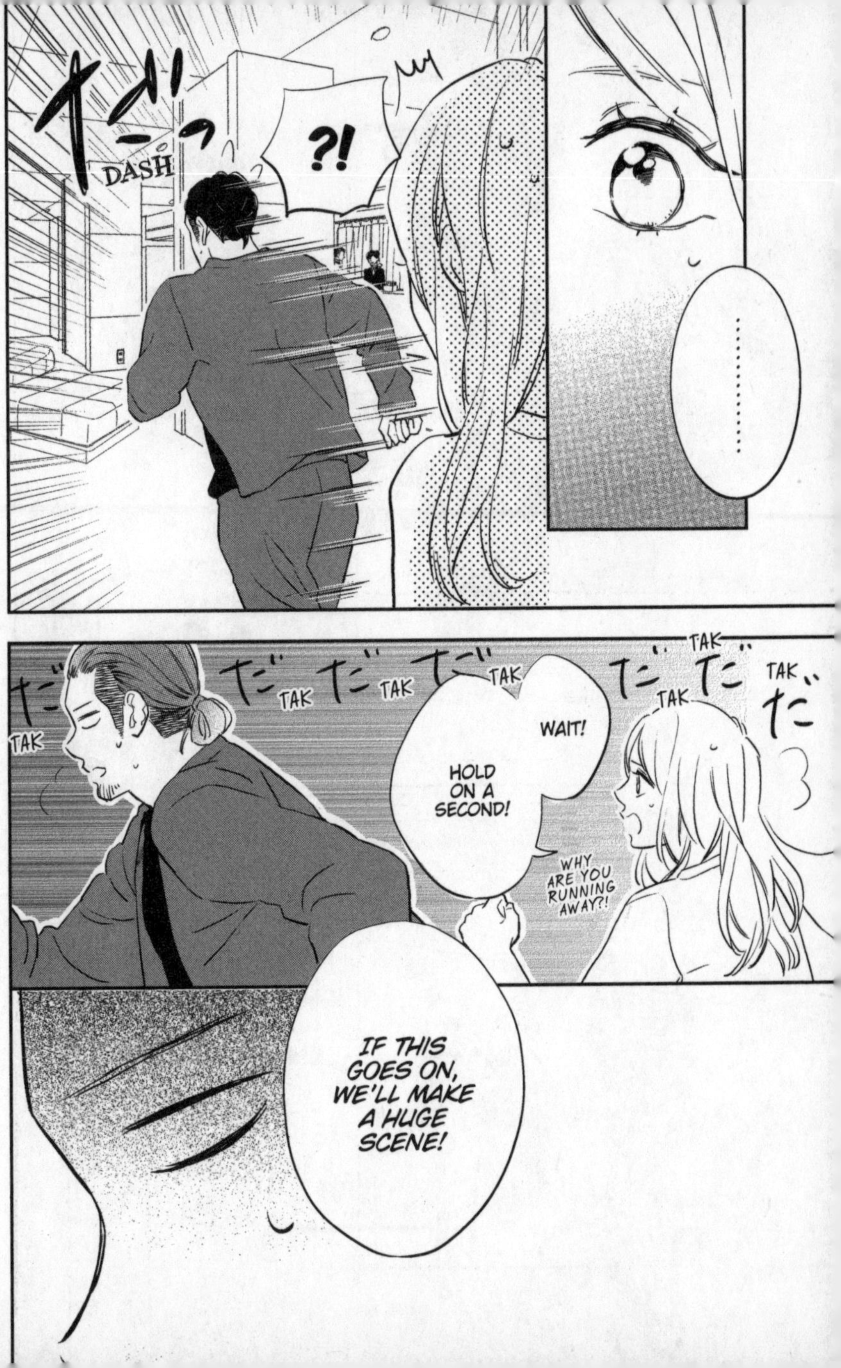
......
DASH
?!
TAK TAK TAK TAK
WAIT!
HOLD ON A SECOND!
WHY ARE YOU RUNNING AWAY?!
TAK TAK TAK TAK
IF THIS GOES ON, WE'LL MAKE A HUGE SCENE!

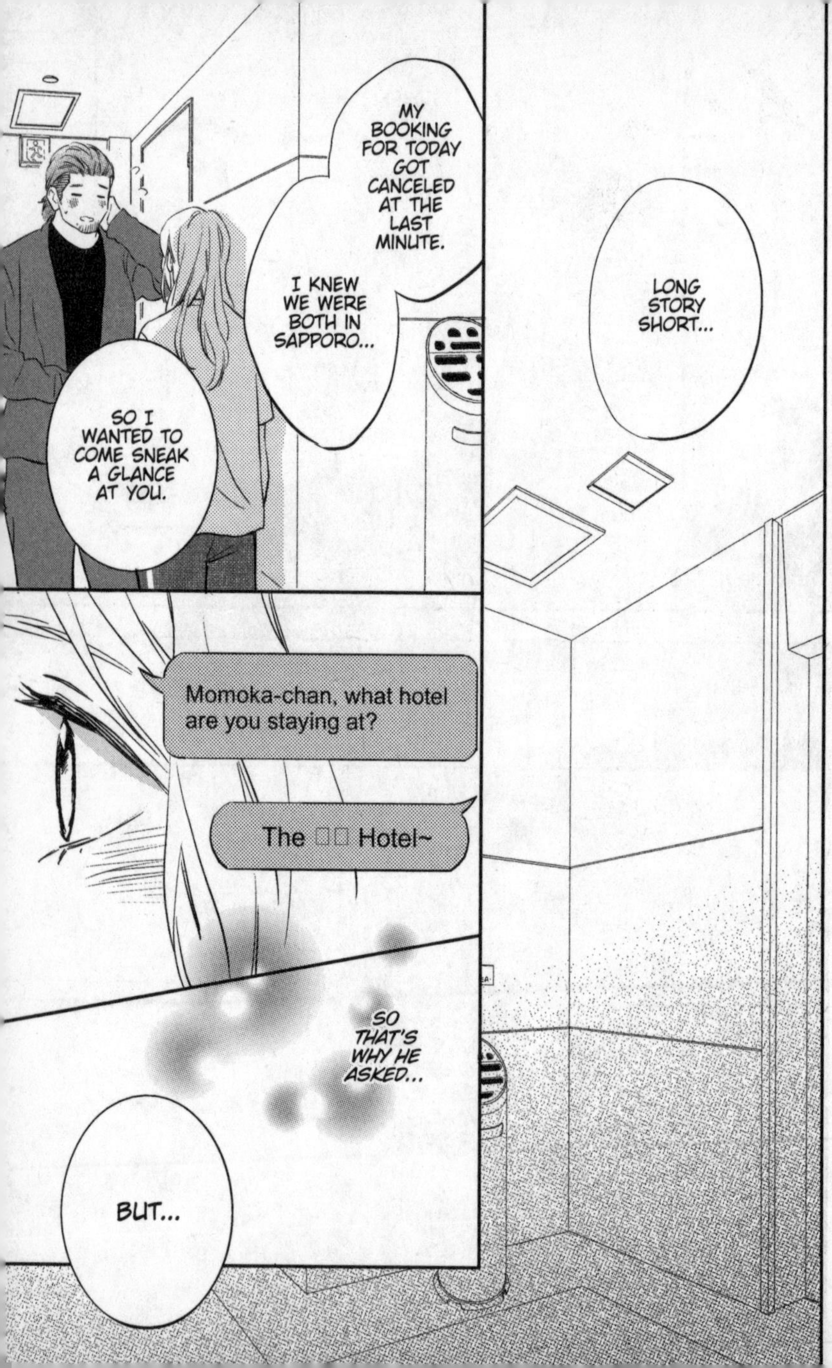
LONG STORY SHORT...
MY BOOKING FOR TODAY GOT CANCELED AT THE LAST MINUTE.
I KNEW WE WERE BOTH IN SAPPORO...
SO I WANTED TO COME SNEAK A GLANCE AT YOU.
Momoka-chan, what hotel are you staying at?
The □□ Hotel~
SO THAT'S WHY HE ASKED...
BUT...

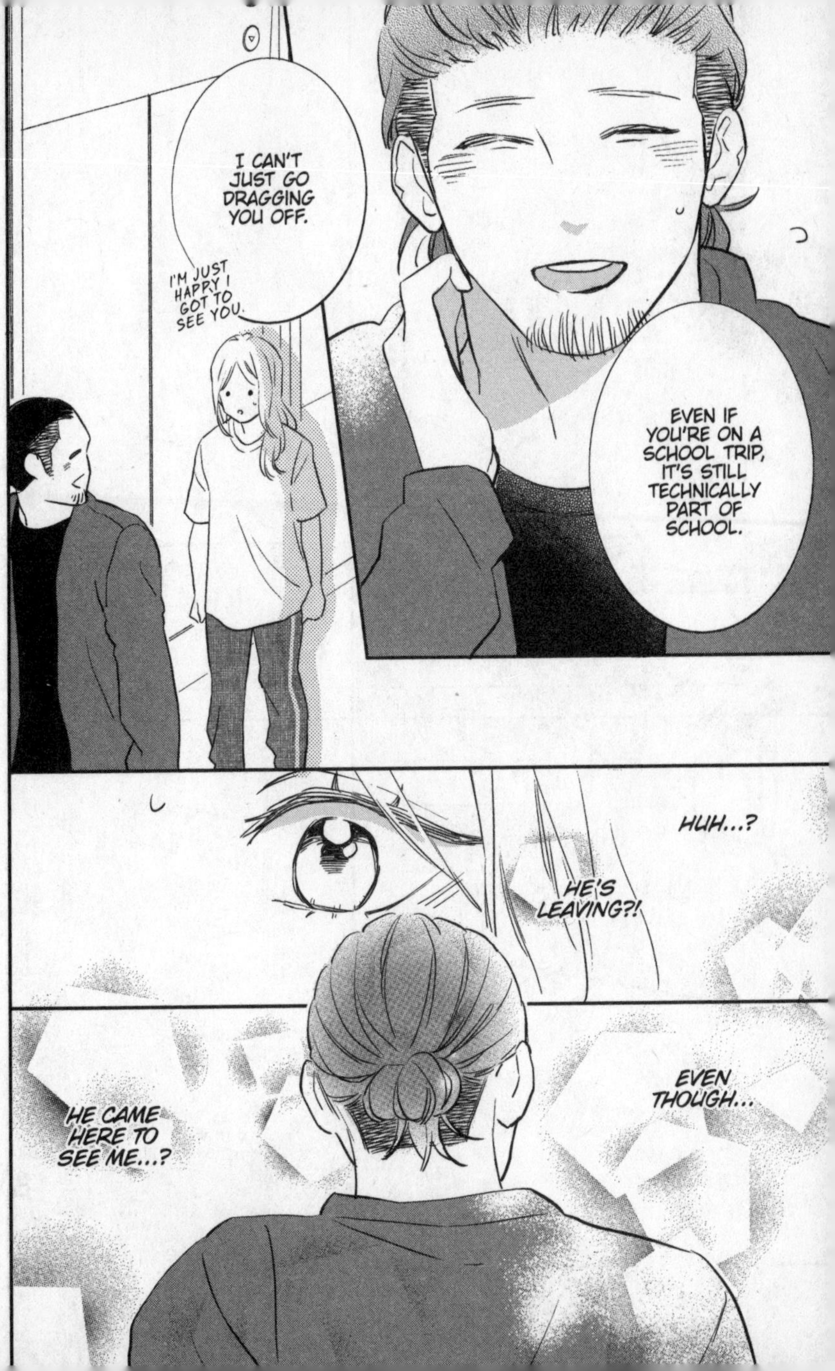
EVEN IF YOU'RE ON A SCHOOL TRIP, IT'S STILL TECHNICALLY PART OF SCHOOL.
I CAN'T JUST GO DRAGGING YOU OFF.
I'M JUST HAPPY I GOT TO SEE YOU.
HUH...?
HE'S LEAVING?!
EVEN THOUGH...
HE CAME HERE TO SEE ME...?

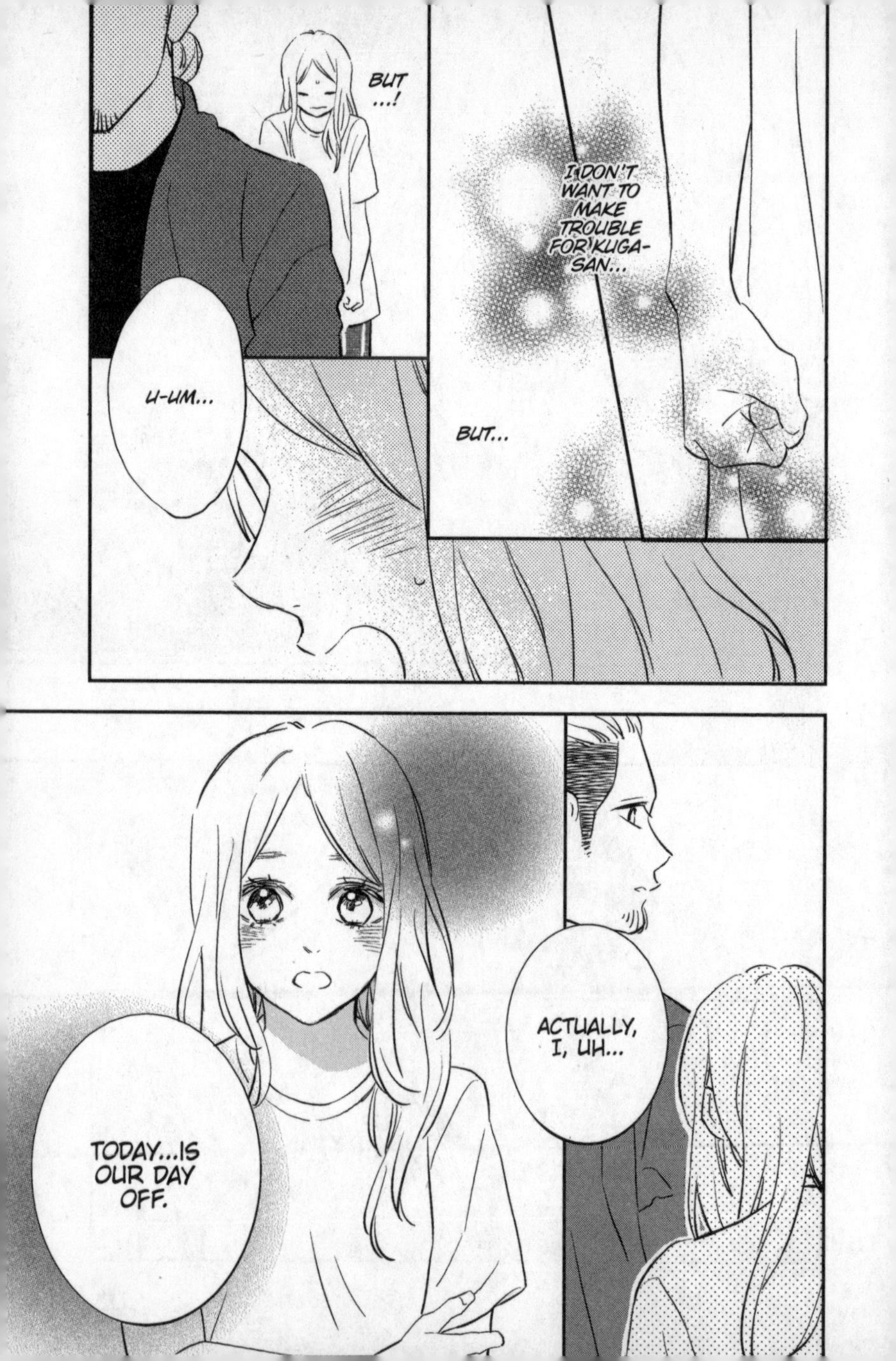

I DON'T WANT TO MAKE TROUBLE FOR KUGA-SAN...
BUT...
BUT ...!
U-UM...
ACTUALLY, I, UH...
TODAY...IS OUR DAY OFF.

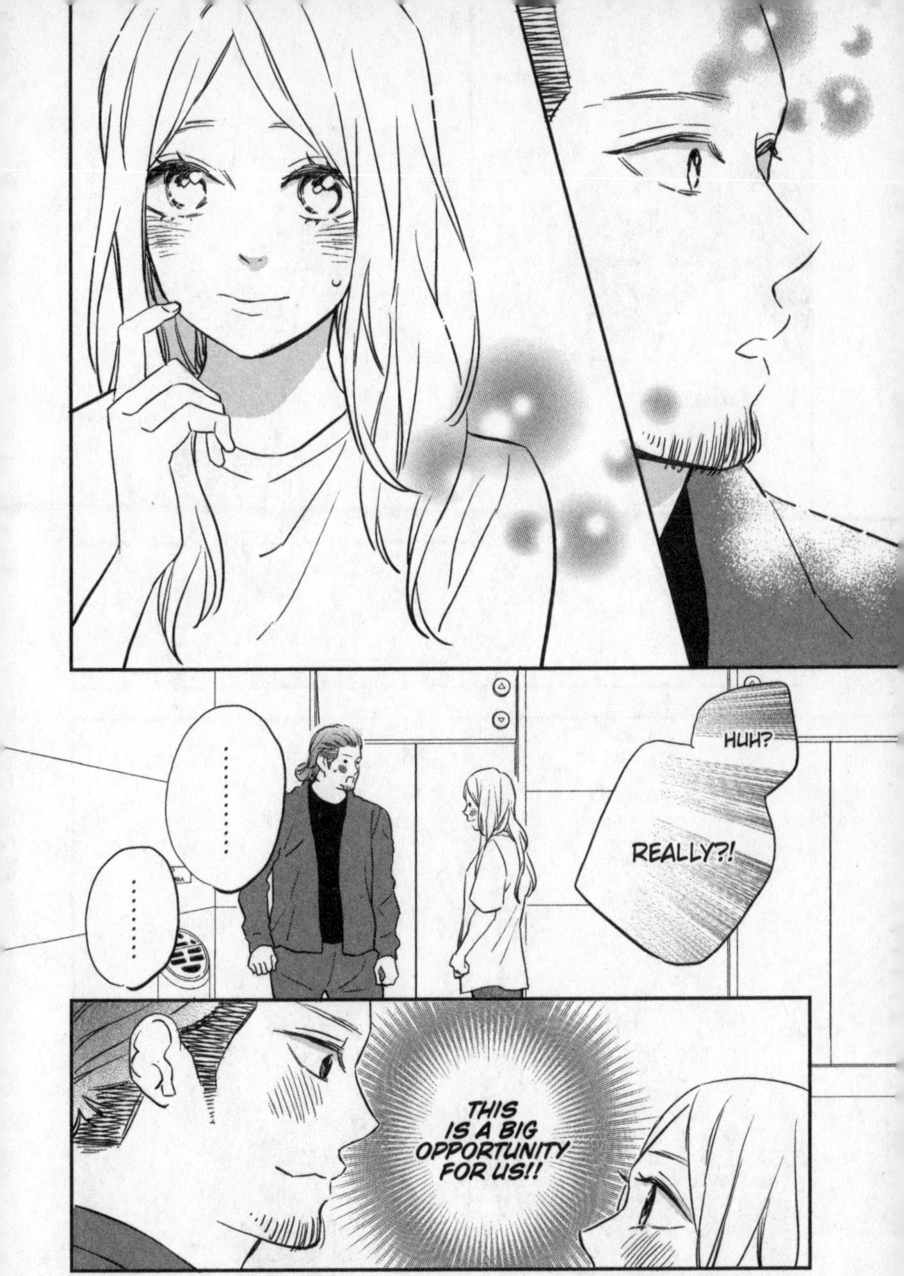

HUH? REALLY?!
....
......
THIS IS A BIG OPPORTUNITY FOR US!!

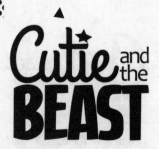

Cutie and the BEAST

Cutie and the BEAST

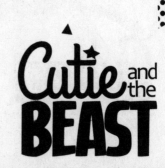

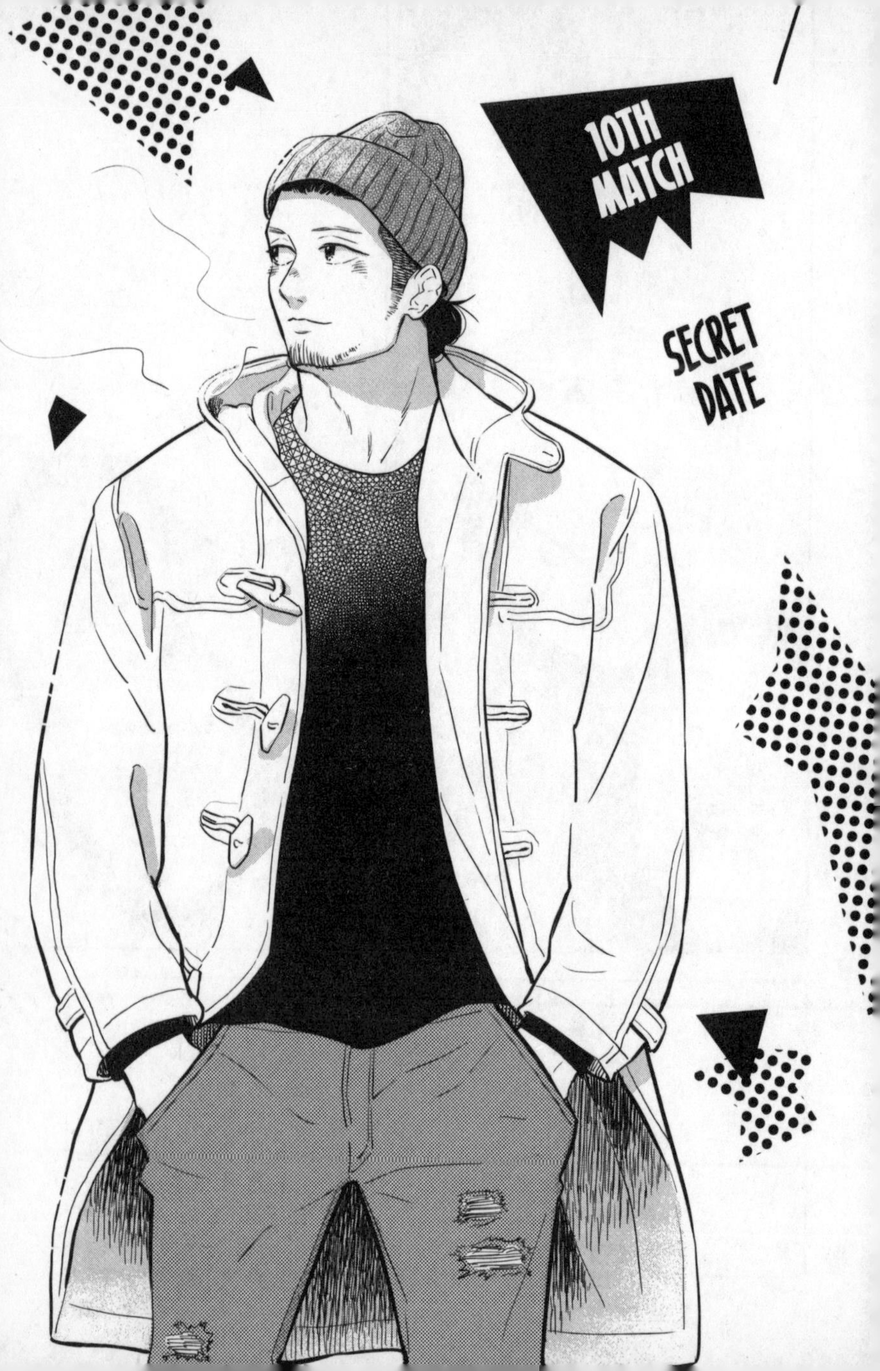
10TH MATCH
SECRET DATE

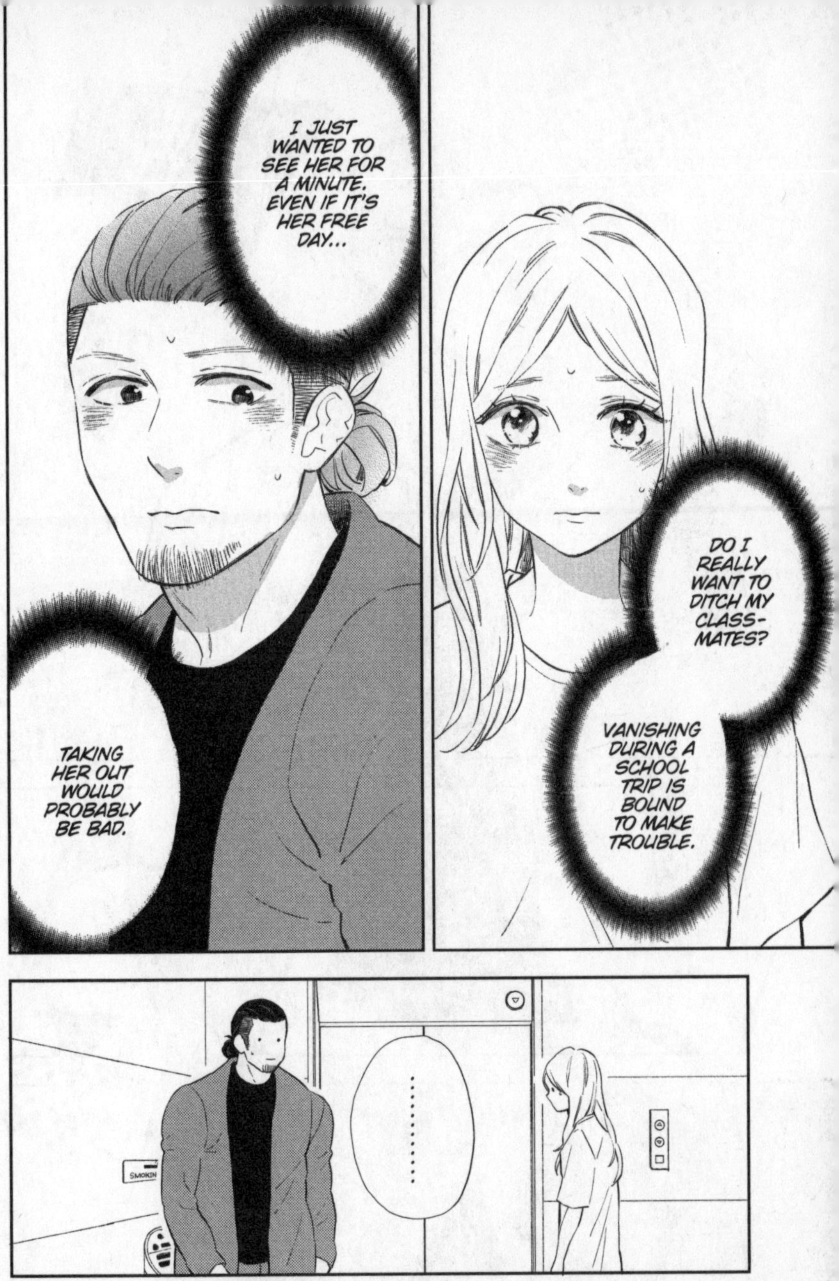
DO I REALLY WANT TO DITCH MY CLASS-MATES?
VANISHING DURING A SCHOOL TRIP IS BOUND TO MAKE TROUBLE.
I JUST WANTED TO SEE HER FOR A MINUTE. EVEN IF IT'S HER FREE DAY...
TAKING HER OUT WOULD PROBABLY BE BAD.
......
SMOKIN

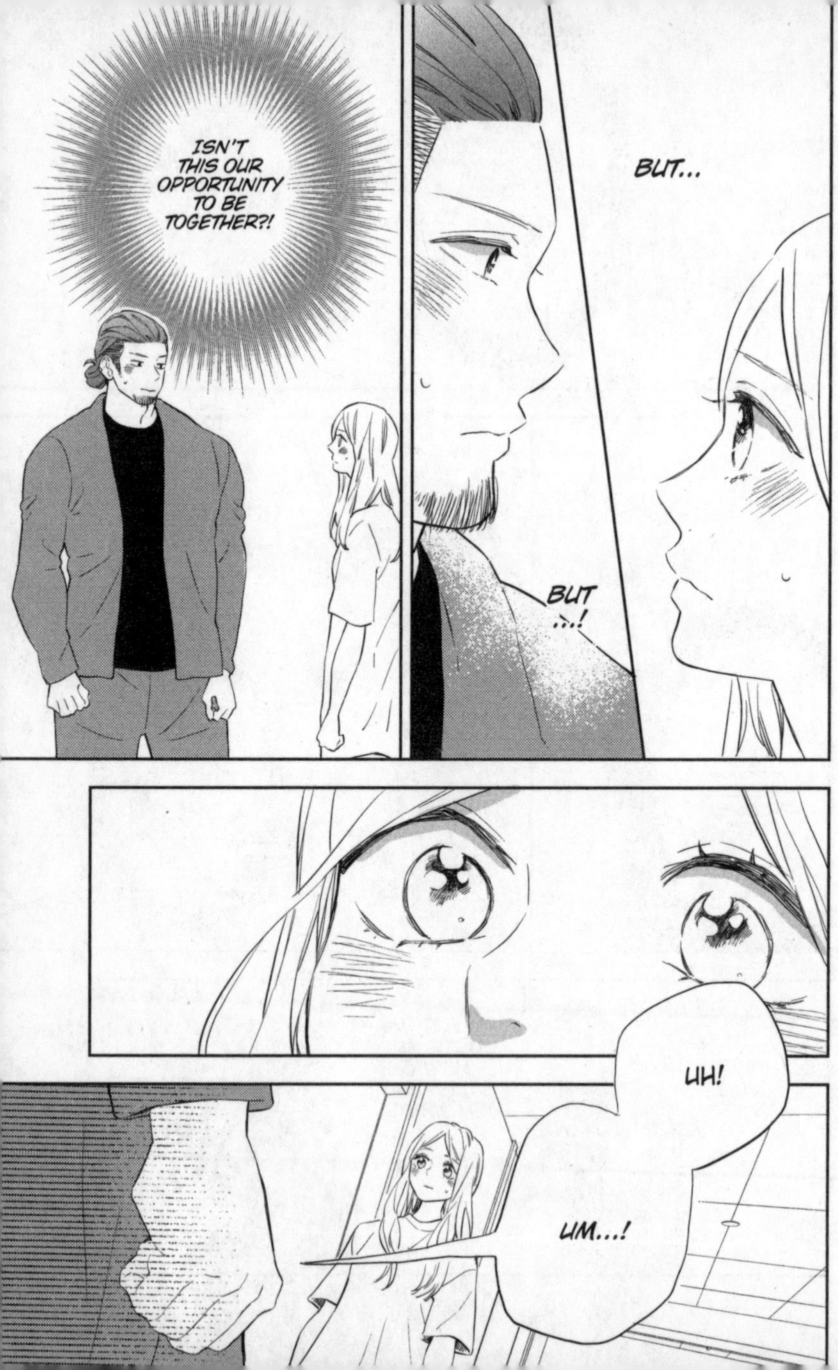
BUT...
BUT ...!
ISN'T THIS OUR OPPORTUNITY TO BE TOGETHER?!
UH!
UM...!

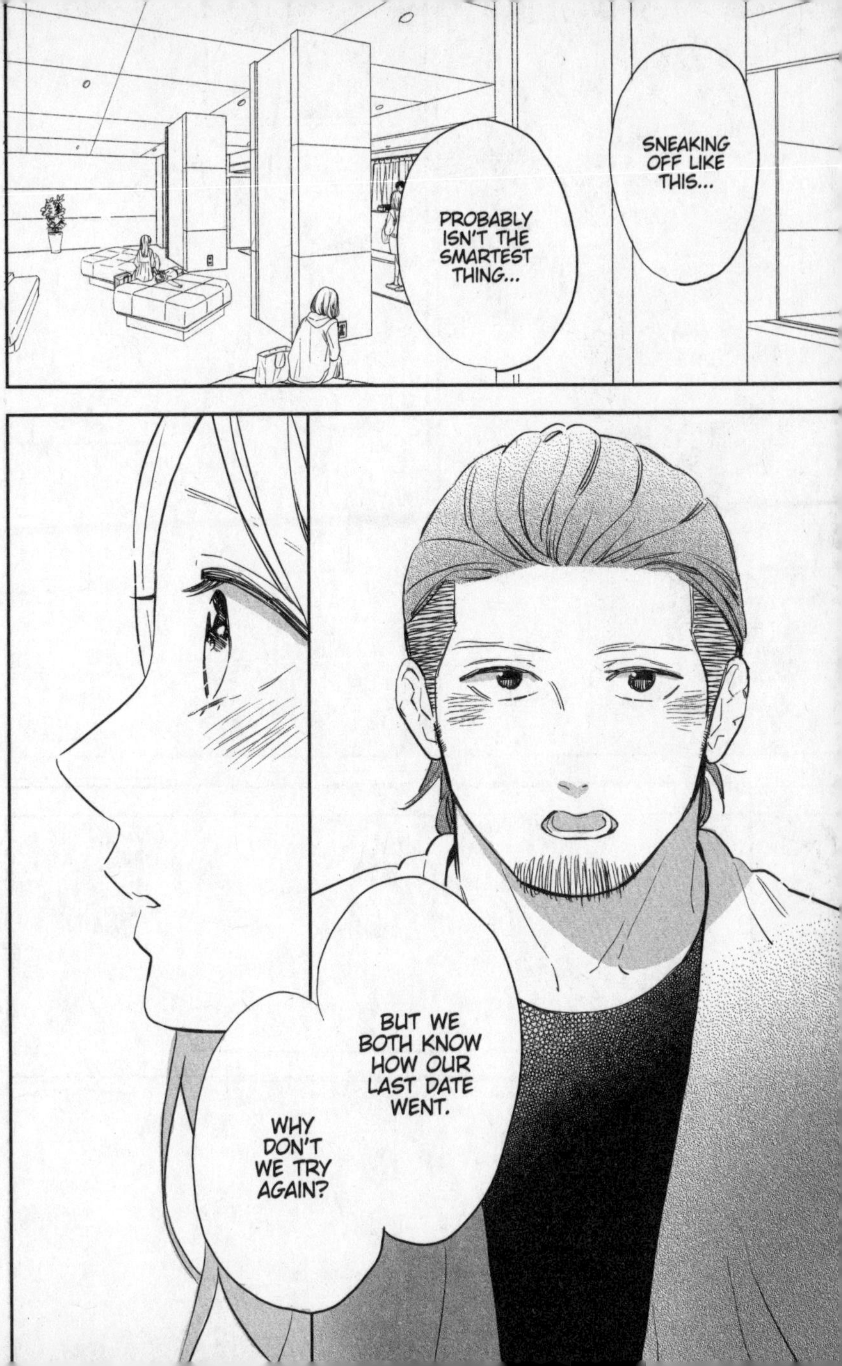
SNEAKING OFF LIKE THIS...
PROBABLY ISN'T THE SMARTEST THING...
BUT WE BOTH KNOW HOW OUR LAST DATE WENT.
WHY DON'T WE TRY AGAIN?

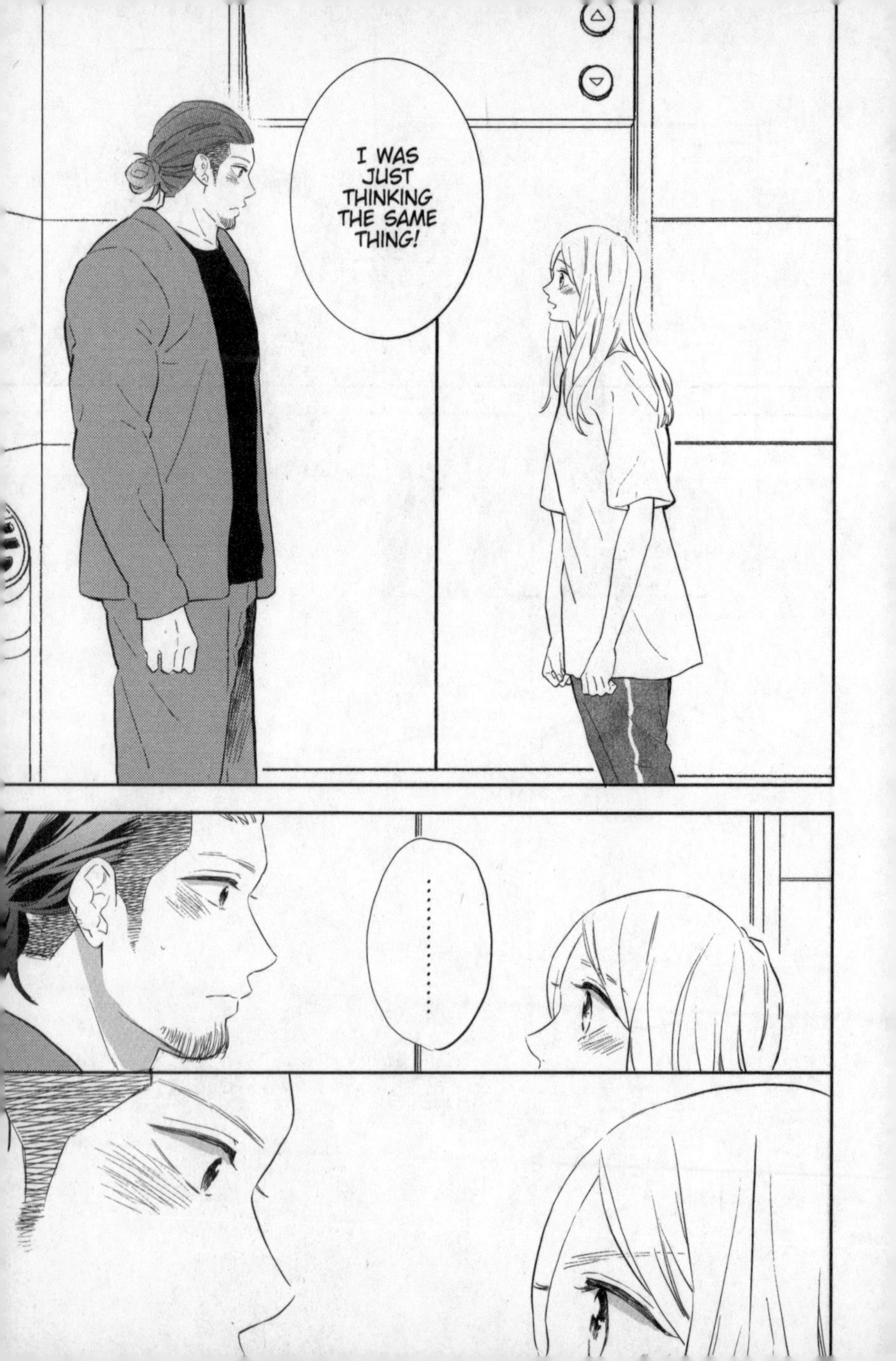
I WAS JUST THINKING THE SAME THING!
......

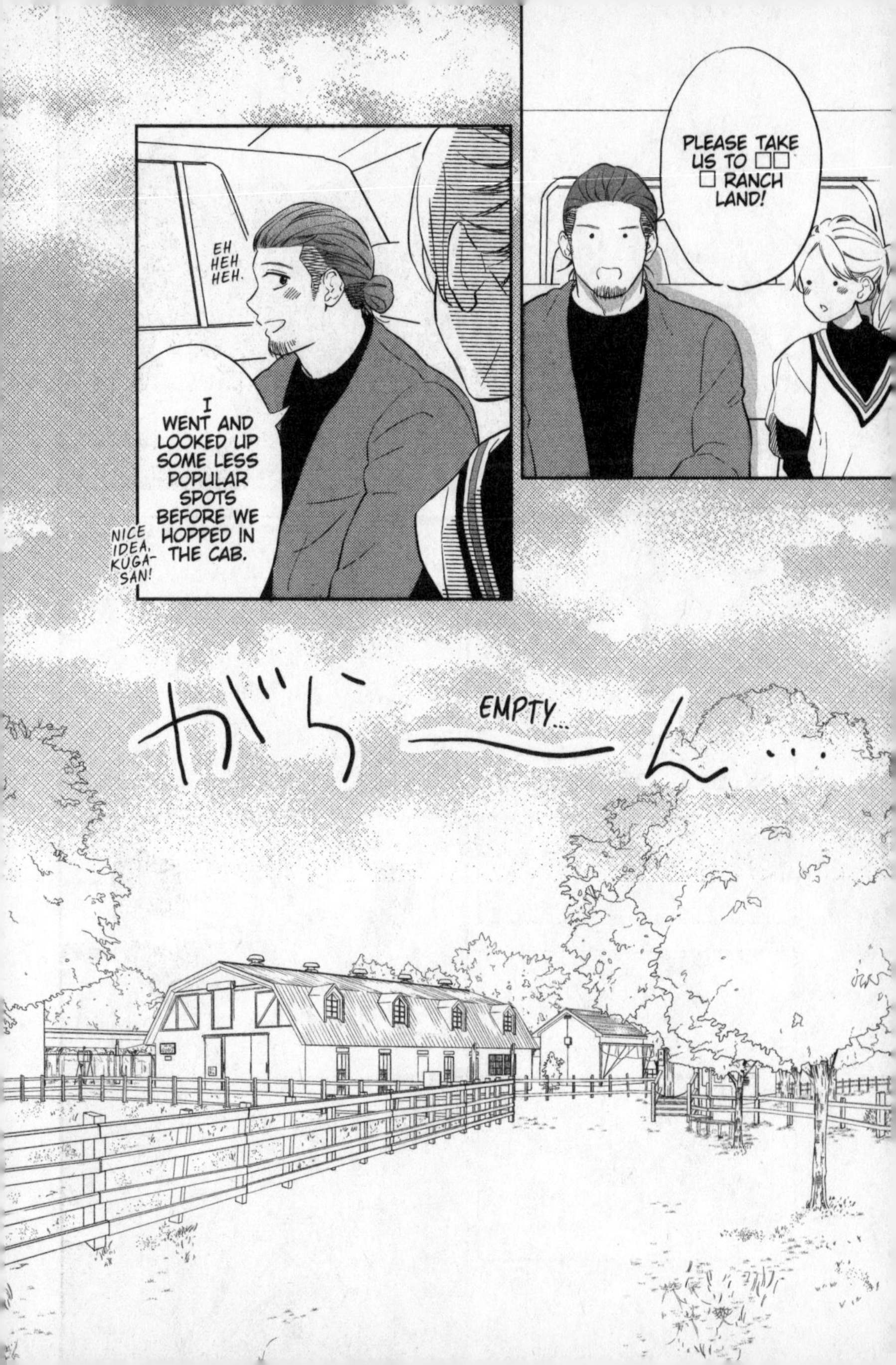
PLEASE TAKE US TO □□ □ RANCH LAND!
EH HEH HEH.
I WENT AND LOOKED UP SOME LESS POPULAR SPOTS BEFORE WE HOPPED IN THE CAB.
NICE IDEA, KUGA-SAN!
がらーん…
EMPTY...

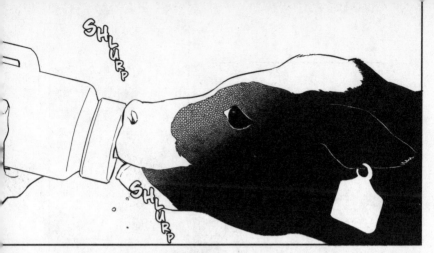

SH
VRP

SH
VRP

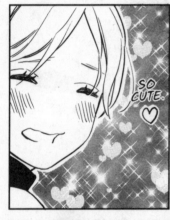

SO
CUTE. ♥

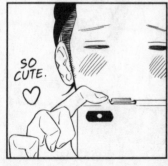

SO
CUTE.
♥

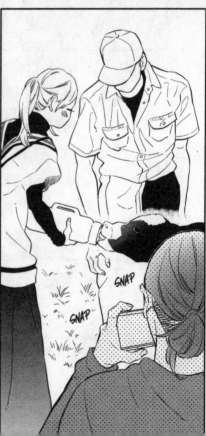

SNAP

SNAP

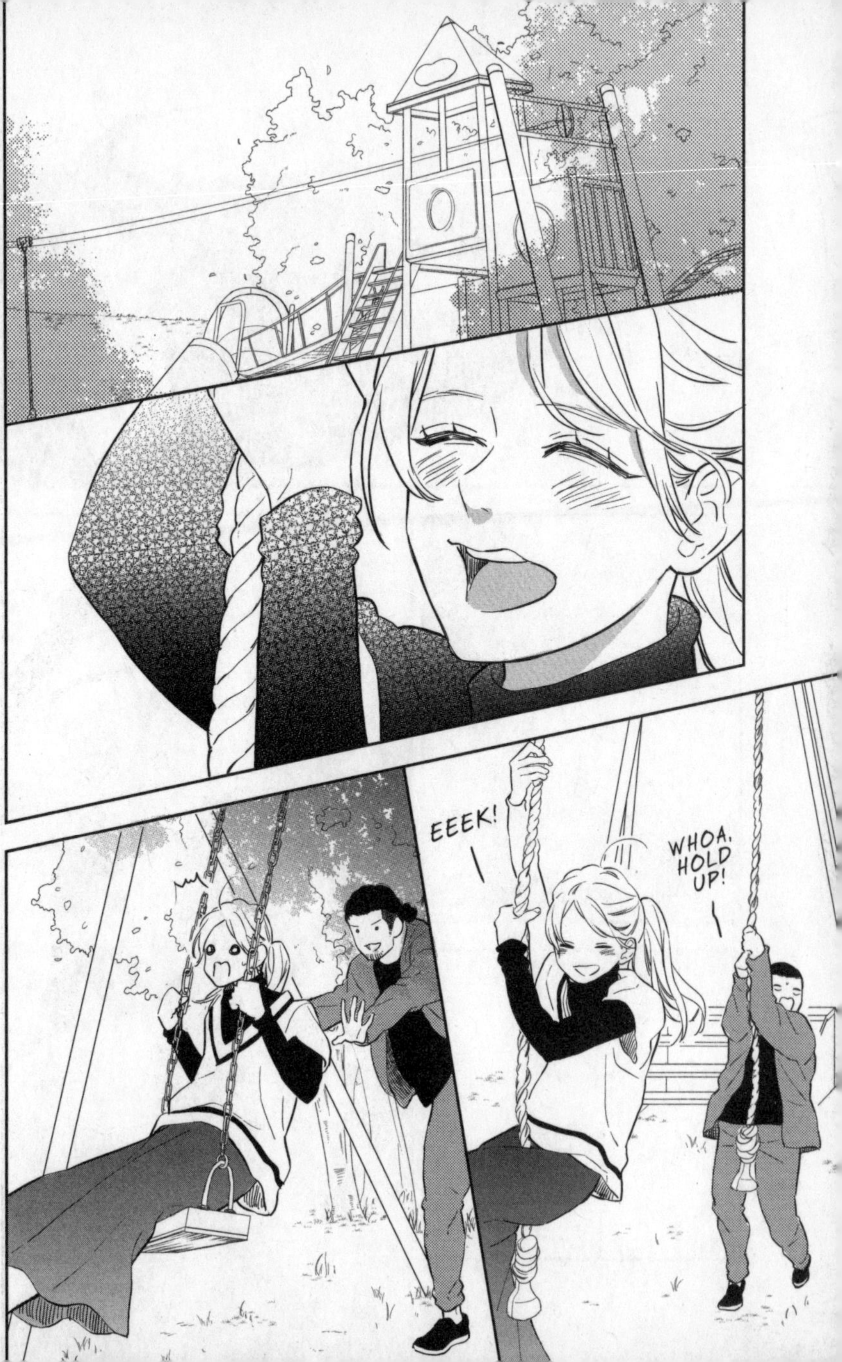
WHOA, HOLD UP!
EEEK!

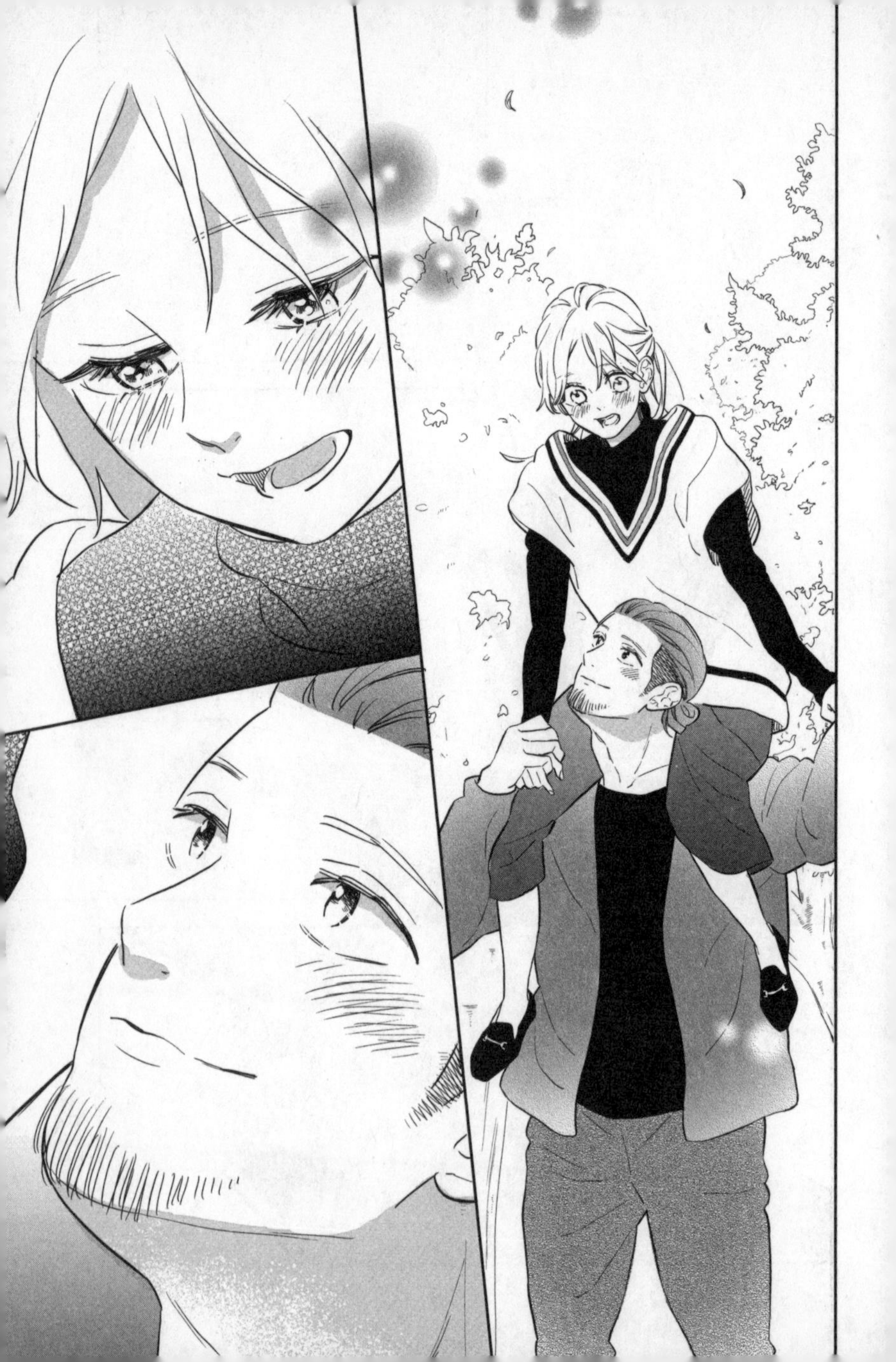

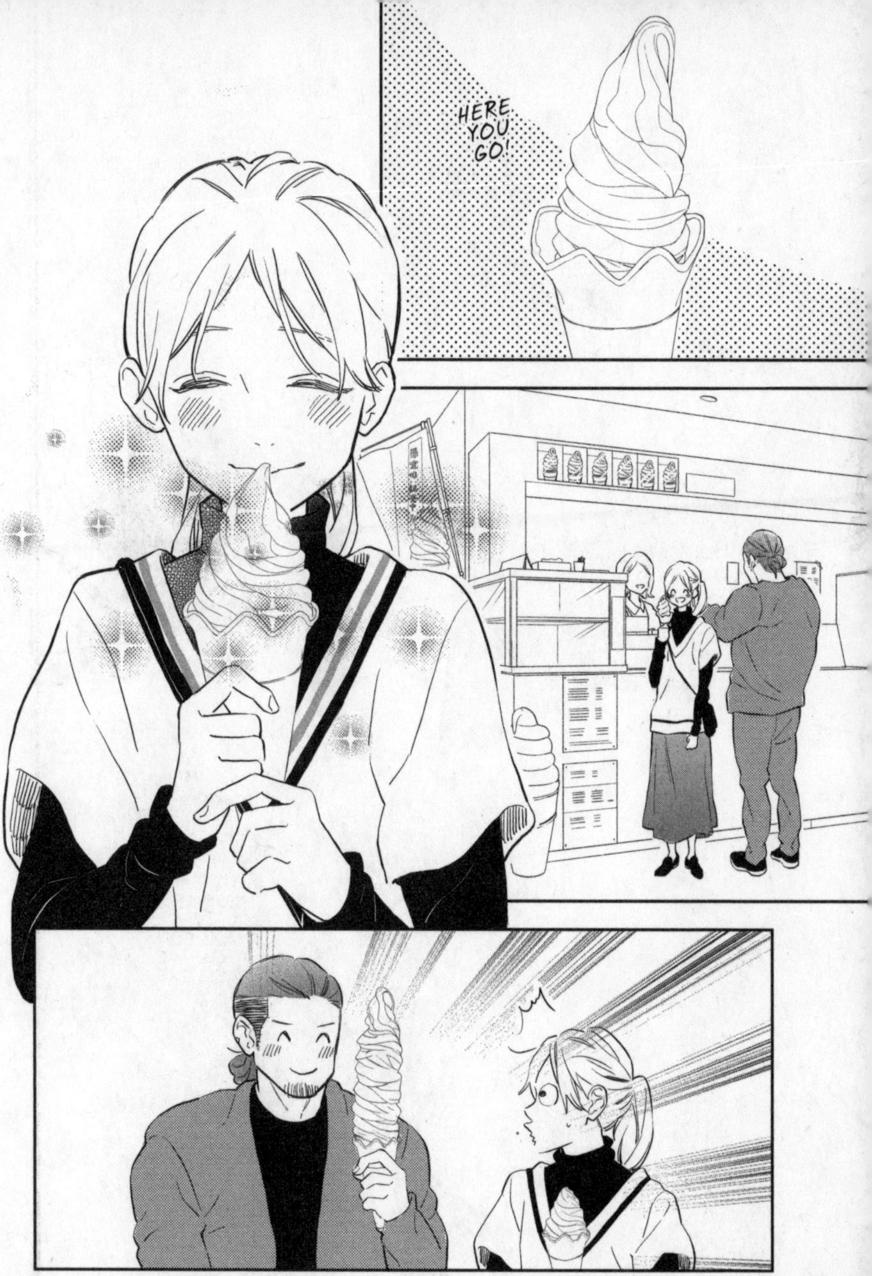
HERE YOU GO!

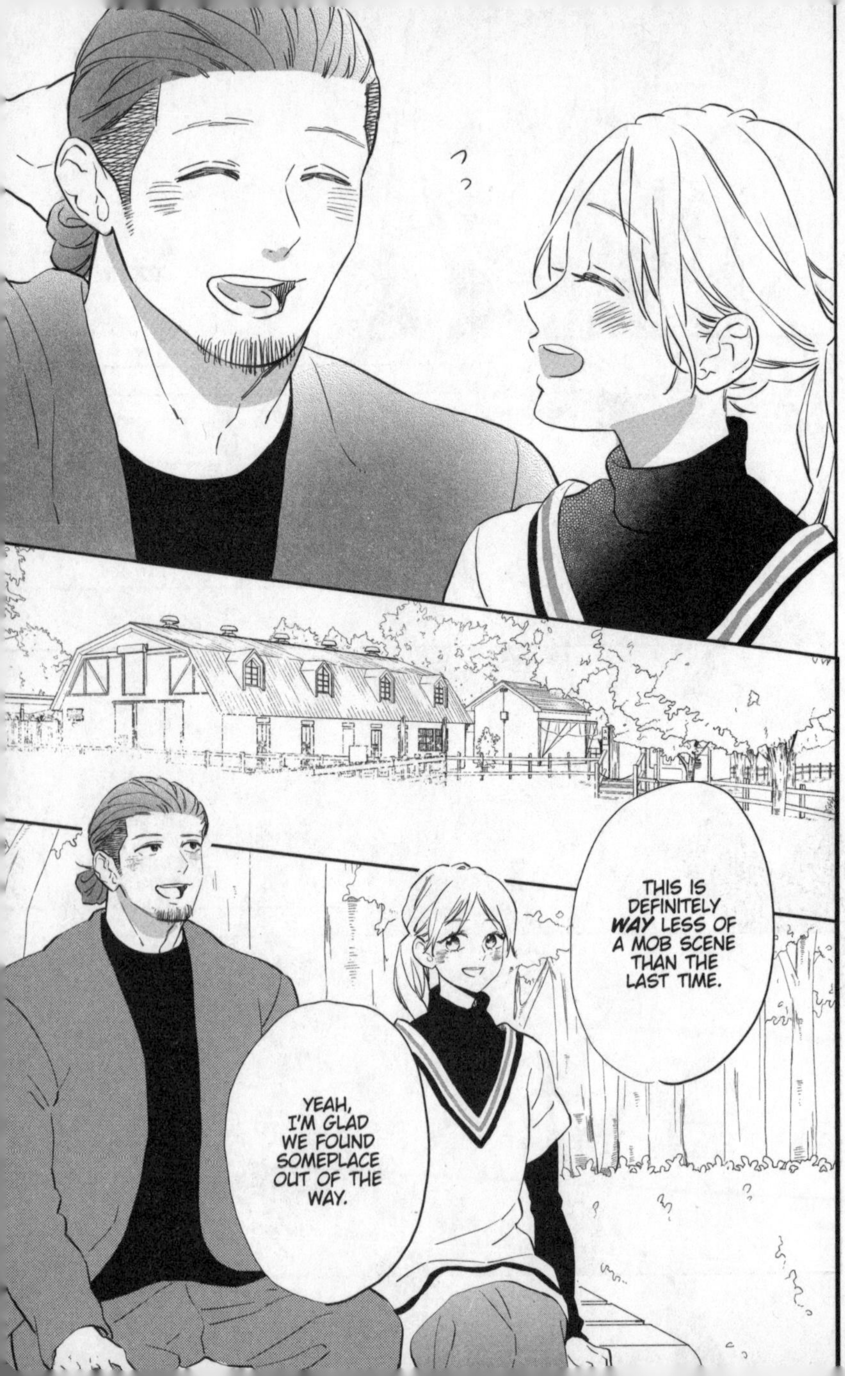
THIS IS DEFINITELY *WAY* LESS OF A MOB SCENE THAN THE LAST TIME.
YEAH, I'M GLAD WE FOUND SOMEPLACE OUT OF THE WAY.

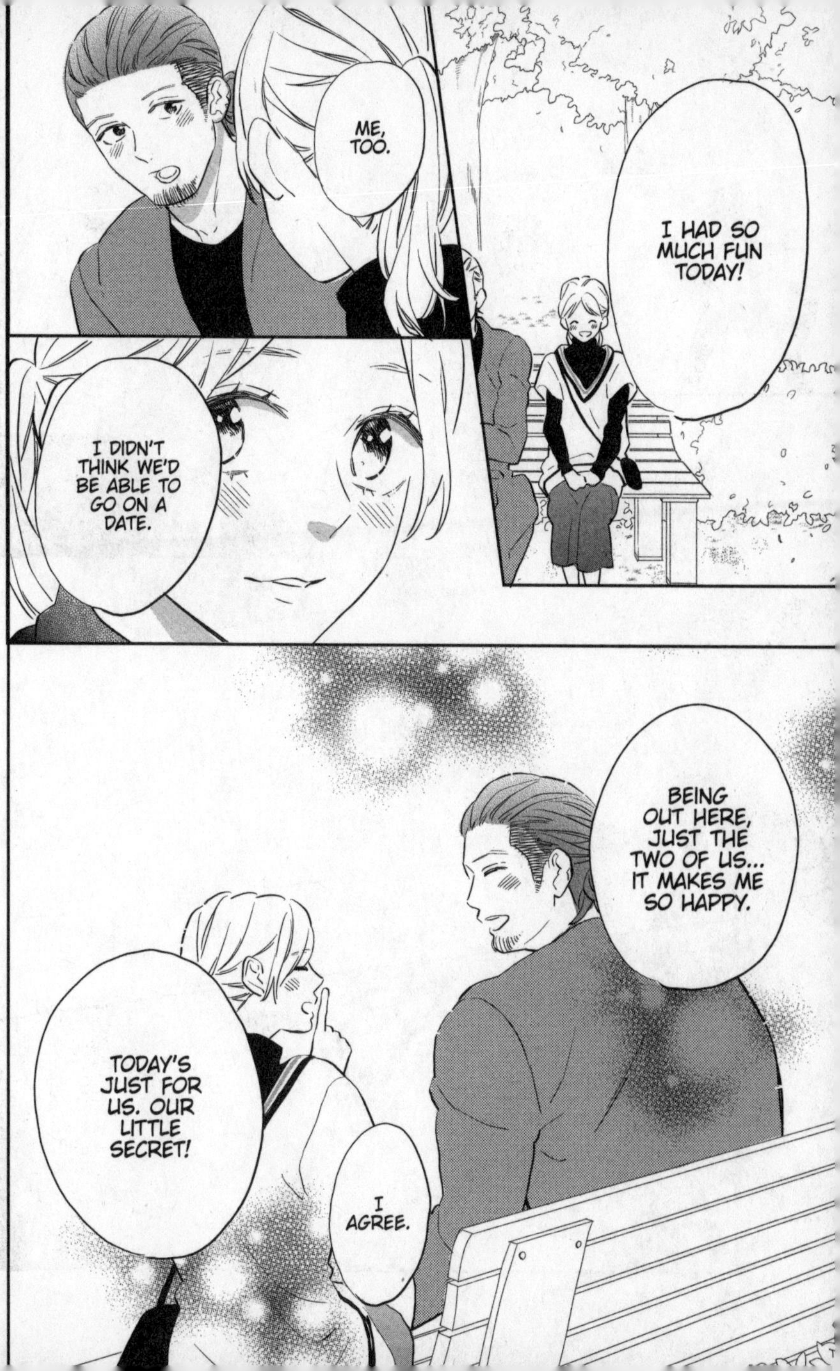
I HAD SO MUCH FUN TODAY!
ME, TOO.
I DIDN'T THINK WE'D BE ABLE TO GO ON A DATE.
BEING OUT HERE, JUST THE TWO OF US... IT MAKES ME SO HAPPY.
TODAY'S JUST FOR US. OUR LITTLE SECRET!
I AGREE.

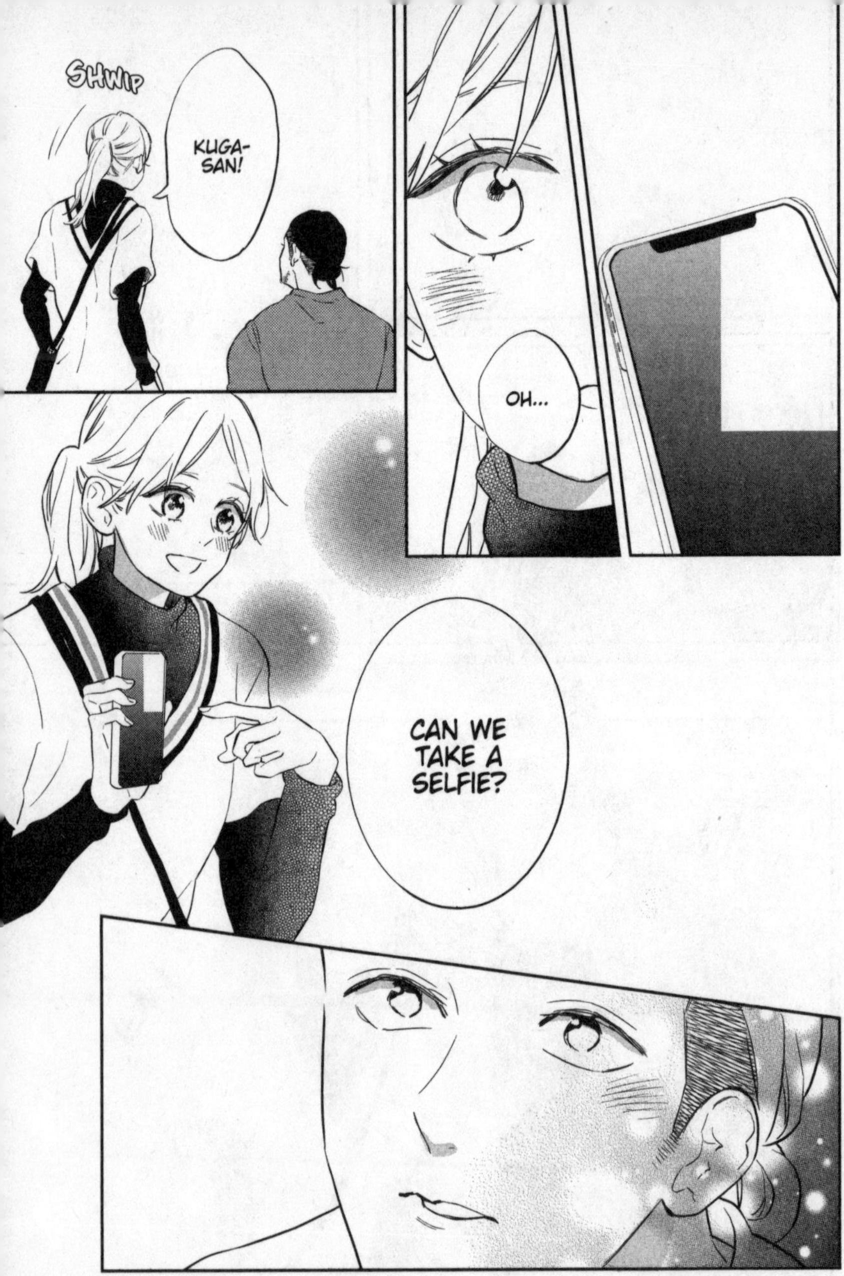
OH...
SHWIP
KUGA-SAN!
CAN WE TAKE A SELFIE?

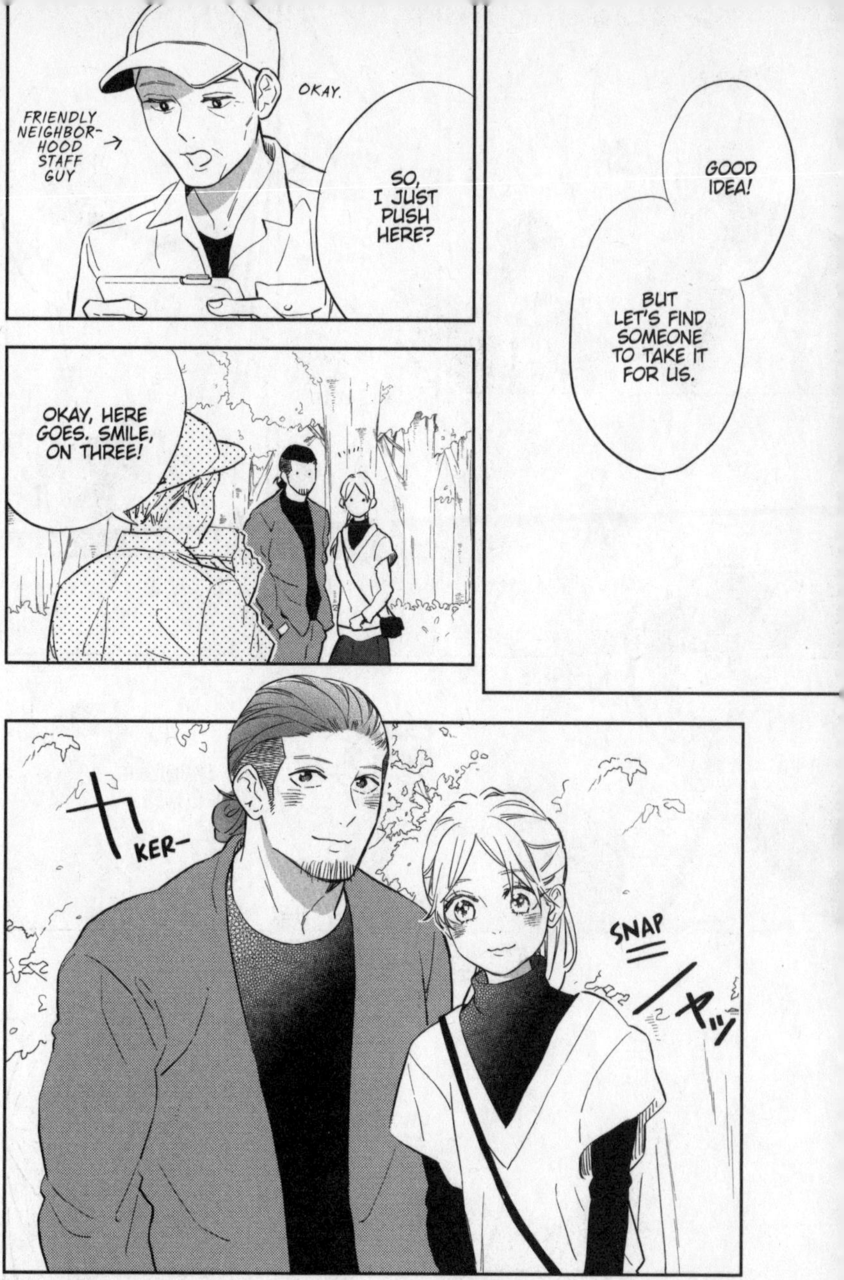
GOOD IDEA!
BUT LET'S FIND SOMEONE TO TAKE IT FOR US.
OKAY.
FRIENDLY NEIGHBORHOOD STAFF GUY
SO, I JUST PUSH HERE?
OKAY, HERE GOES. SMILE, ON THREE!
カ KER-
シャッ SNAP

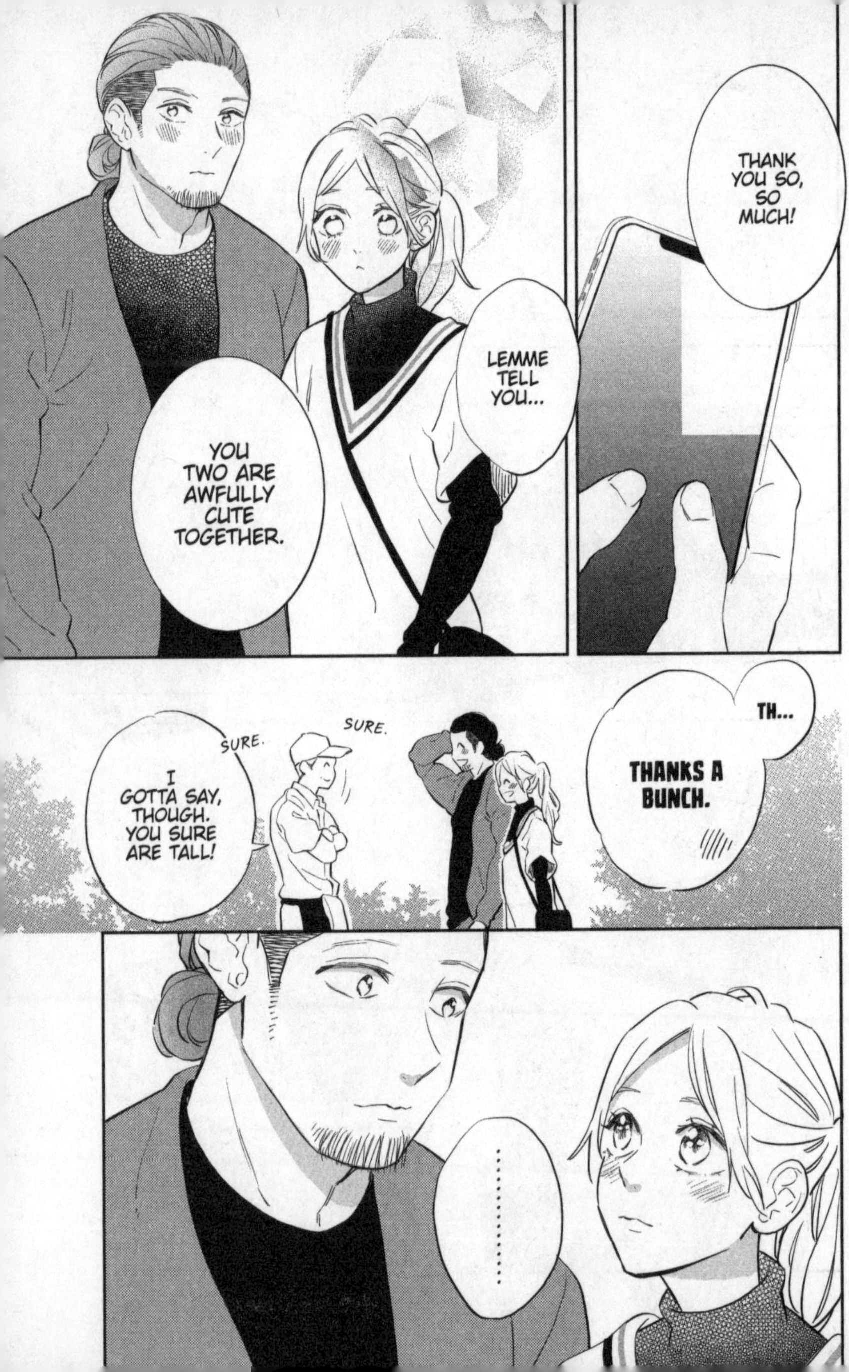
THANK YOU SO, SO MUCH!
LEMME TELL YOU...
YOU TWO ARE AWFULLY CUTE TOGETHER.
TH...
THANKS A BUNCH.
SURE.
SURE.
I GOTTA SAY, THOUGH. YOU SURE ARE TALL!
......

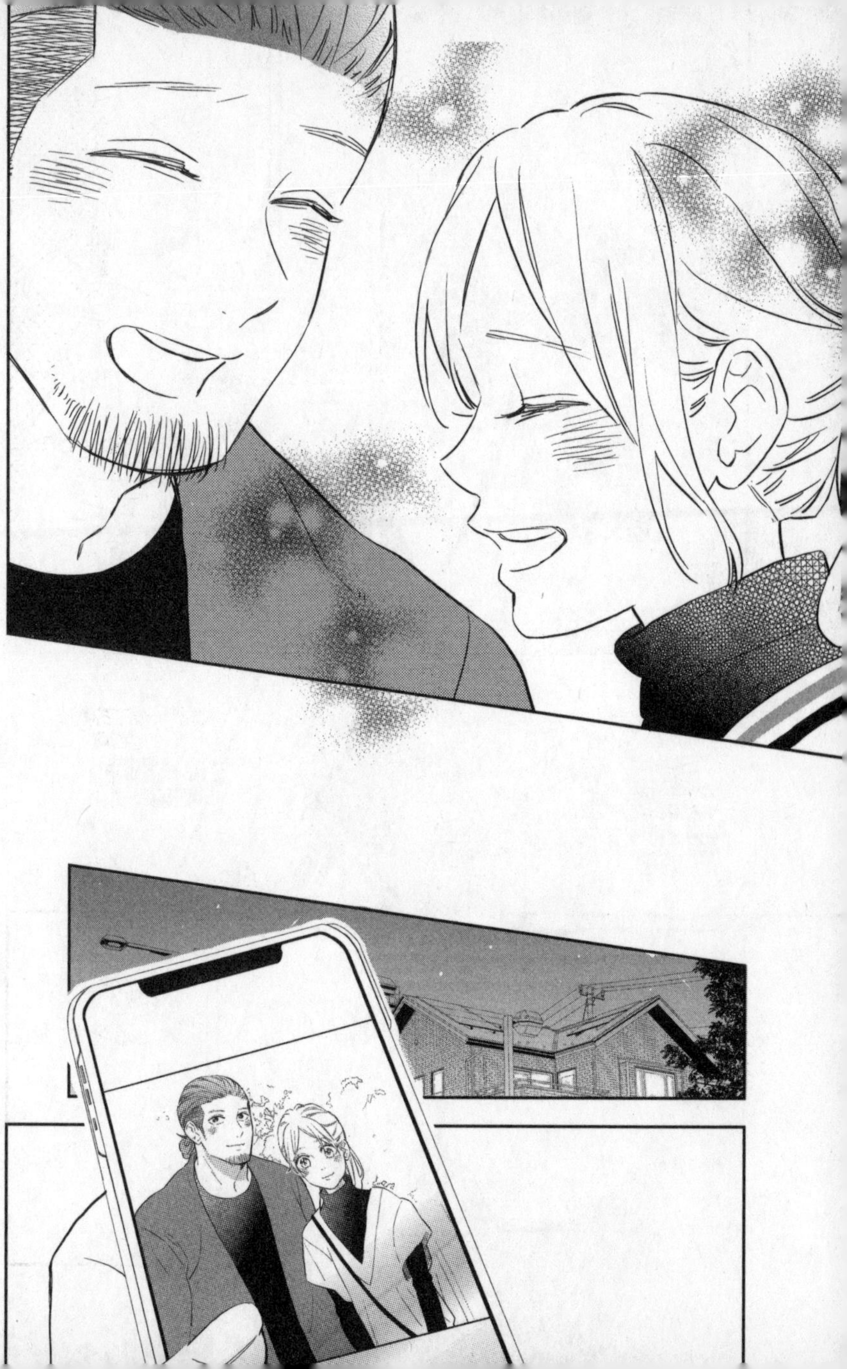

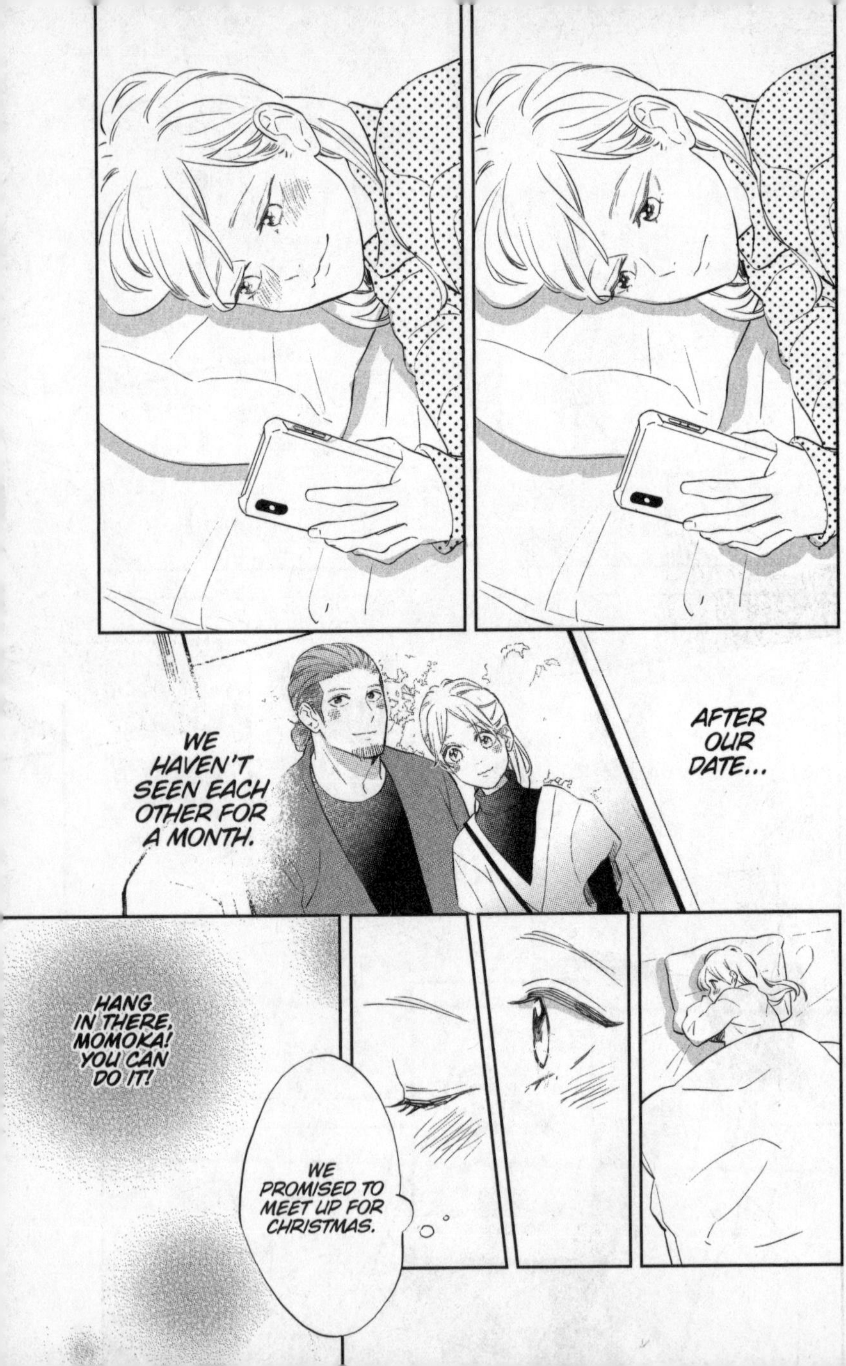
AFTER OUR DATE...
WE HAVEN'T SEEN EACH OTHER FOR A MONTH.
WE PROMISED TO MEET UP FOR CHRISTMAS.
HANG IN THERE, MOMOKA! YOU CAN DO IT!

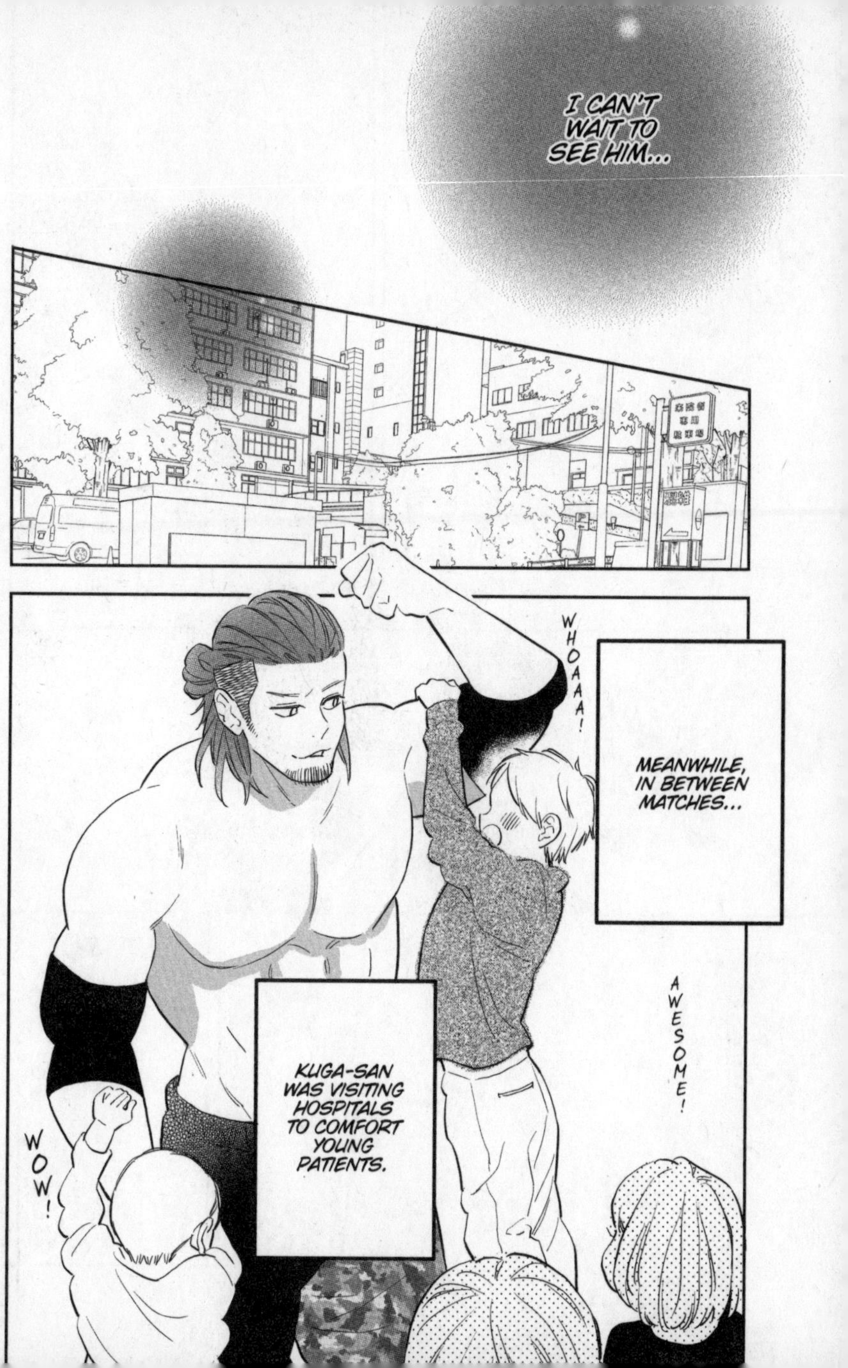
I CAN'T WAIT TO SEE HIM...
MEANWHILE, IN BETWEEN MATCHES...
WHOAAA!
AWESOME!
KUGA-SAN WAS VISITING HOSPITALS TO COMFORT YOUNG PATIENTS.
WOW!

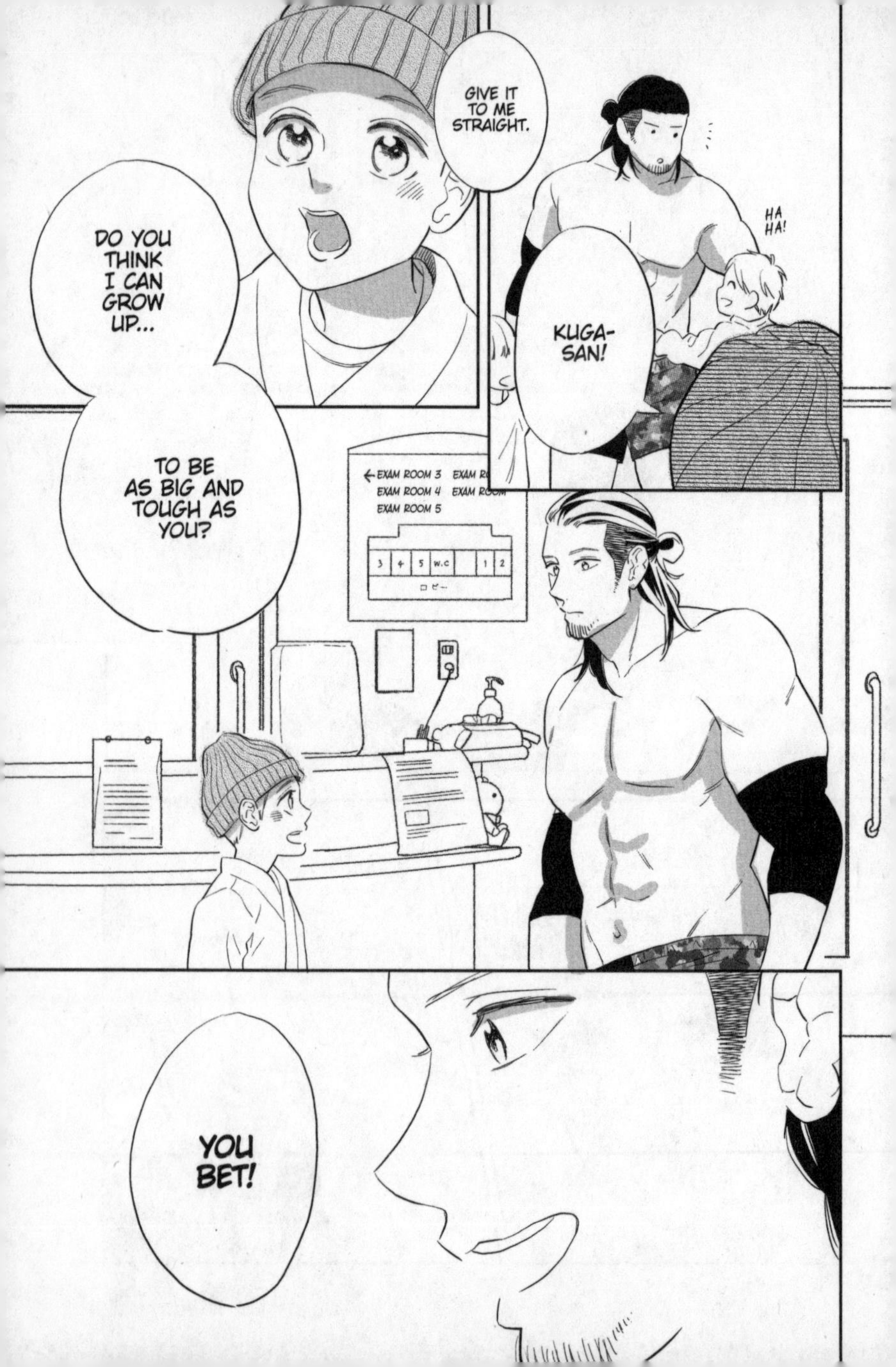
HA HA!
KUGA-SAN!
GIVE IT TO ME STRAIGHT.
DO YOU THINK I CAN GROW UP...
← EXAM ROOM 3
EXAM ROOM 4
EXAM ROOM 5
TO BE AS BIG AND TOUGH AS YOU?
YOU BET!

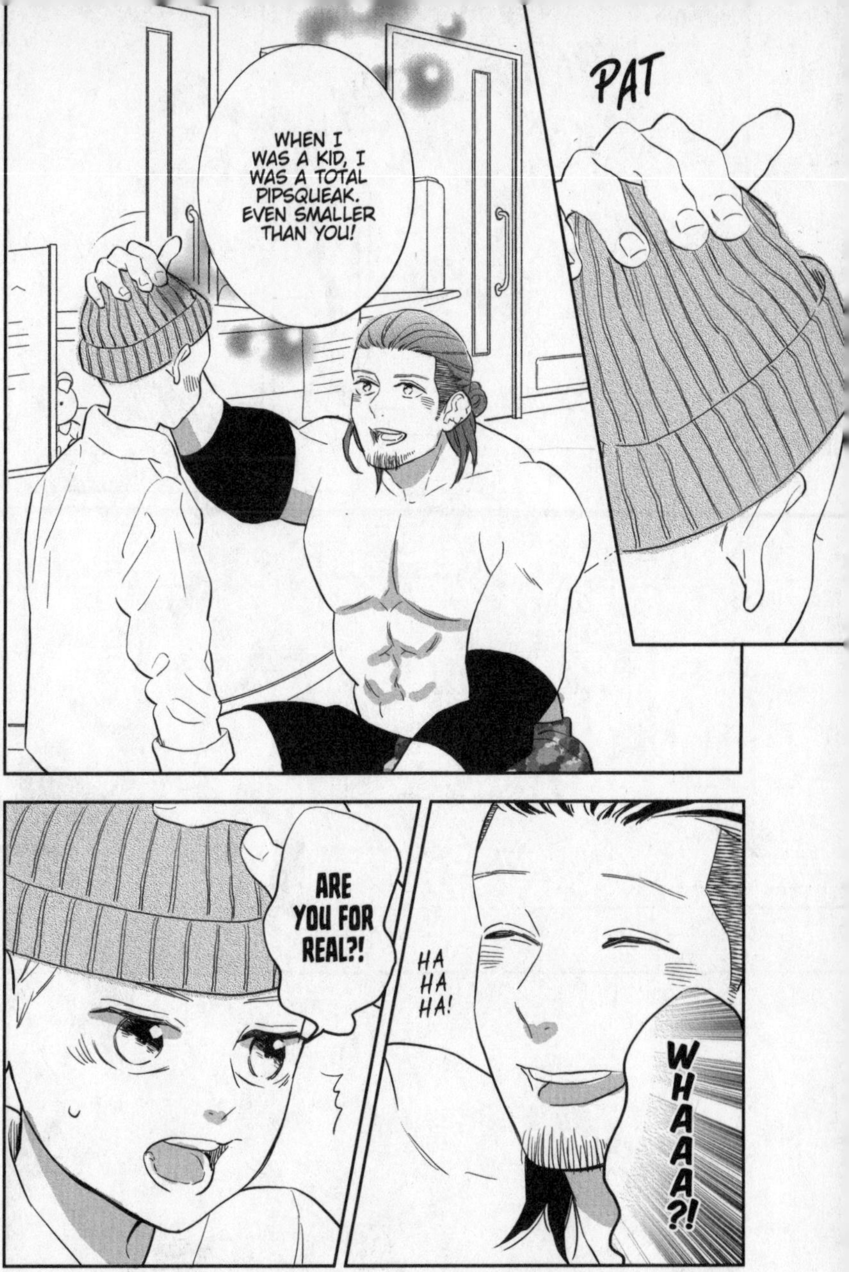
PAT
WHEN I WAS A KID, I WAS A TOTAL PIPSQUEAK. EVEN SMALLER THAN YOU!
HA HA HA!
WHAAAA?!
ARE YOU FOR REAL?!

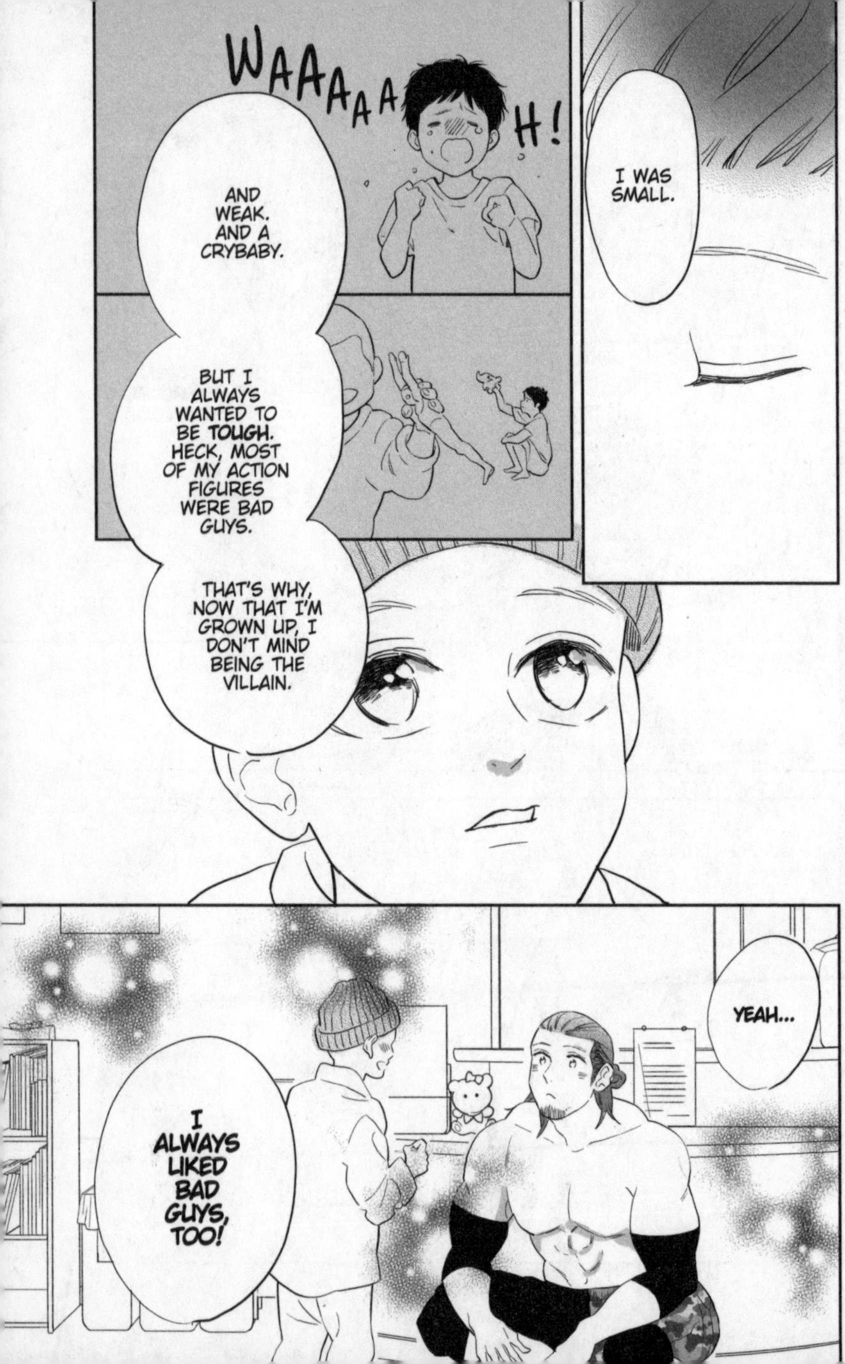
I WAS SMALL.
AND WEAK. AND A CRYBABY.
WAAAAAH!
BUT I ALWAYS WANTED TO BE TOUGH. HECK, MOST OF MY ACTION FIGURES WERE BAD GUYS.
THAT'S WHY, NOW THAT I'M GROWN UP, I DON'T MIND BEING THE VILLAIN.
YEAH...
I ALWAYS LIKED BAD GUYS, TOO!

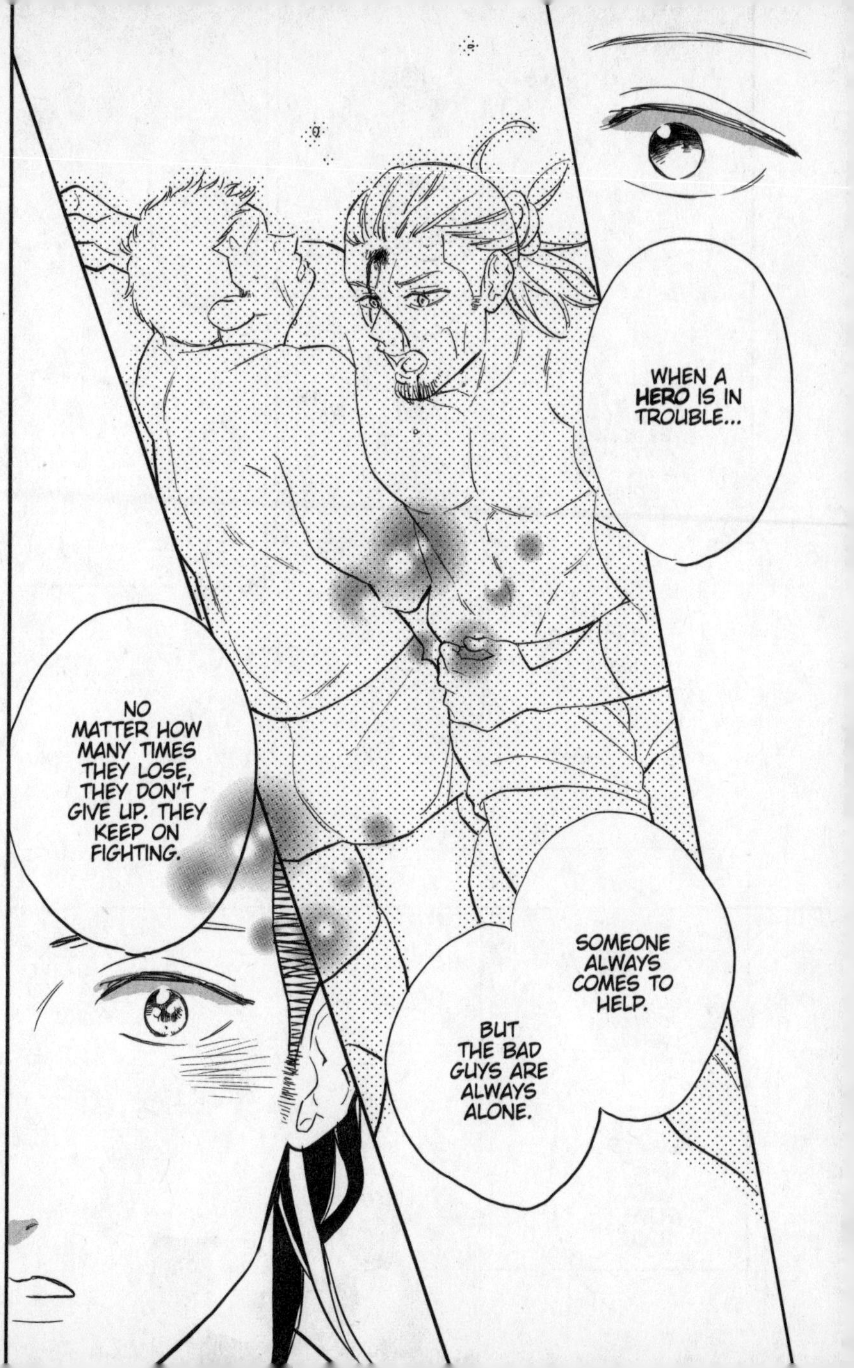
WHEN A HERO IS IN TROUBLE...
SOMEONE ALWAYS COMES TO HELP.
BUT THE BAD GUYS ARE ALWAYS ALONE.
NO MATTER HOW MANY TIMES THEY LOSE, THEY DON'T GIVE UP. THEY KEEP ON FIGHTING.

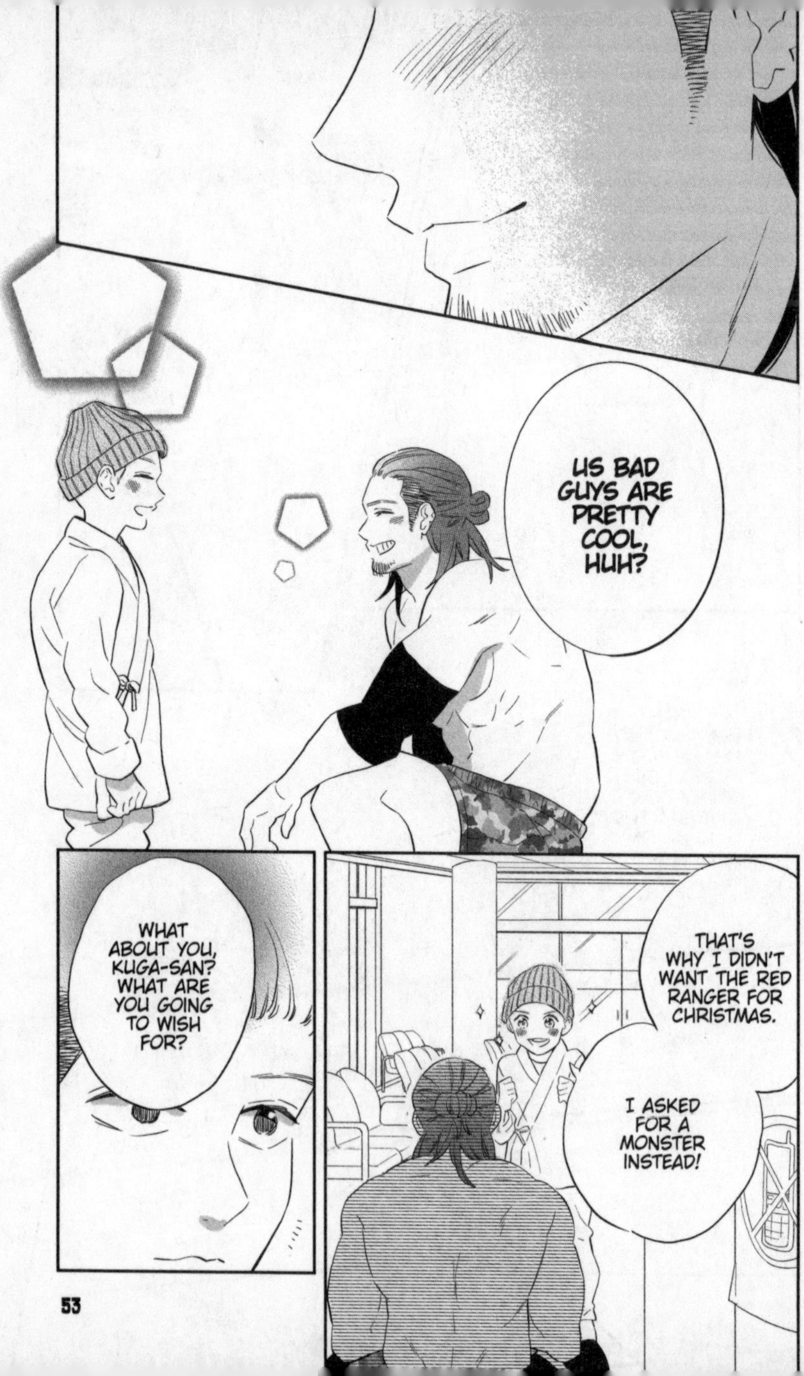
US BAD GUYS ARE PRETTY COOL, HUH?
THAT'S WHY I DIDN'T WANT THE RED RANGER FOR CHRISTMAS.
I ASKED FOR A MONSTER INSTEAD!
WHAT ABOUT YOU, KUGA-SAN? WHAT ARE YOU GOING TO WISH FOR?

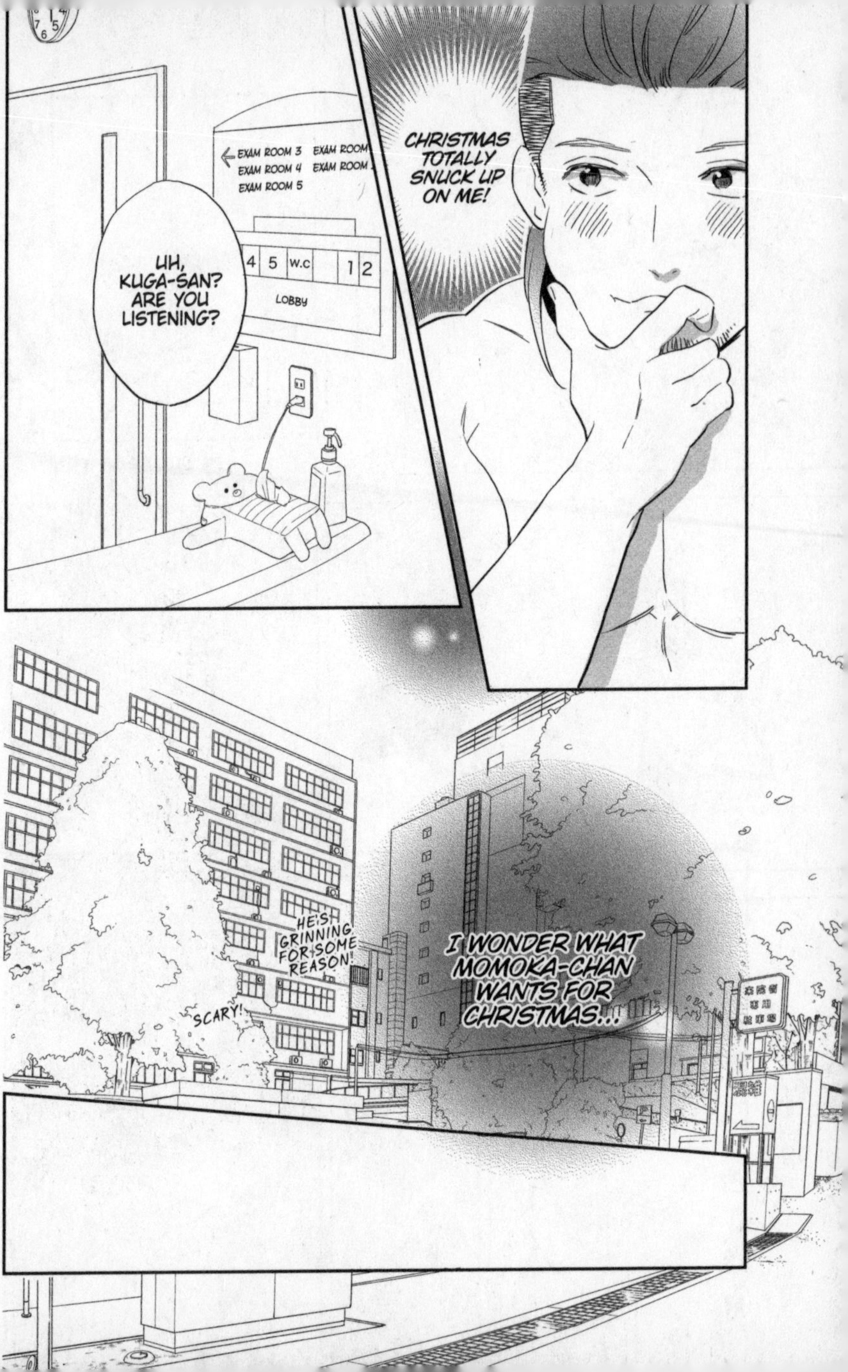
CHRISTMAS TOTALLY SNUCK UP ON ME!
EXAM ROOM 3
EXAM ROOM 4
EXAM ROOM 5
LOBBY
UH, KUGA-SAN? ARE YOU LISTENING?
I WONDER WHAT MOMOKA-CHAN WANTS FOR CHRISTMAS...
HE'S GRINNING FOR SOME REASON!
SCARY!

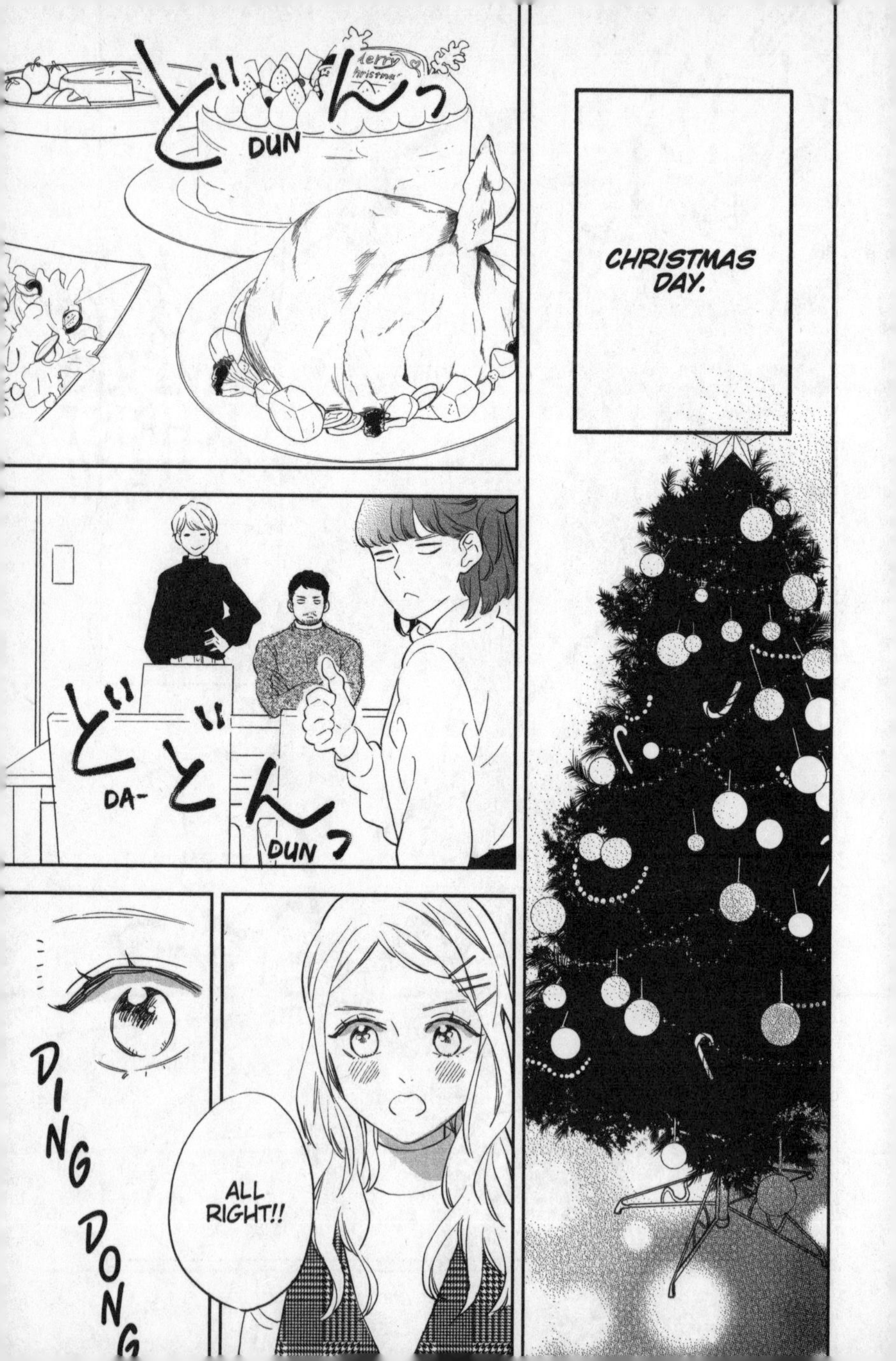
CHRISTMAS DAY.
DUN
DA-DUN
ALL RIGHT!!
DING DONG

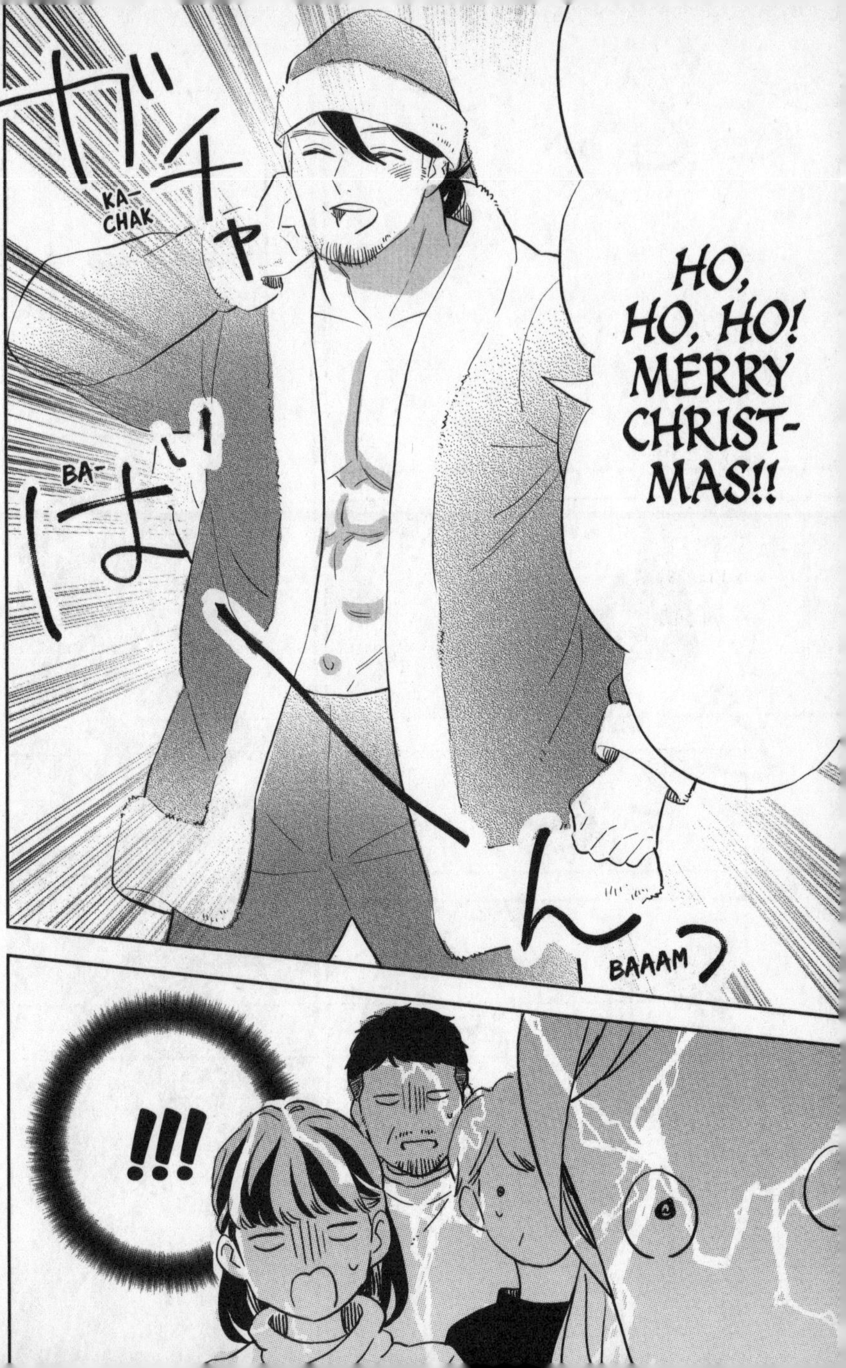
HO, HO, HO! MERRY CHRIST-MAS!!
ガチャ
KA-CHAK
ばーん
BA-
BAAAM
!!!

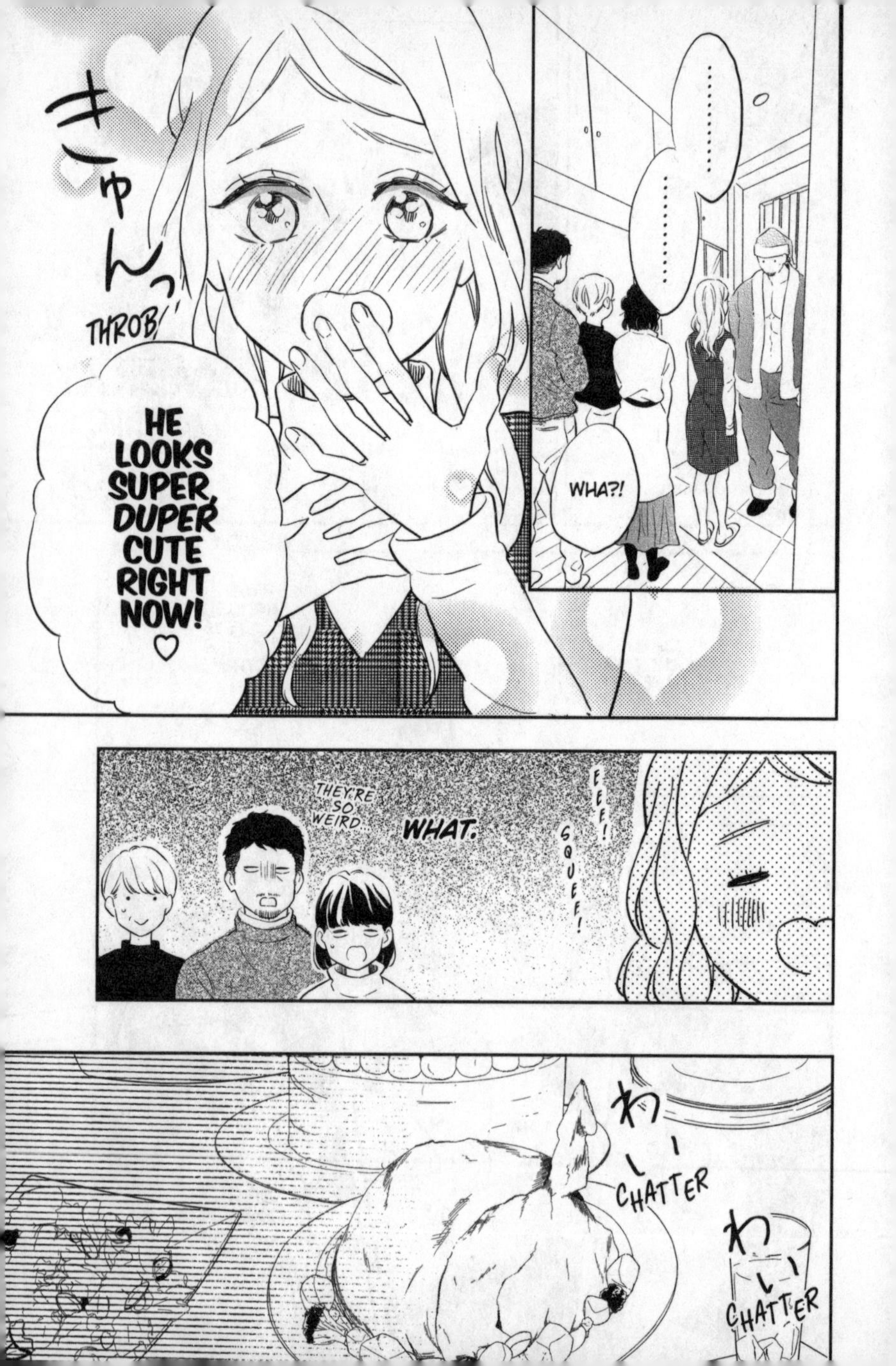
......
......
WHA?!
きゅんっ
THROB
HE LOOKS SUPER DUPER CUTE RIGHT NOW! ♡
EEE! SQUEE!
WHAT.
THEY'RE SO WEIRD.
わいわい
CHATTER
わいわい
CHATTER

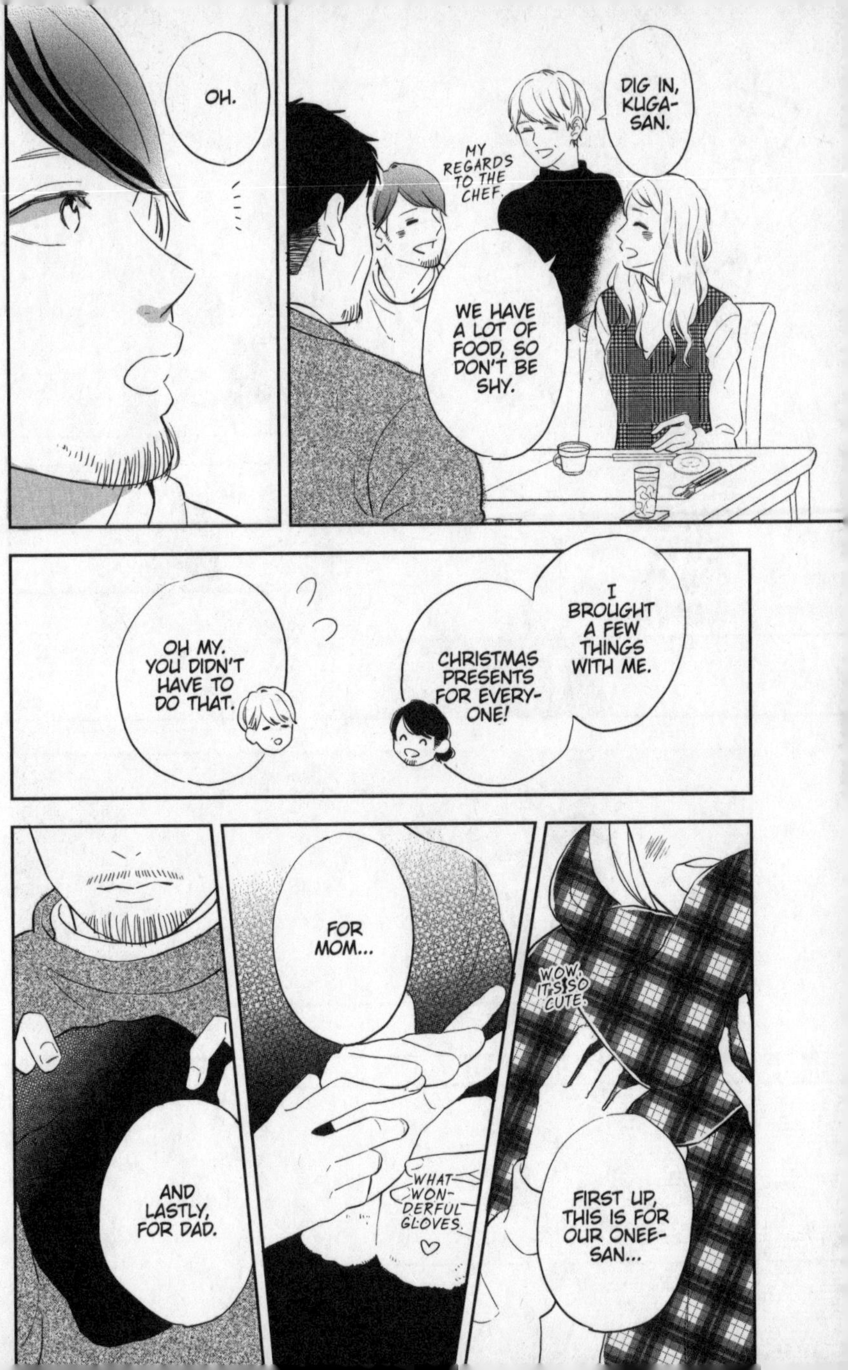
DIG IN, KUGA-SAN.
MY REGARDS TO THE CHEF.
WE HAVE A LOT OF FOOD, SO DON'T BE SHY.
OH.
I BROUGHT A FEW THINGS WITH ME.
CHRISTMAS PRESENTS FOR EVERY-ONE!
OH MY. YOU DIDN'T HAVE TO DO THAT.
FIRST UP, THIS IS FOR OUR ONEE-SAN...
WOW, IT'S SO CUTE.
FOR MOM...
WHAT WON-DERFUL GLOVES.
AND LASTLY, FOR DAD.

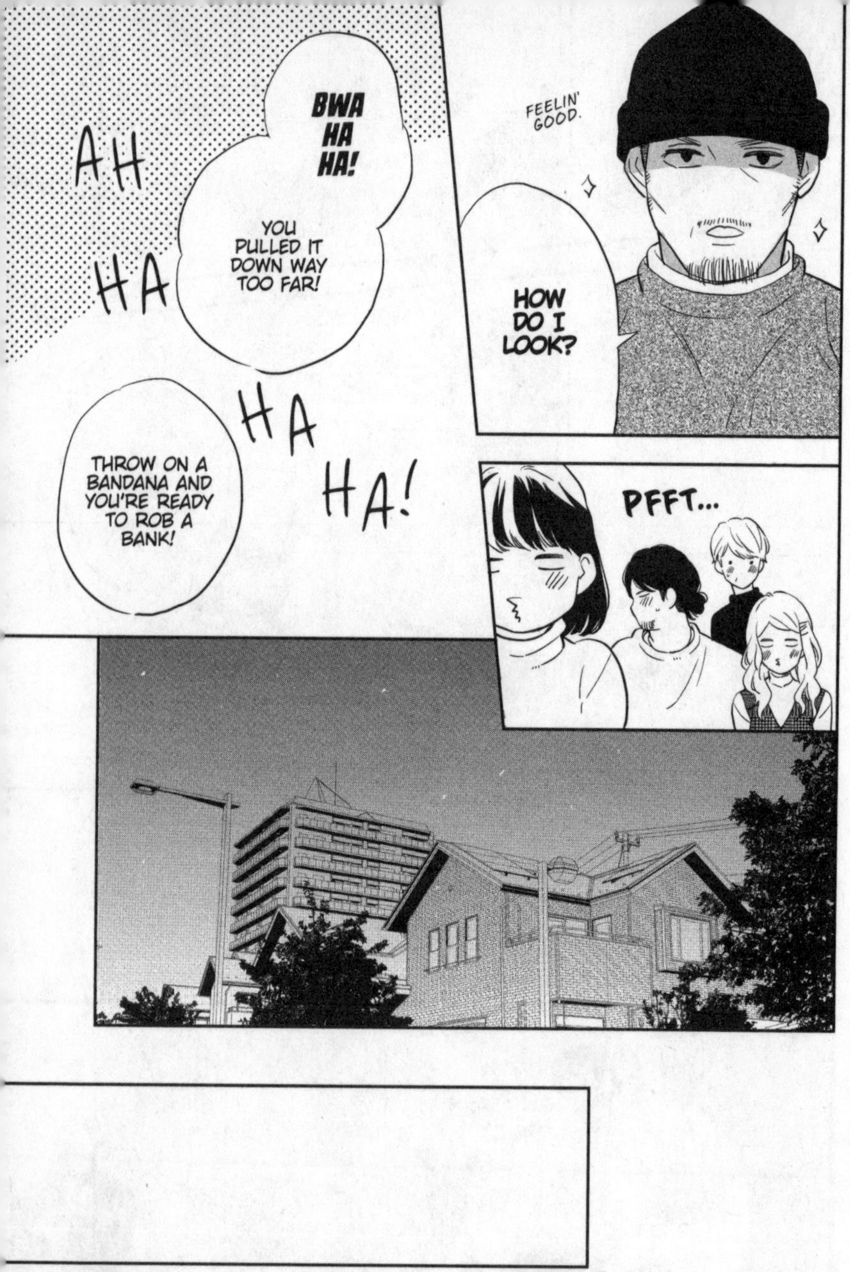
FEELIN' GOOD.
HOW DO I LOOK?
BWA HA HA!
YOU PULLED IT DOWN WAY TOO FAR!
AH HA HA HA!
THROW ON A BANDANA AND YOU'RE READY TO ROB A BANK!
PFFT...

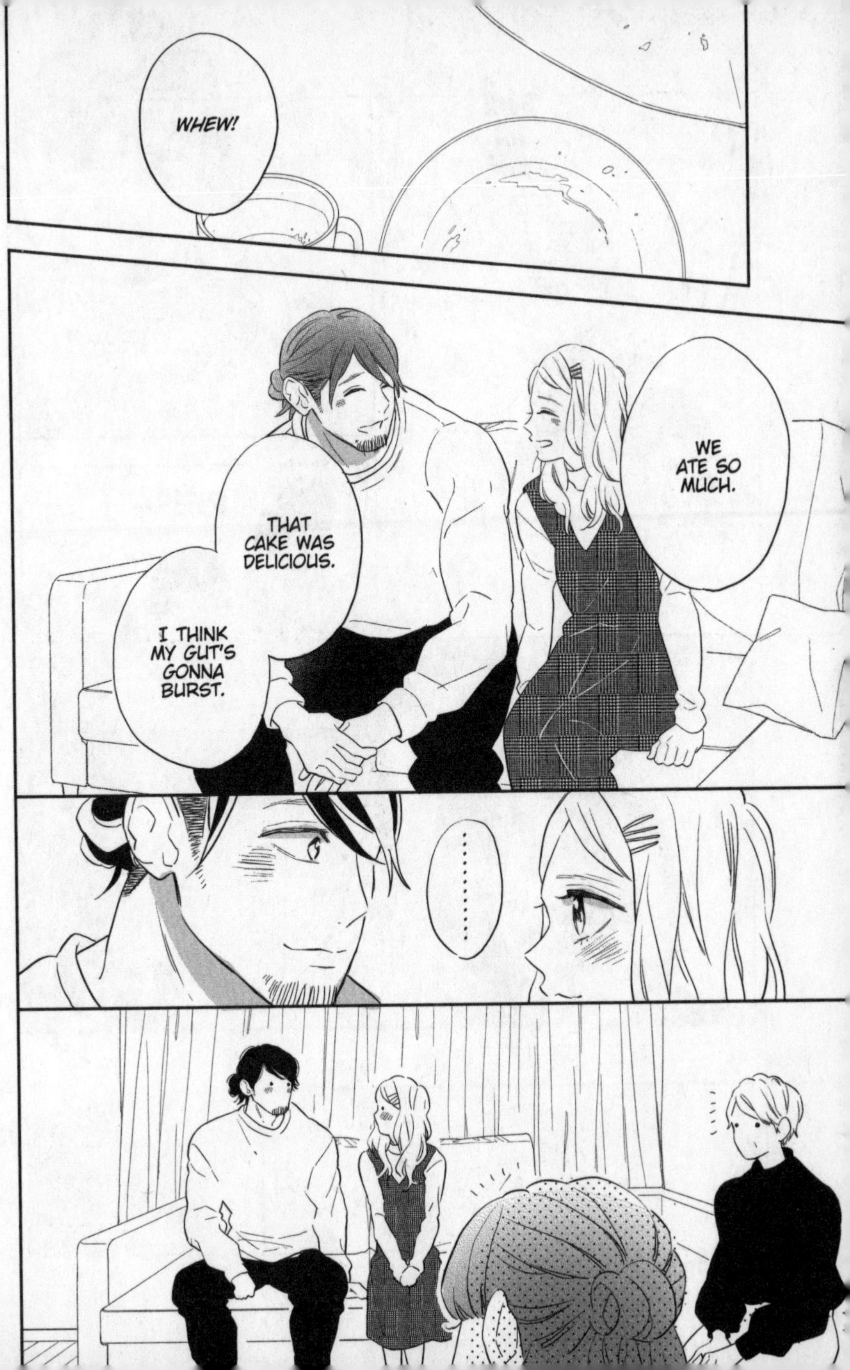
WHEW!
WE ATE SO MUCH.
THAT CAKE WAS DELICIOUS.
I THINK MY GUT'S GONNA BURST.
......

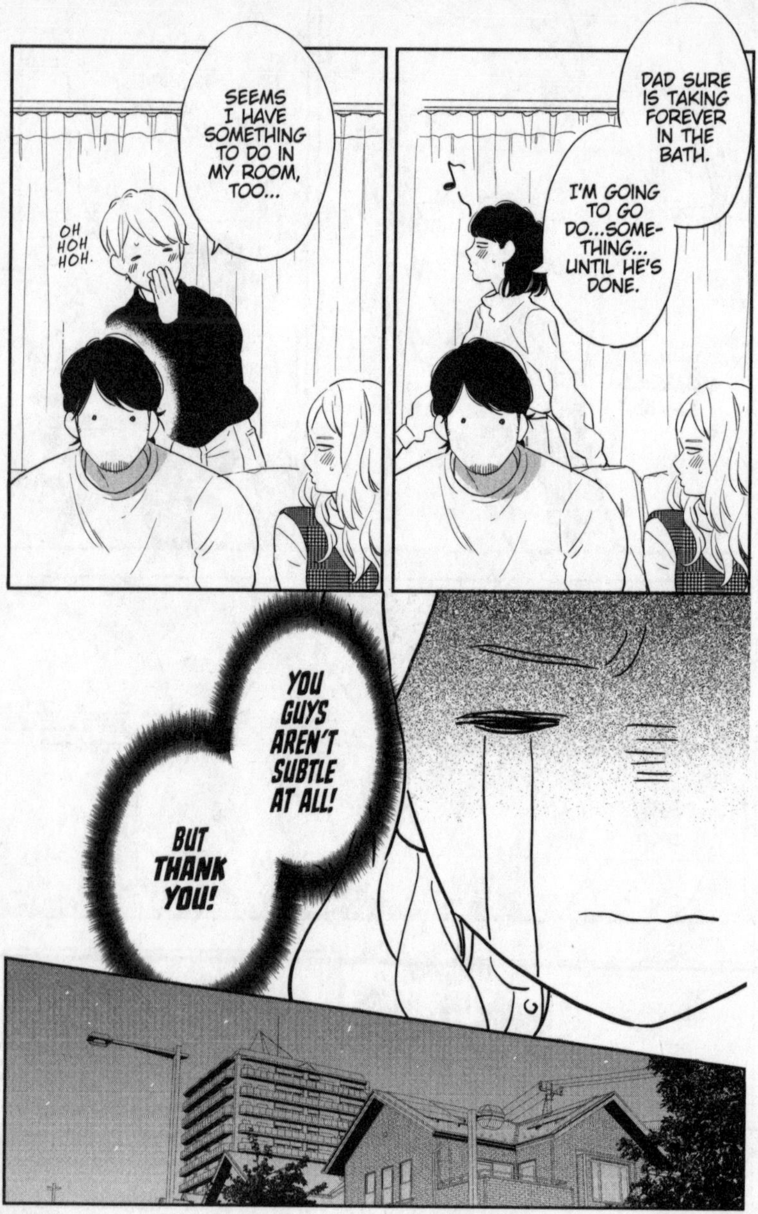
DAD SURE IS TAKING FOREVER IN THE BATH.
I'M GOING TO GO DO...SOME-THING... UNTIL HE'S DONE.
SEEMS I HAVE SOMETHING TO DO IN MY ROOM, TOO...
OH HOH HOH.
YOU GUYS AREN'T SUBTLE AT ALL!
BUT THANK YOU!

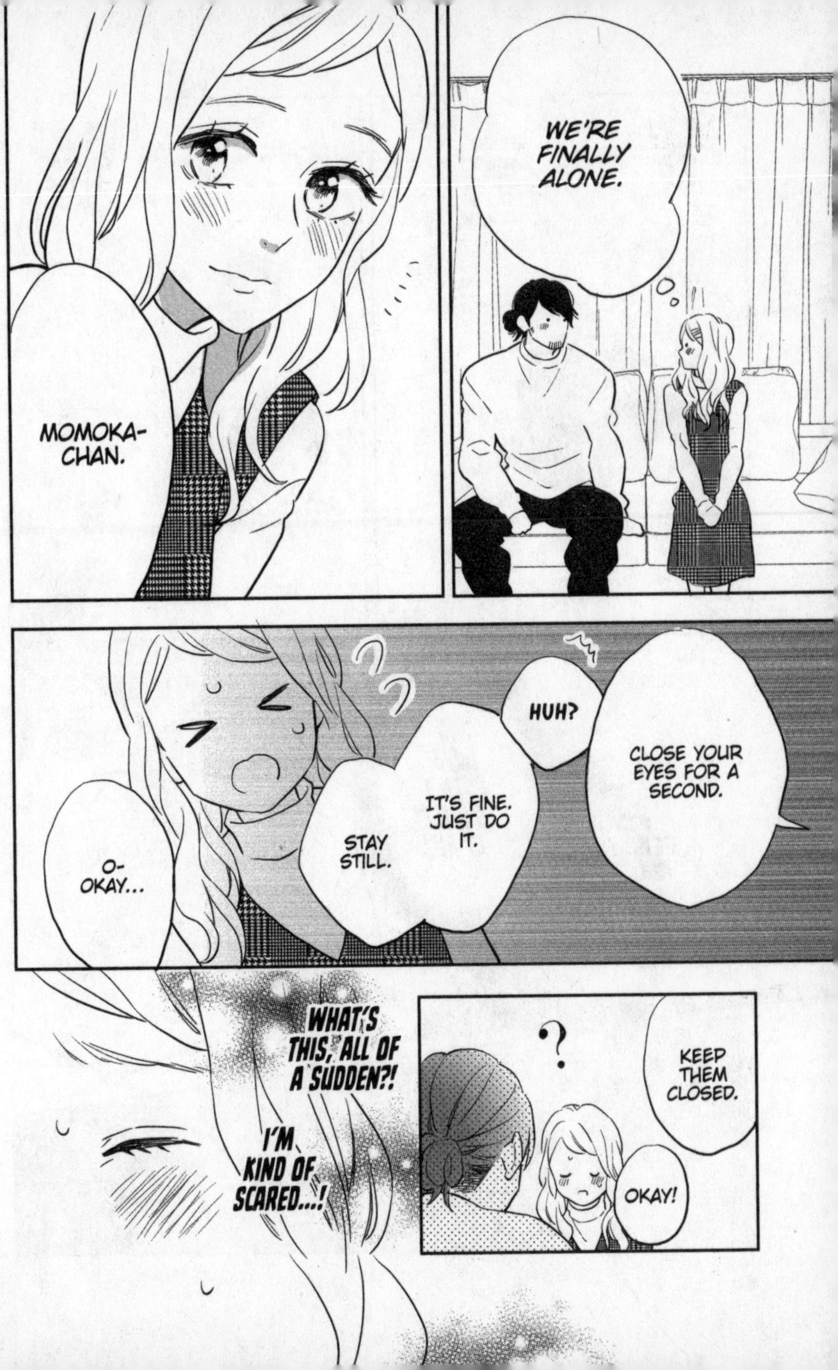
WE'RE FINALLY ALONE.
MOMOKA-CHAN.
CLOSE YOUR EYES FOR A SECOND.
HUH?
IT'S FINE. JUST DO IT.
STAY STILL.
O-OKAY...
KEEP THEM CLOSED.
OKAY!
WHAT'S THIS, ALL OF A SUDDEN?!
I'M KIND OF SCARED...!

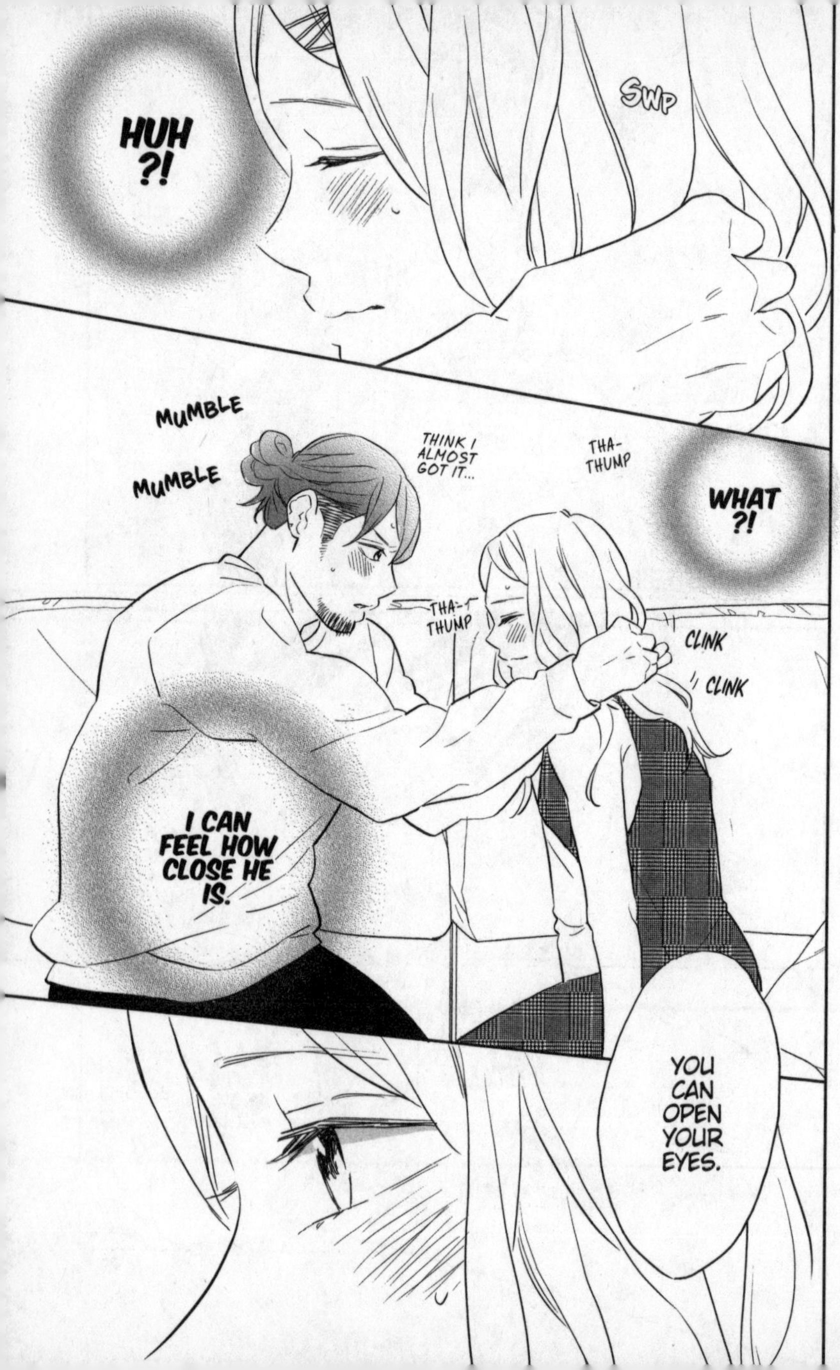
SWP
HUH?!
WHAT?!
THA-THUMP
THINK I ALMOST GOT IT...
MUMBLE
MUMBLE
CLINK
CLINK
THA-THUMP
I CAN FEEL HOW CLOSE HE IS.
YOU CAN OPEN YOUR EYES.

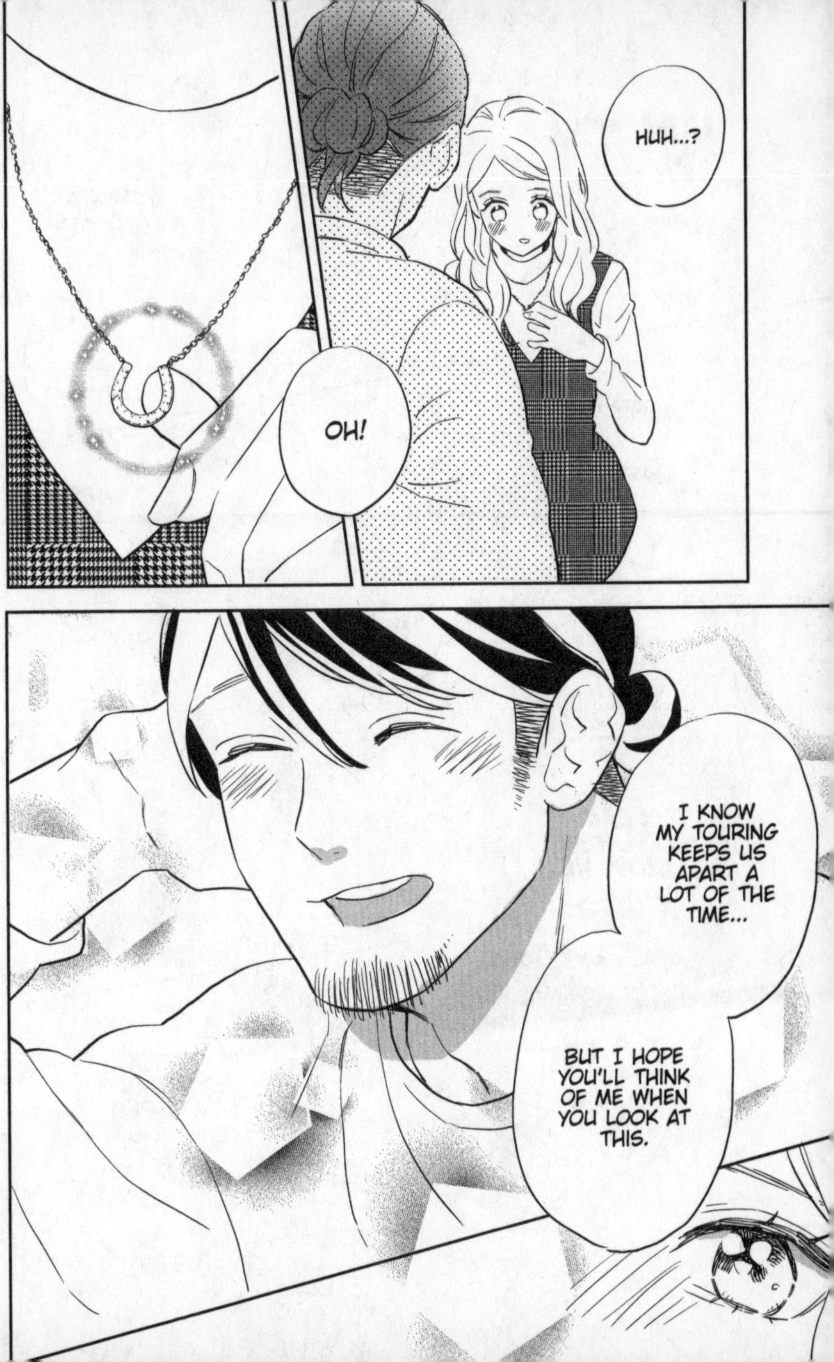
HUH...?
OH!
I KNOW MY TOURING KEEPS US APART A LOT OF THE TIME...
BUT I HOPE YOU'LL THINK OF ME WHEN YOU LOOK AT THIS.

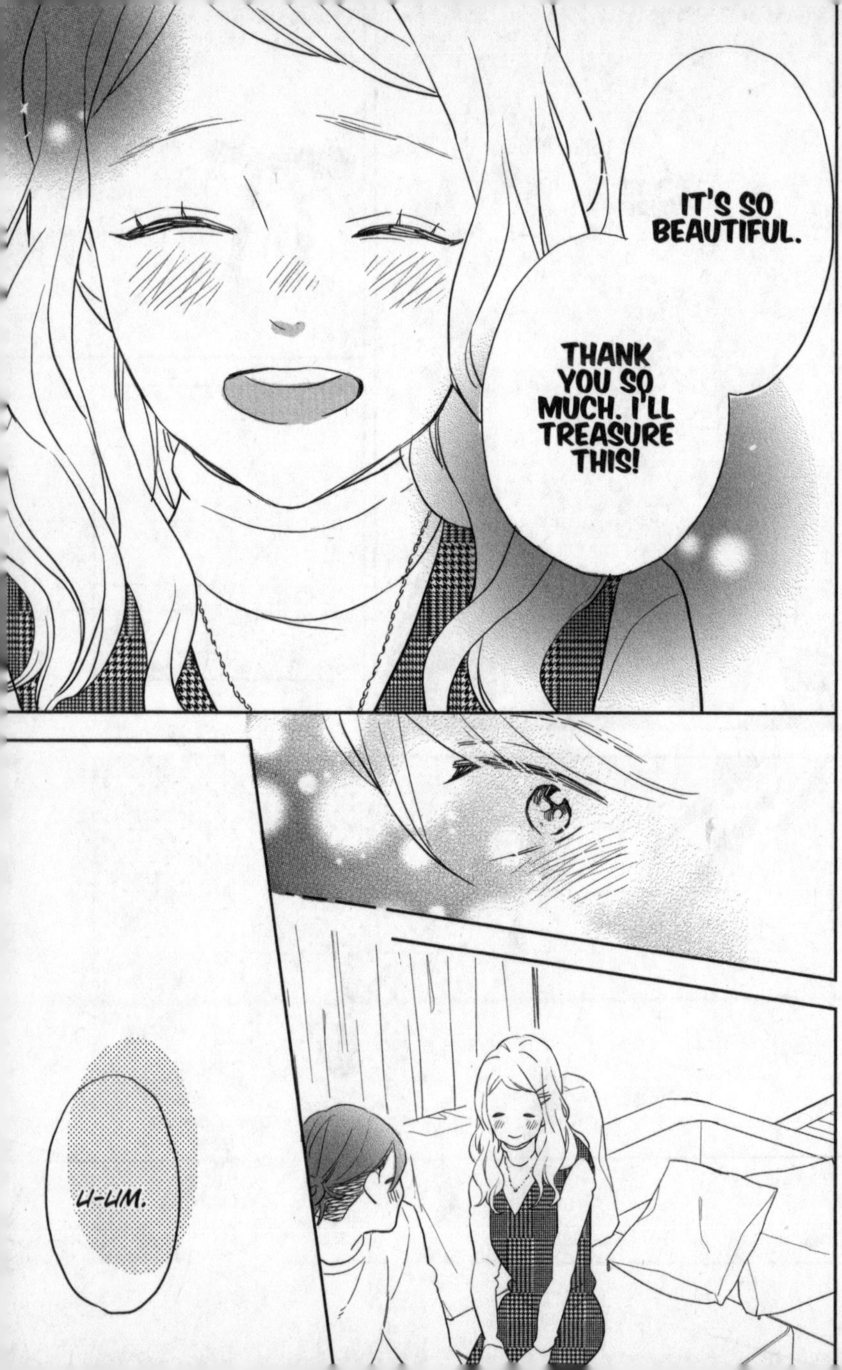
IT'S SO BEAUTIFUL.
THANK YOU SO MUCH. I'LL TREASURE THIS!
U-UM.

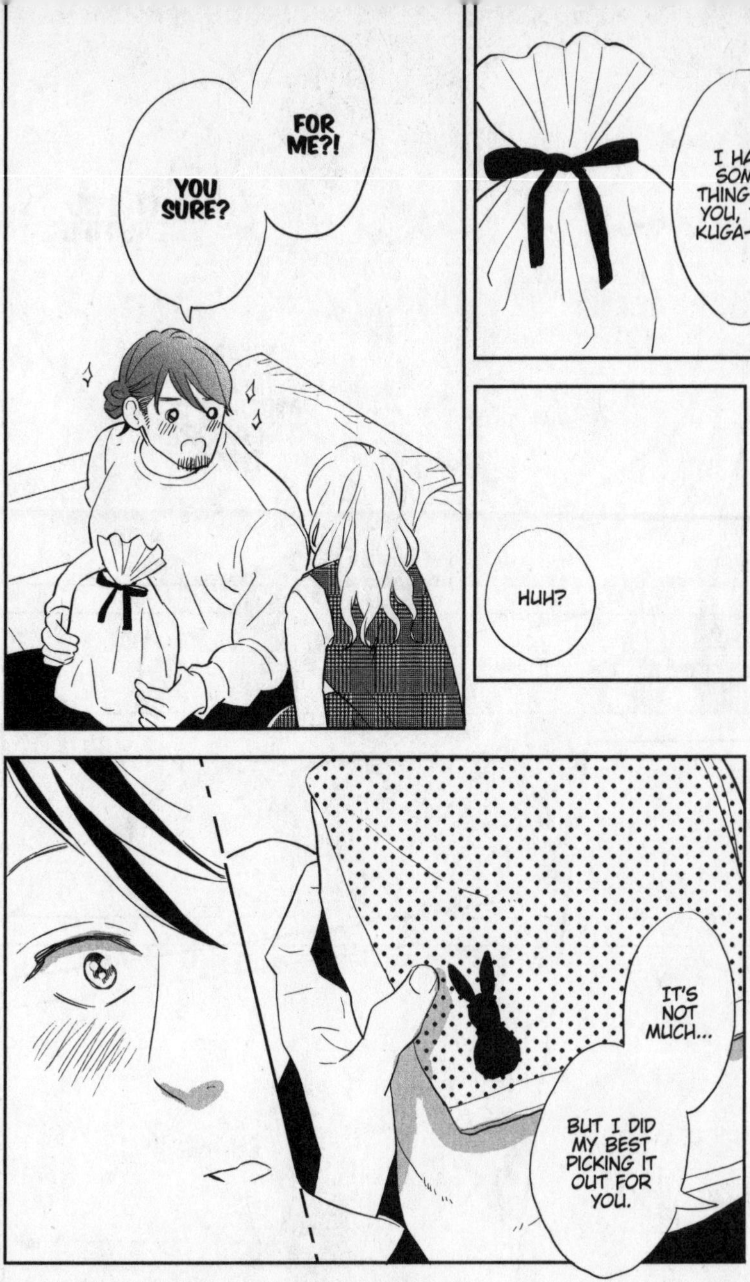
I HAVE SOME-THING FOR YOU, TOO, KUGA-SAN.
HUH?
FOR ME?!
YOU SURE?
IT'S NOT MUCH...
BUT I DID MY BEST PICKING IT OUT FOR YOU.

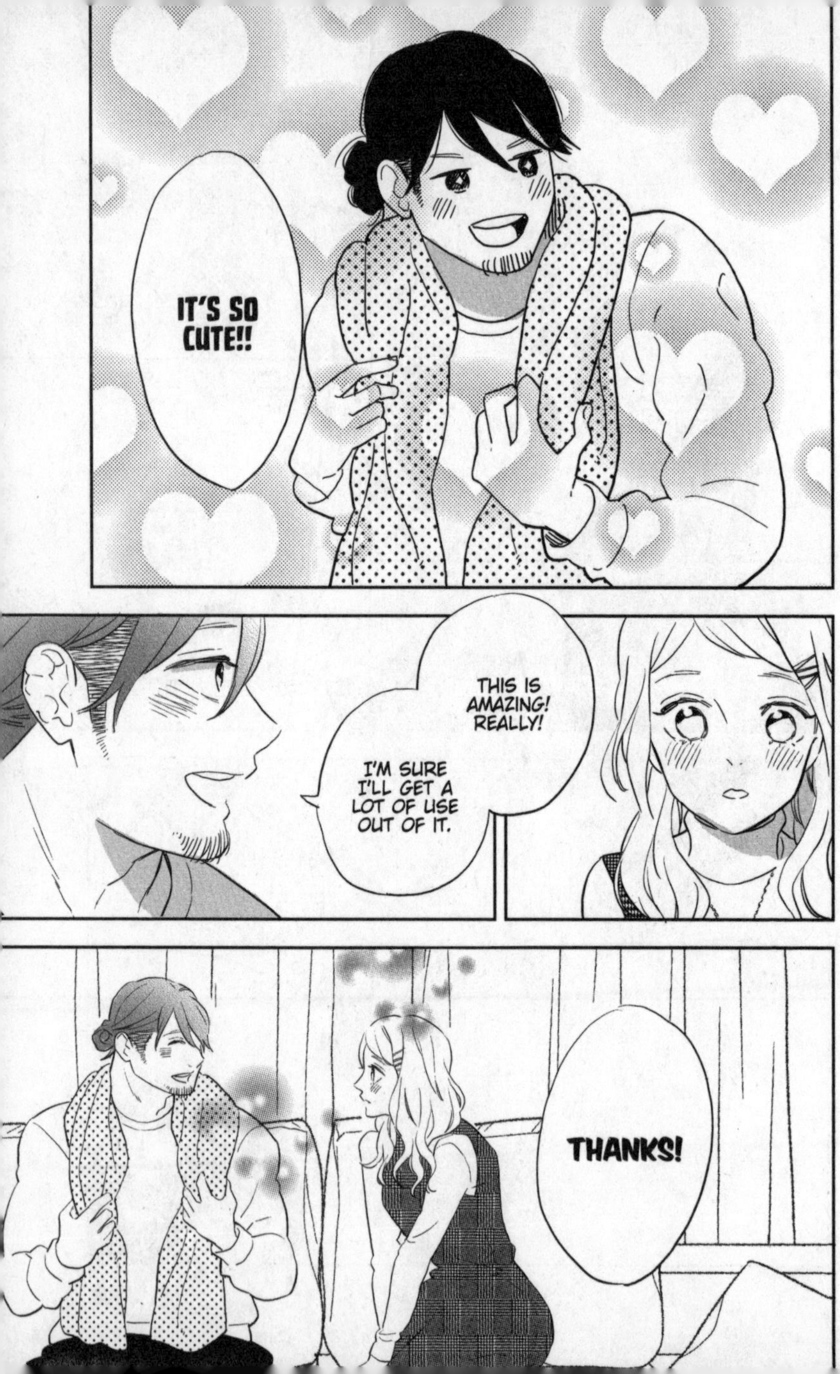
IT'S SO CUTE!!
THIS IS AMAZING! REALLY!
I'M SURE I'LL GET A LOT OF USE OUT OF IT.
THANKS!

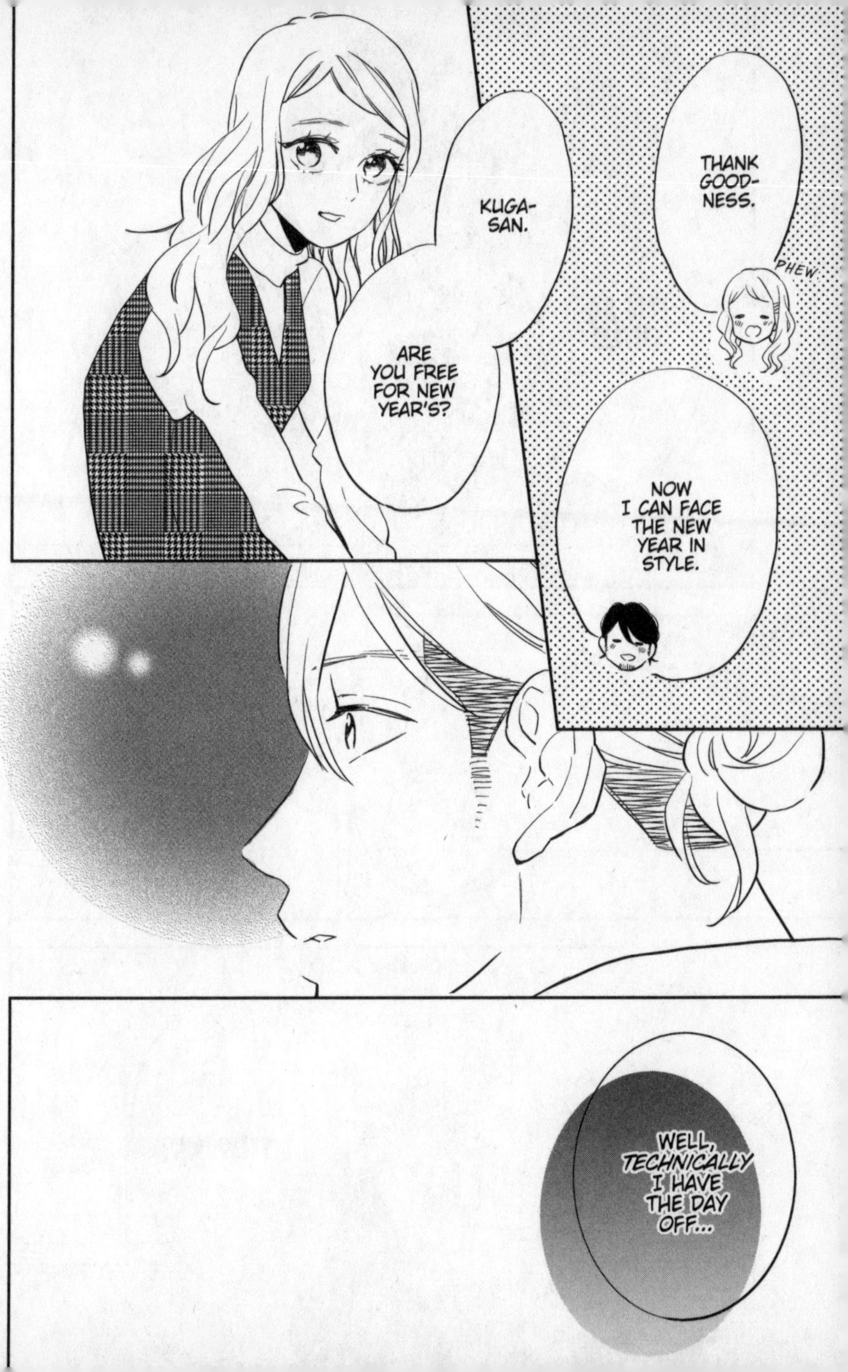
THANK GOOD-NESS.
PHEW
NOW I CAN FACE THE NEW YEAR IN STYLE.
KUGA-SAN.
ARE YOU FREE FOR NEW YEAR'S?
WELL, TECHNICALLY I HAVE THE DAY OFF...

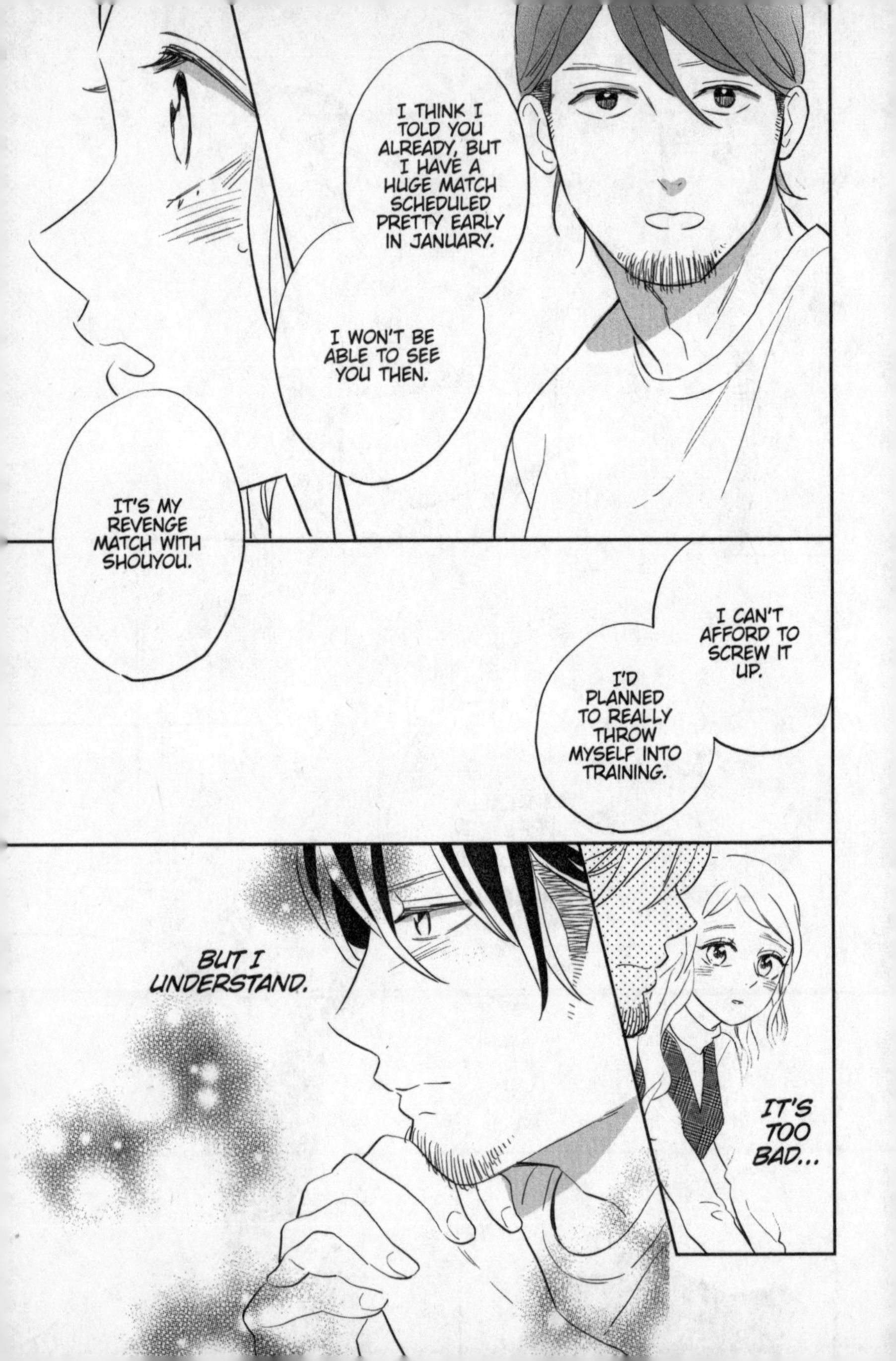

I THINK I TOLD YOU ALREADY, BUT I HAVE A HUGE MATCH SCHEDULED PRETTY EARLY IN JANUARY.
I WON'T BE ABLE TO SEE YOU THEN.
IT'S MY REVENGE MATCH WITH SHOUYOU.
I CAN'T AFFORD TO SCREW IT UP.
I'D PLANNED TO REALLY THROW MYSELF INTO TRAINING.
IT'S TOO BAD...
BUT I UNDERSTAND.

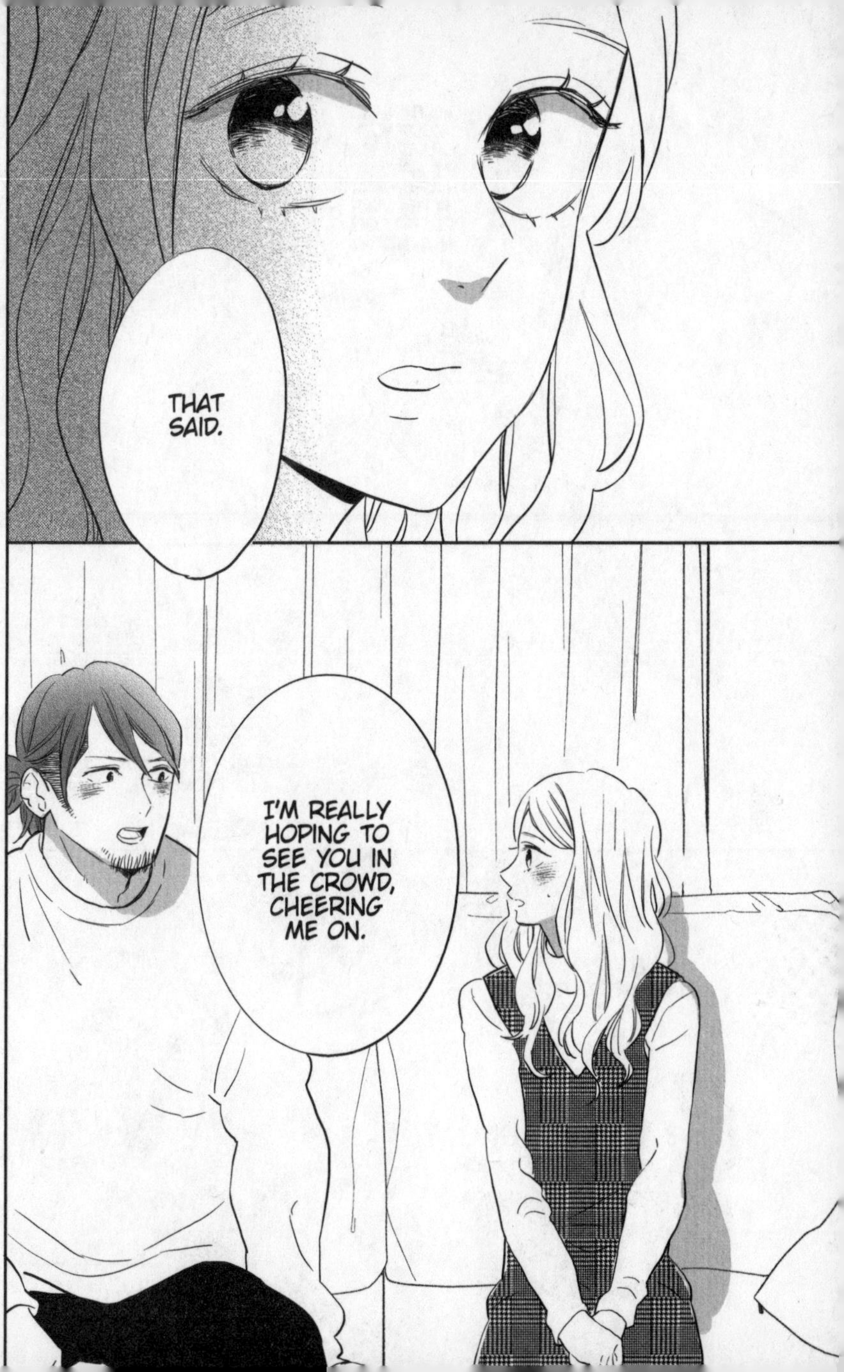
THAT SAID.
I'M REALLY HOPING TO SEE YOU IN THE CROWD, CHEERING ME ON.

Cutie and the BEAST

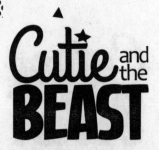

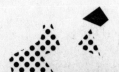

Cutie and the BEAST

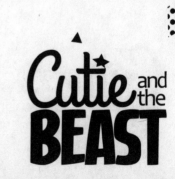

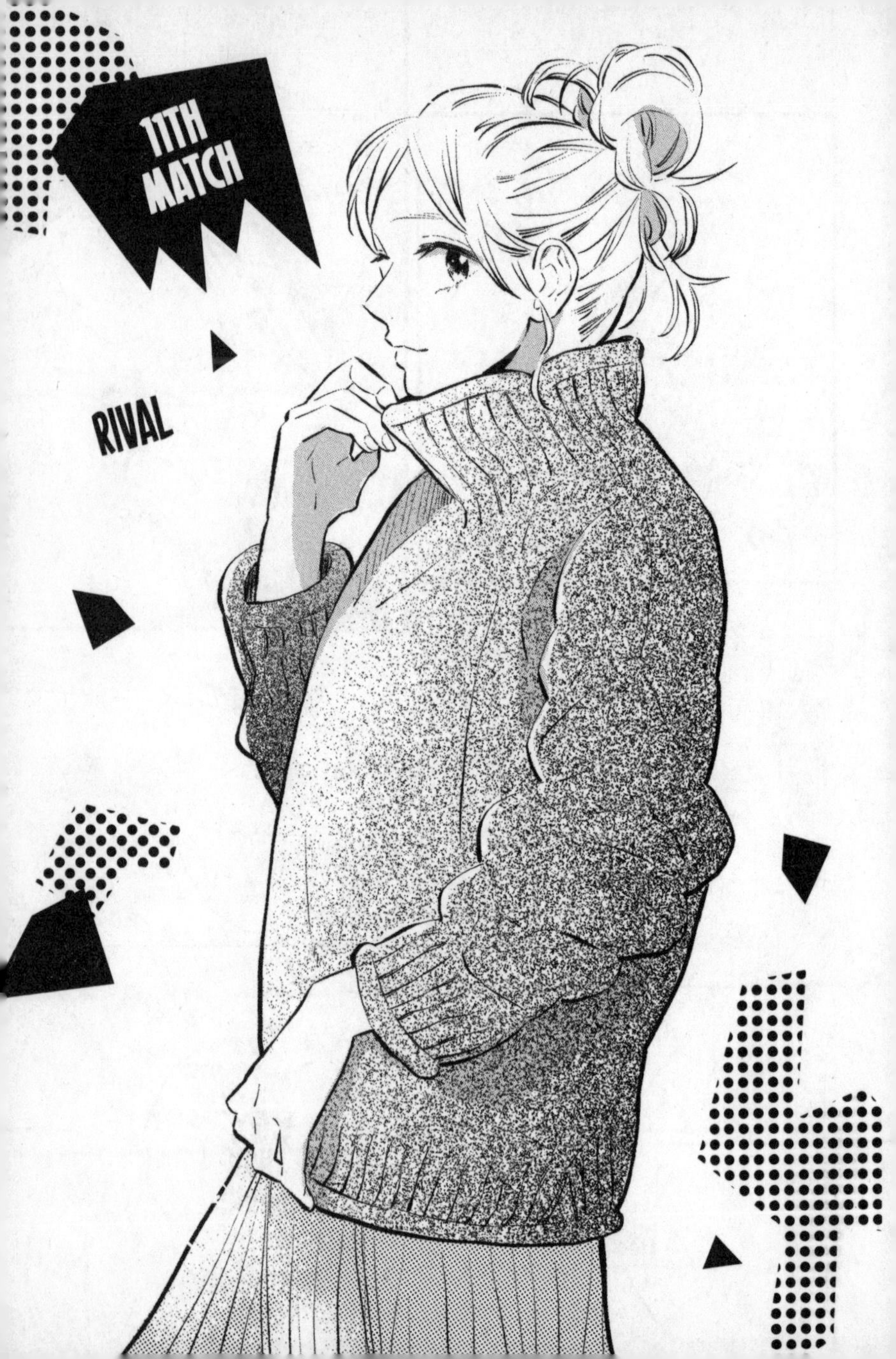
11TH
MATCH
RIVAL

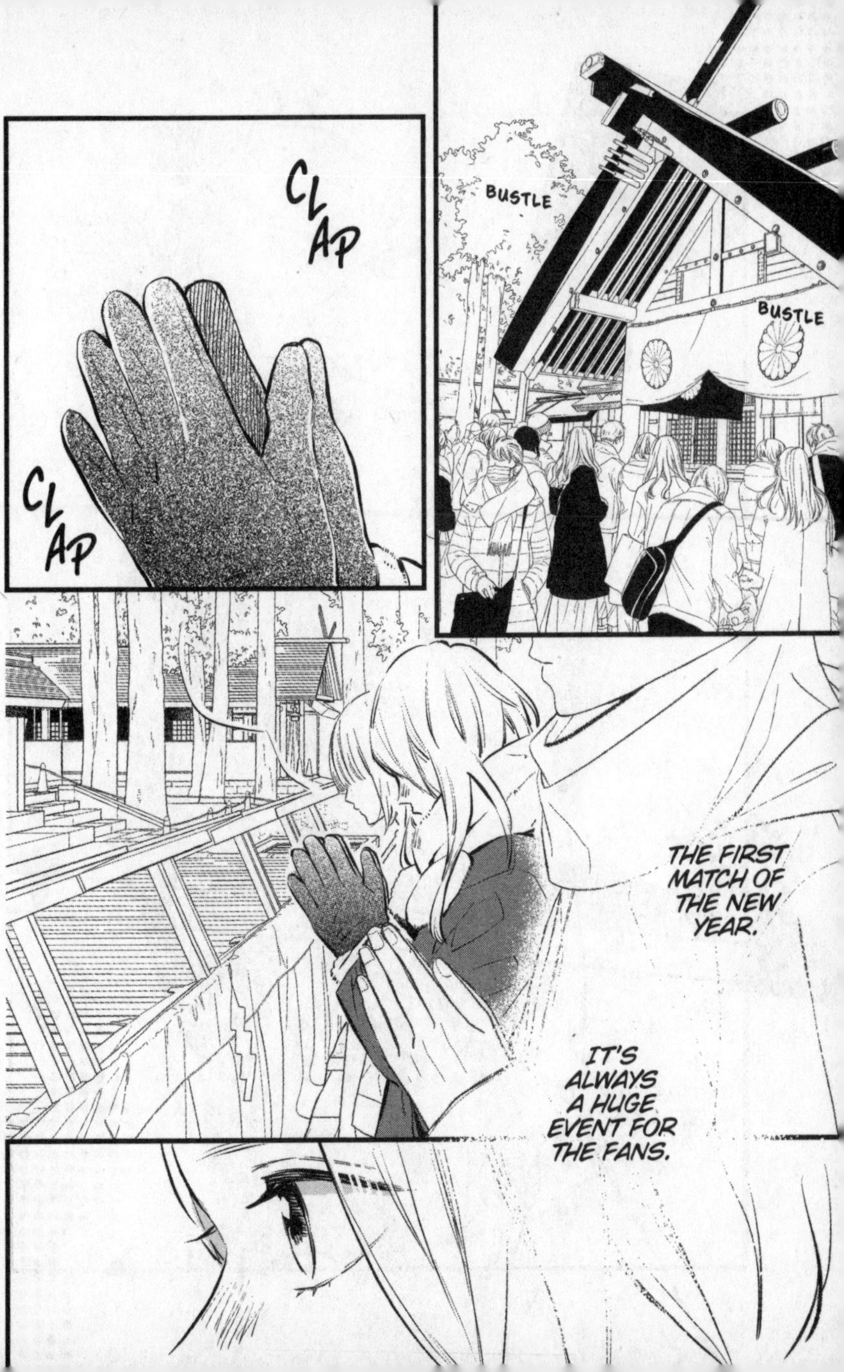
BUSTLE
BUSTLE
CLAP
CLAP
THE FIRST MATCH OF THE NEW YEAR.
IT'S ALWAYS A HUGE EVENT FOR THE FANS.

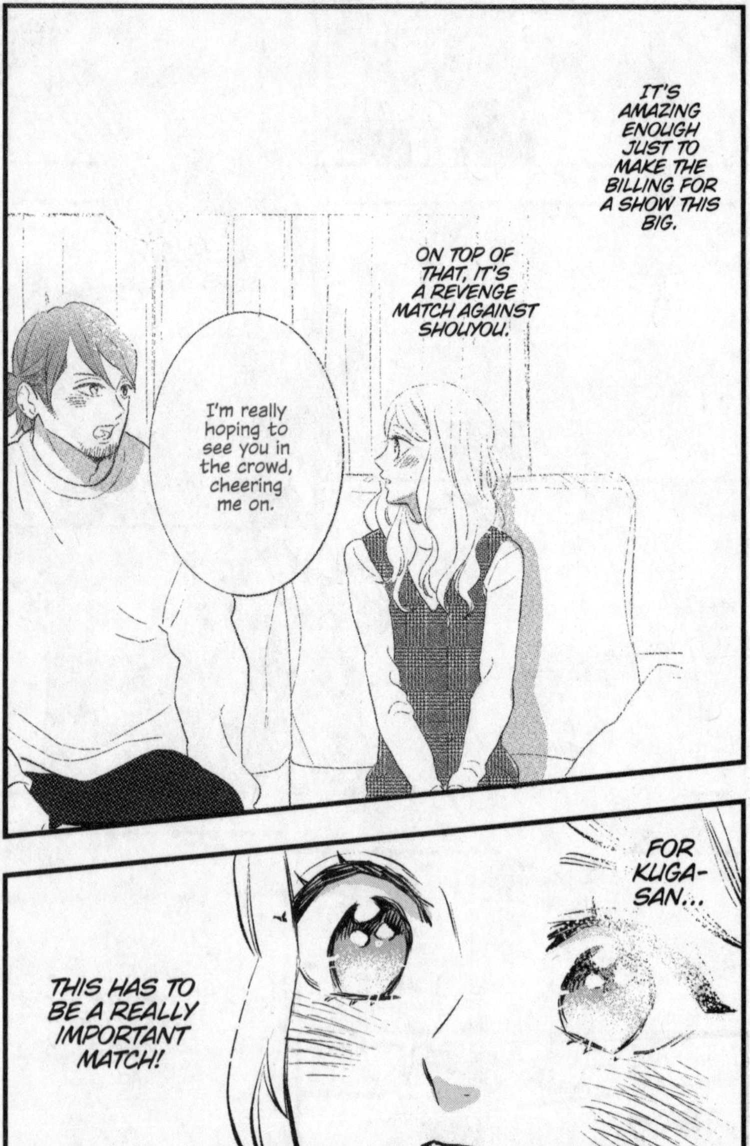
IT'S AMAZING ENOUGH JUST TO MAKE THE BILLING FOR A SHOW THIS BIG.
ON TOP OF THAT, IT'S A REVENGE MATCH AGAINST SHOUYOU.
I'm really hoping to see you in the crowd, cheering me on.
FOR KUGA-SAN...
THIS HAS TO BE A REALLY IMPORTANT MATCH!

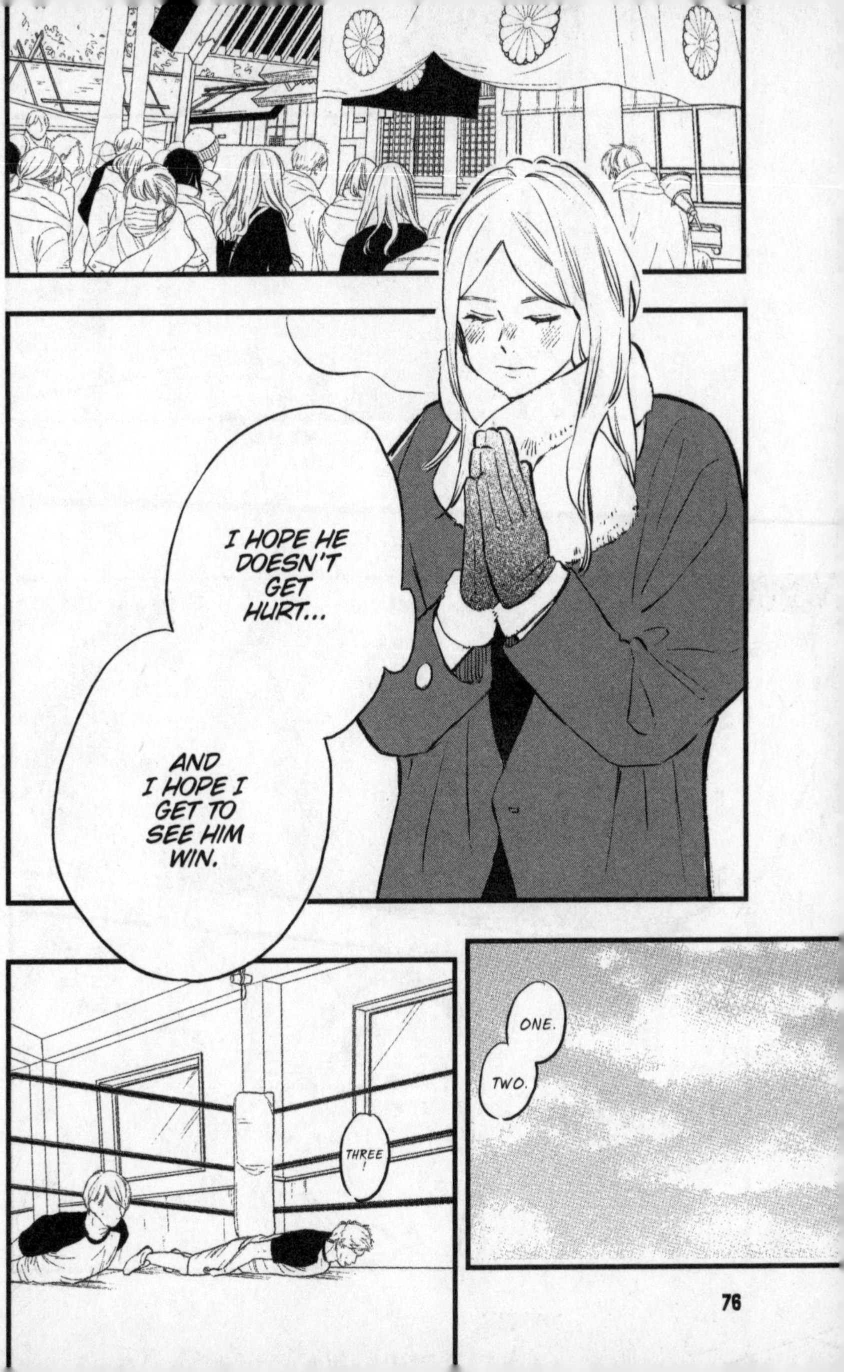
I HOPE HE DOESN'T GET HURT...
AND I HOPE I GET TO SEE HIM WIN.
ONE.
TWO.
THREE!

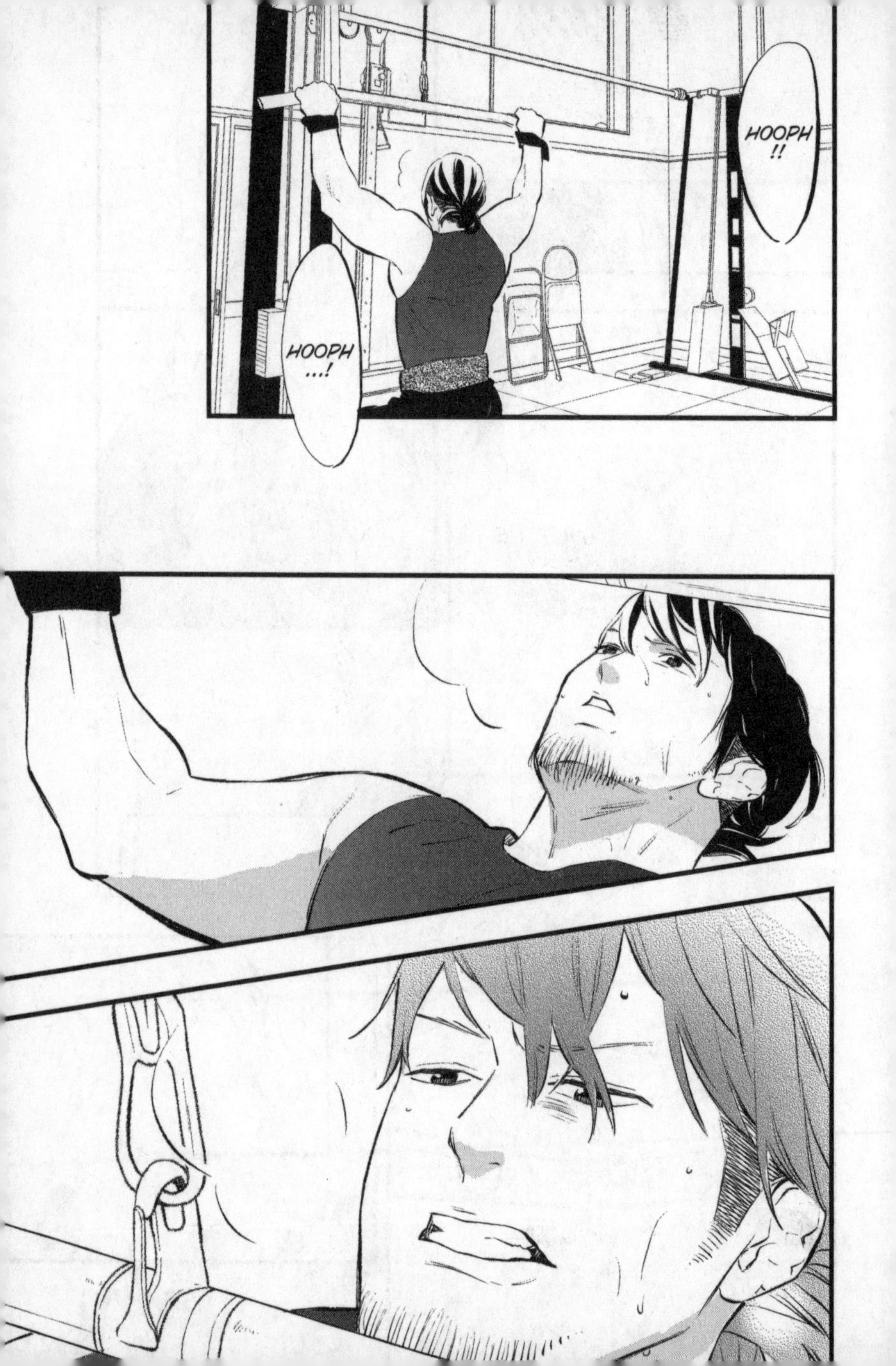
HOOPH !!
HOOPH ...!

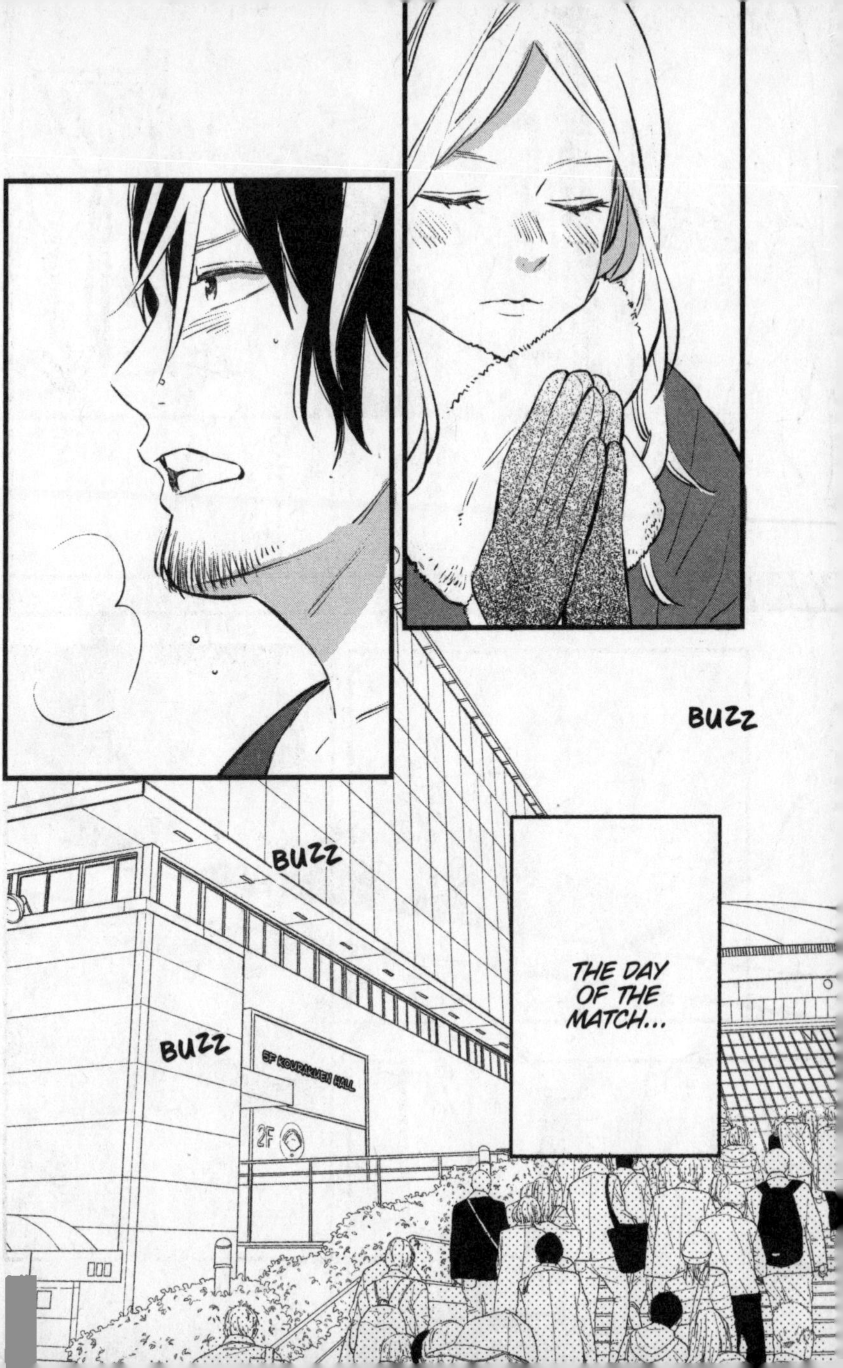
BUZZ
THE DAY OF THE MATCH...
BUZZ
BUZZ
5F KOURAKUEN HALL
2F

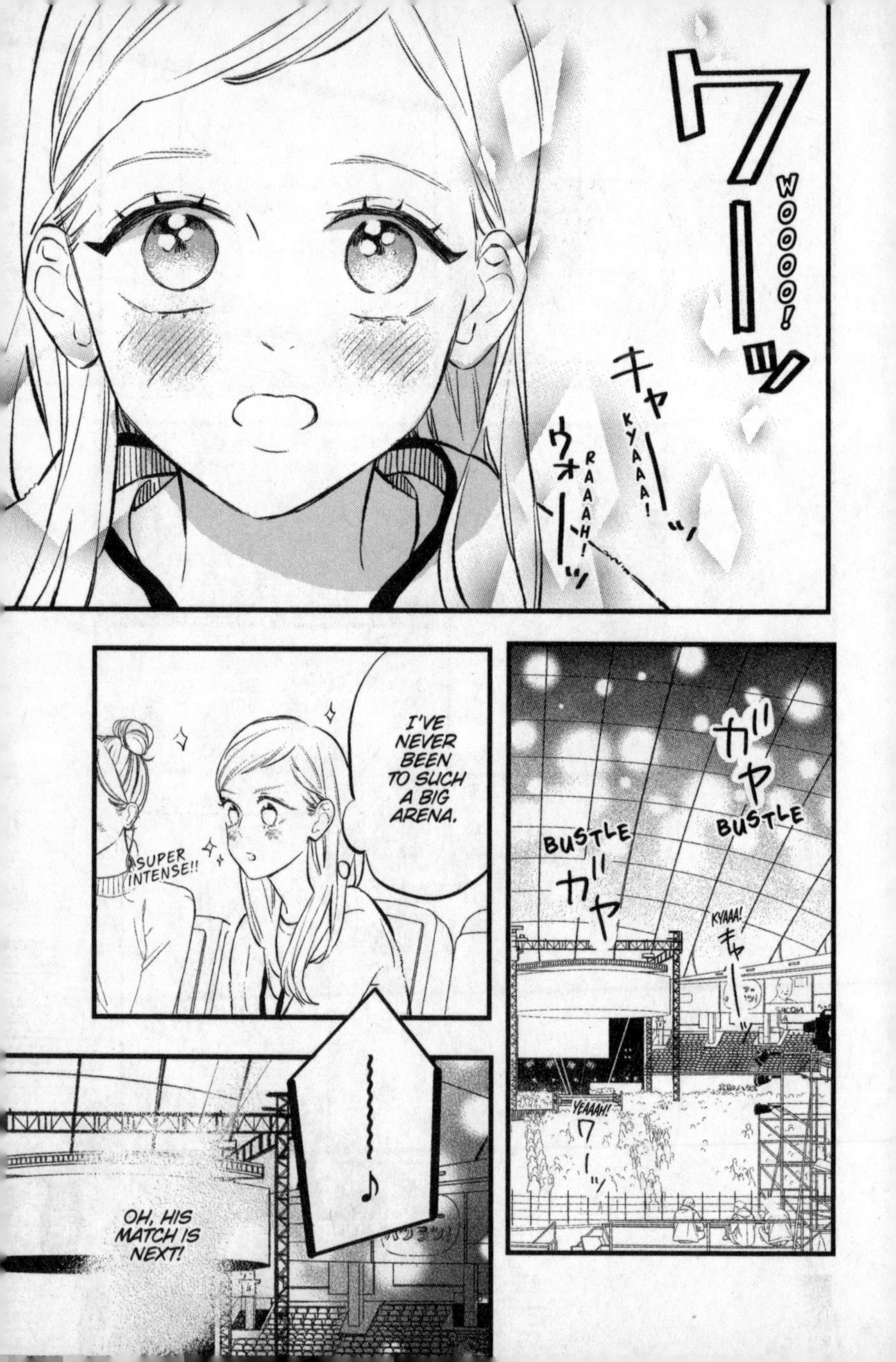

ウーッ
WOOOOO!
キャーッ
KYAAAA!
ウォーッ
RAAAH!
ガヤ
BUSTLE
ガヤ
BUSTLE
KYAAA!
キャーッ
YEAAAH!
ワーッ
I'VE NEVER BEEN TO SUCH A BIG ARENA.
SUPER INTENSE!!
~~~~♪
OH, HIS MATCH IS NEXT!
~~~~

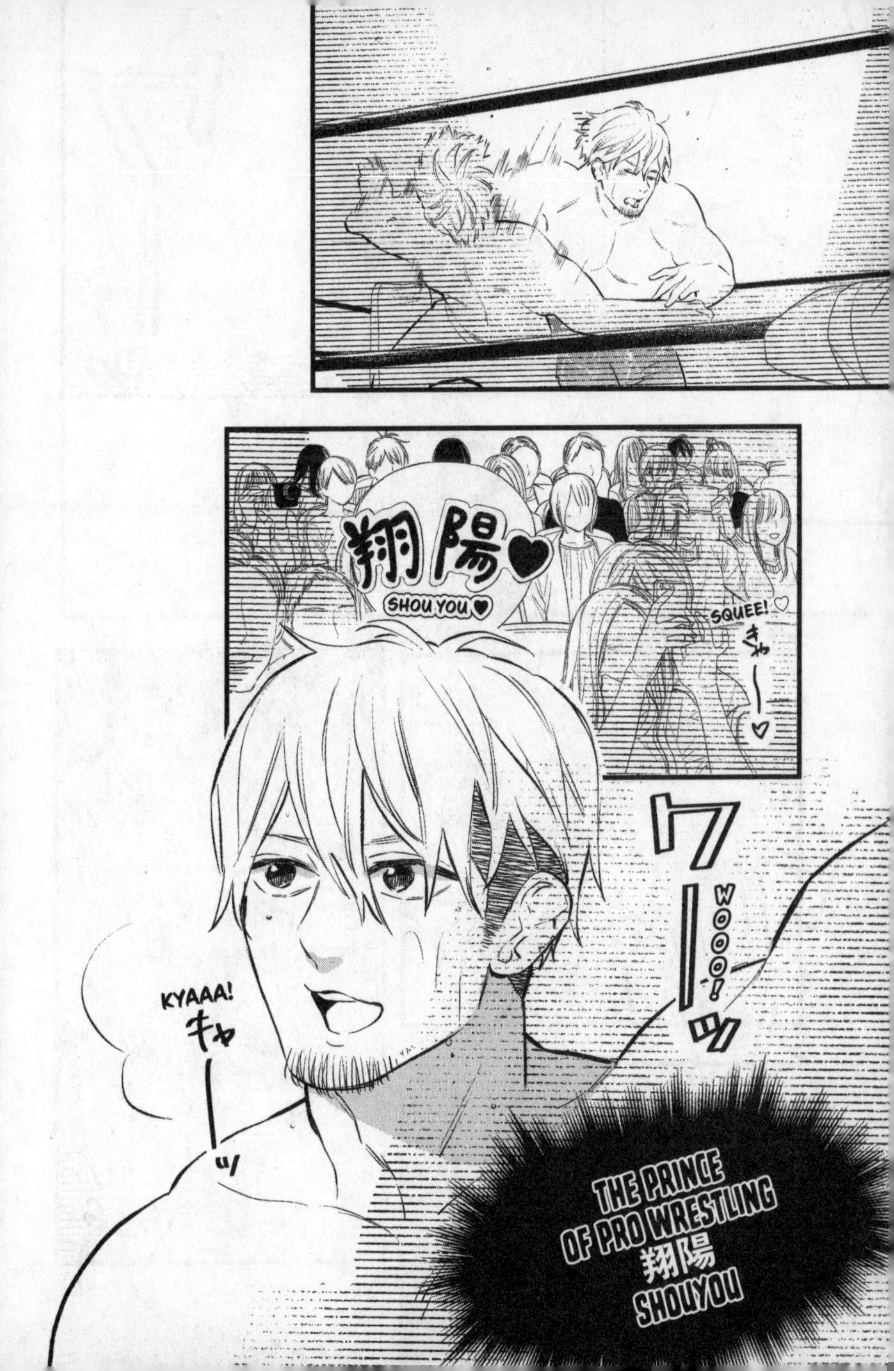
翔陽♥
SHOU YOU♥
SQUEE!♡
きゃ～♡
ワーッ
WOOOO!
KYAAA!
キャーッ
THE PRINCE OF PRO WRESTLING
翔陽
SHOUYOU

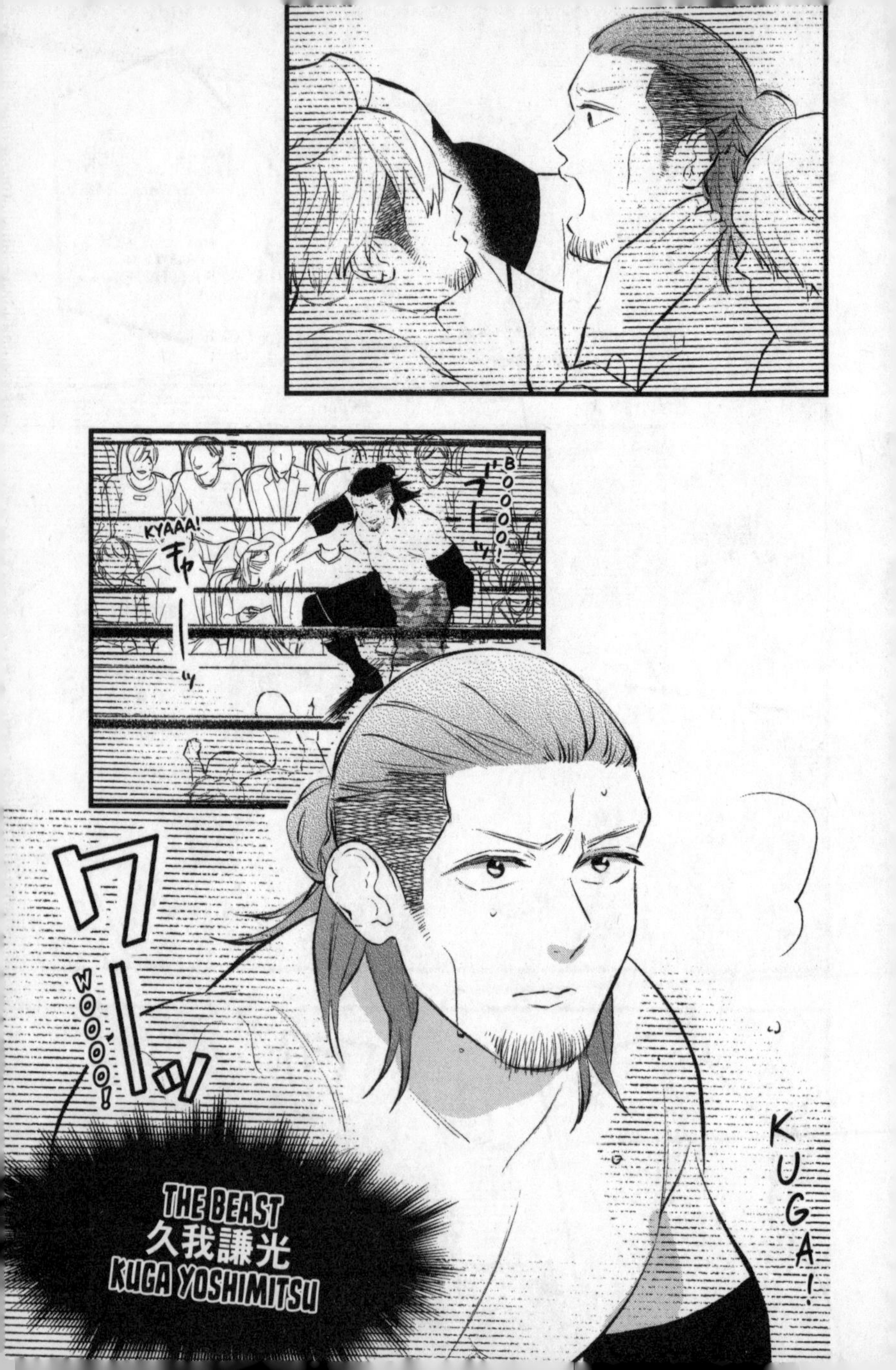
BOOOOO!
KYAAA!
WOOOOO!
KUGA!
THE BEAST
久我謙光
KUGA YOSHIMITSU

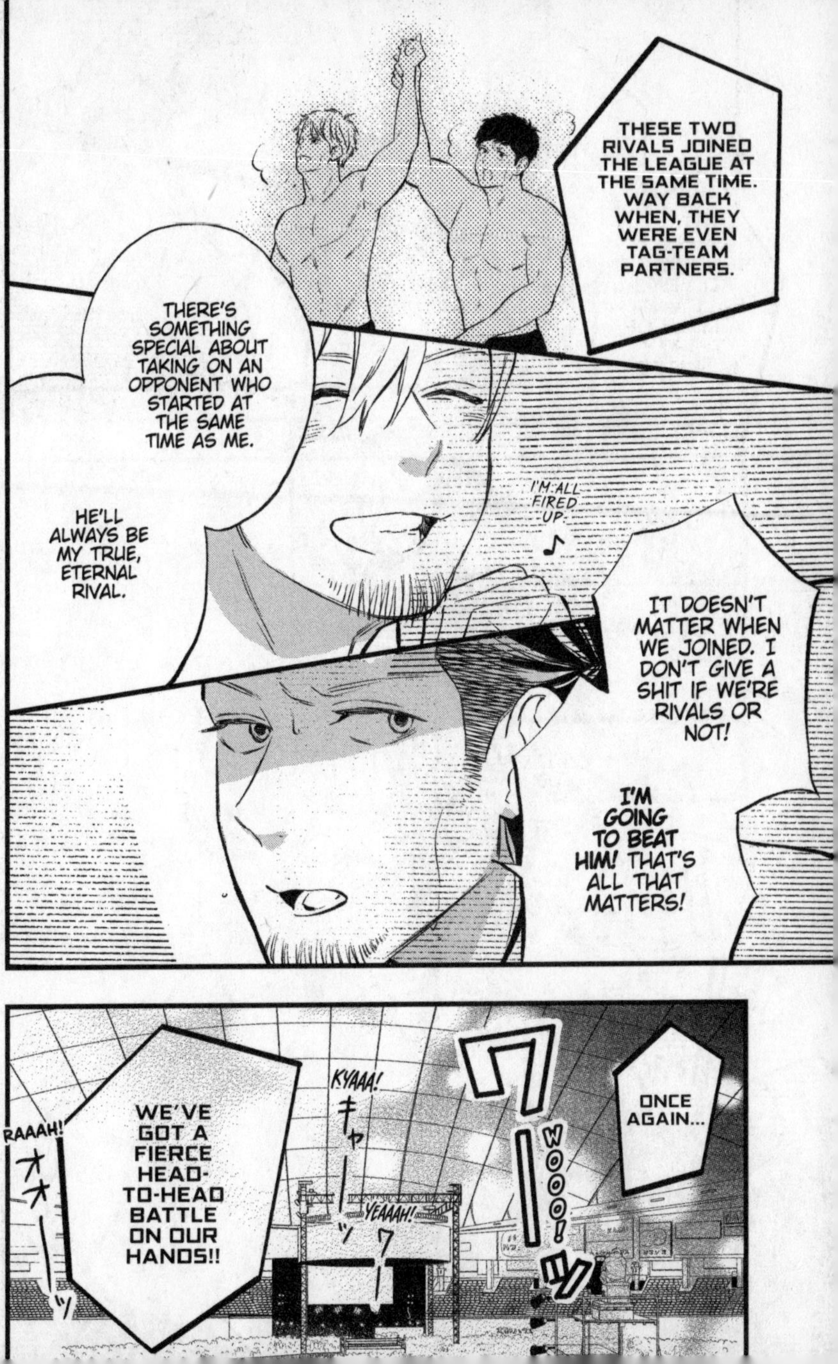
THESE TWO RIVALS JOINED THE LEAGUE AT THE SAME TIME. WAY BACK WHEN, THEY WERE EVEN TAG-TEAM PARTNERS.
THERE'S SOMETHING SPECIAL ABOUT TAKING ON AN OPPONENT WHO STARTED AT THE SAME TIME AS ME.
I'M ALL FIRED UP ♪
HE'LL ALWAYS BE MY TRUE, ETERNAL RIVAL.
IT DOESN'T MATTER WHEN WE JOINED. I DON'T GIVE A SHIT IF WE'RE RIVALS OR NOT!
I'M GOING TO BEAT HIM! THAT'S ALL THAT MATTERS!
ONCE AGAIN...
WOOOO!
ワーーッ
YEAAAH!
ワーー
KYAAA!
キャーーッ
WE'VE GOT A FIERCE HEAD-TO-HEAD BATTLE ON OUR HANDS!!
RAAAH!
オオーーッ

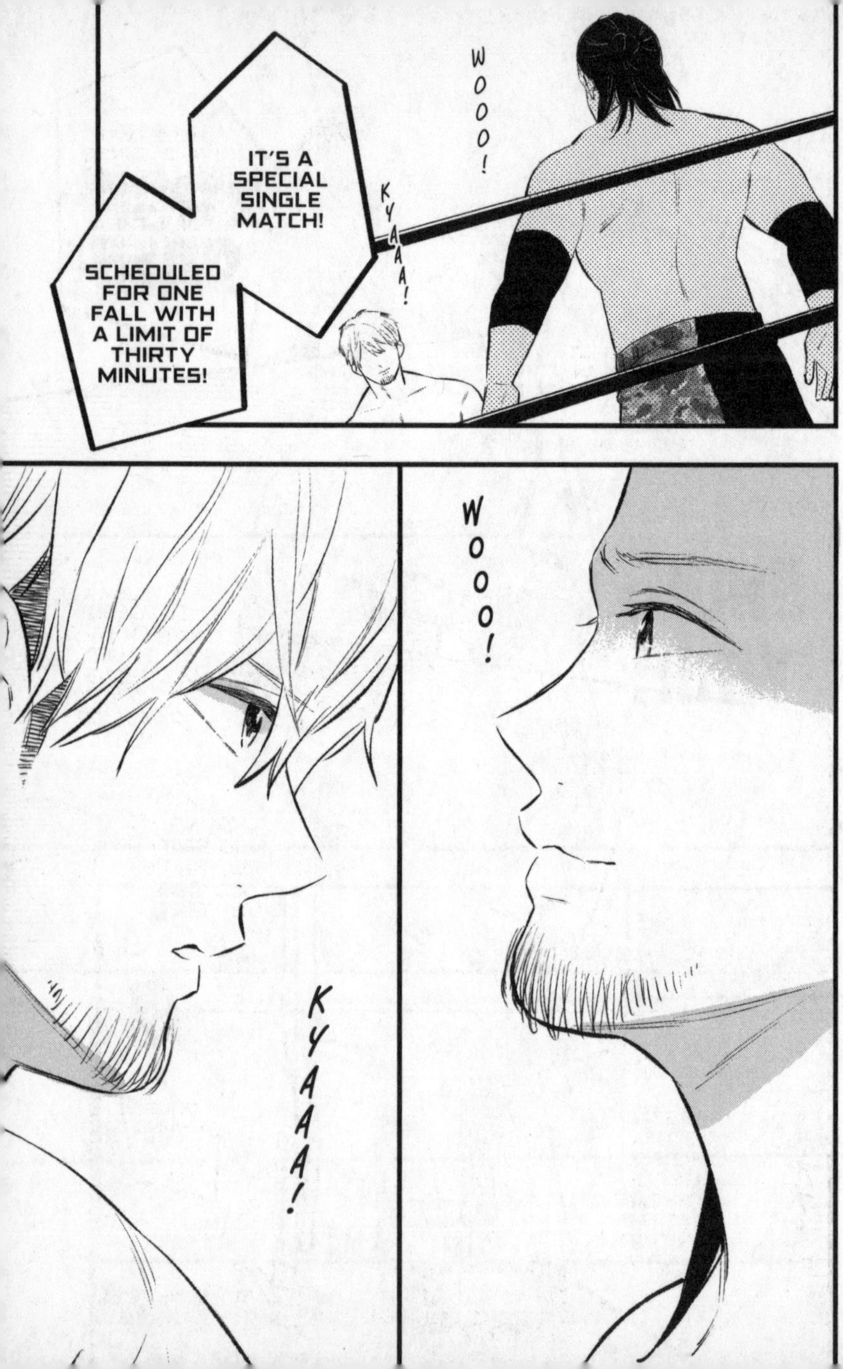
WOOO!
KYAAA!
IT'S A SPECIAL SINGLE MATCH!
SCHEDULED FOR ONE FALL WITH A LIMIT OF THIRTY MINUTES!
WOOO!
KYAAAA!

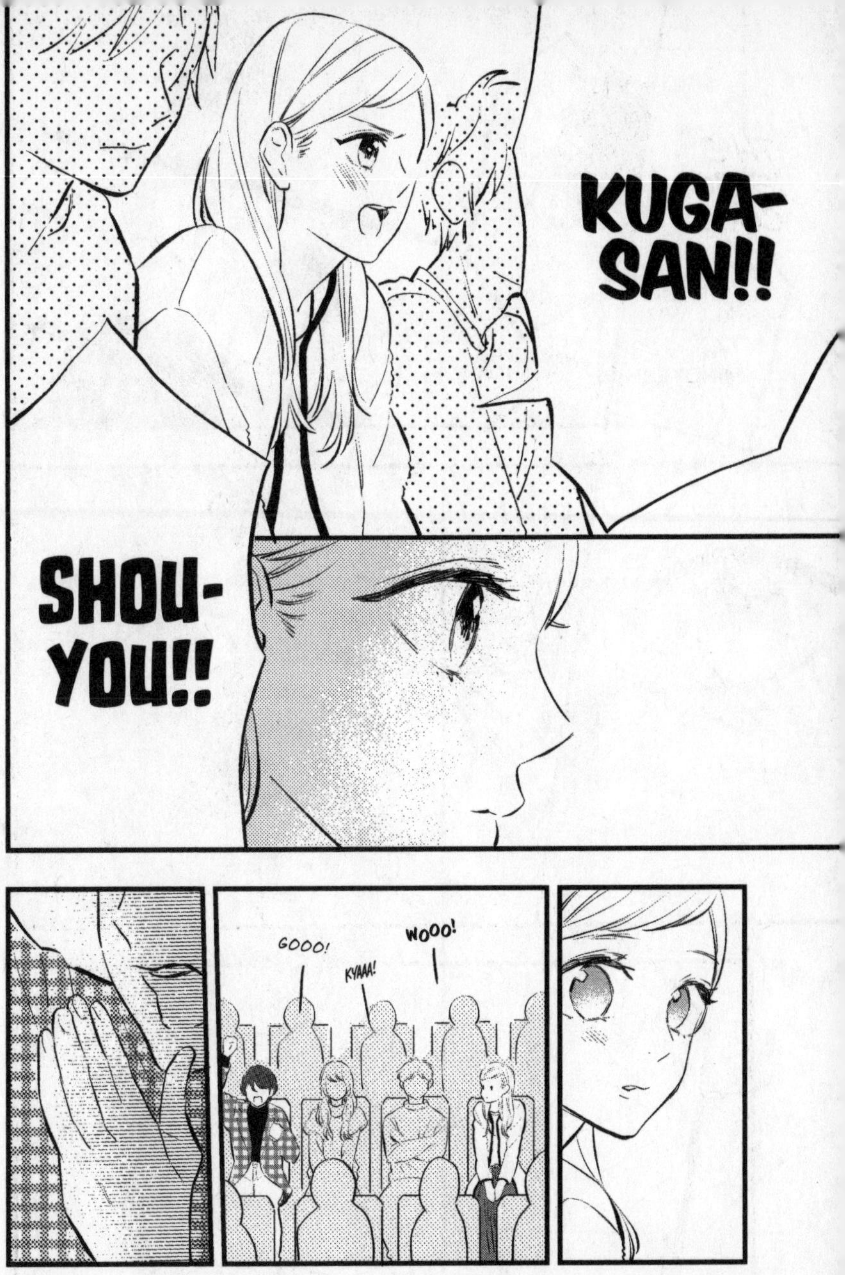
KUGA-SAN!!
SHOU-YOU!!
WOOO!
KYAAA!
GOOO!

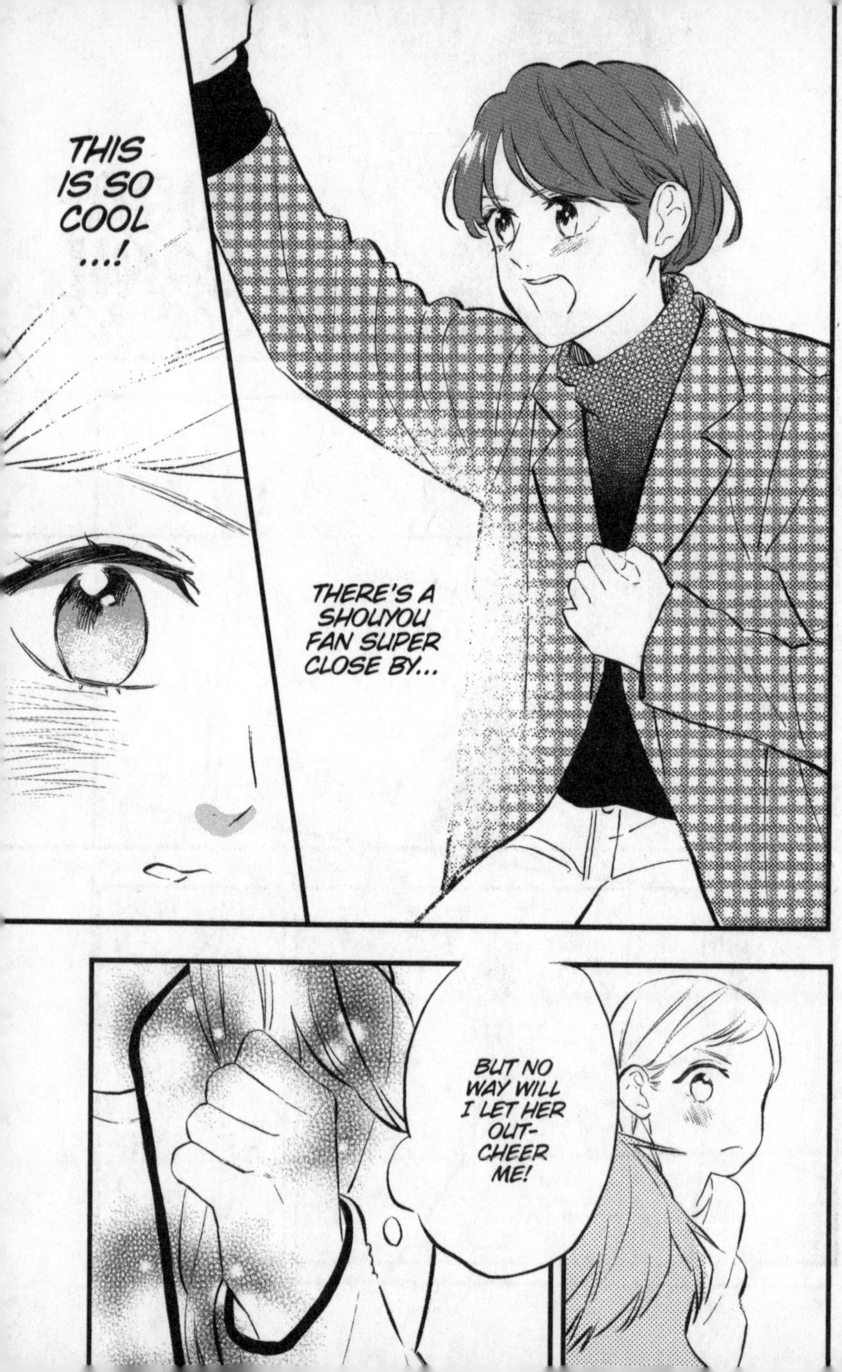
THIS IS SO COOL ...!
THERE'S A SHOUYOU FAN SUPER CLOSE BY...
BUT NO WAY WILL I LET HER OUT-CHEER ME!

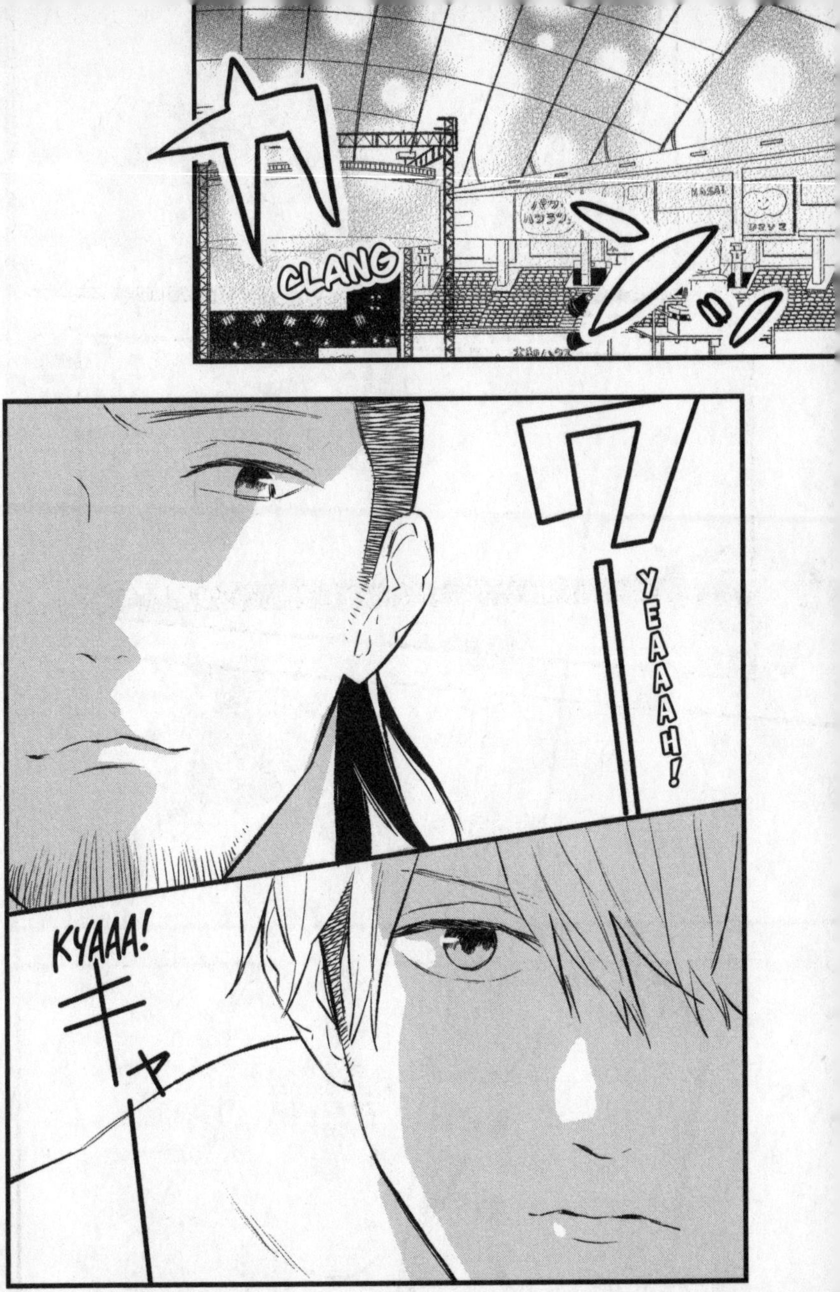
CLANG
YEAAAAH!
KYAAA!

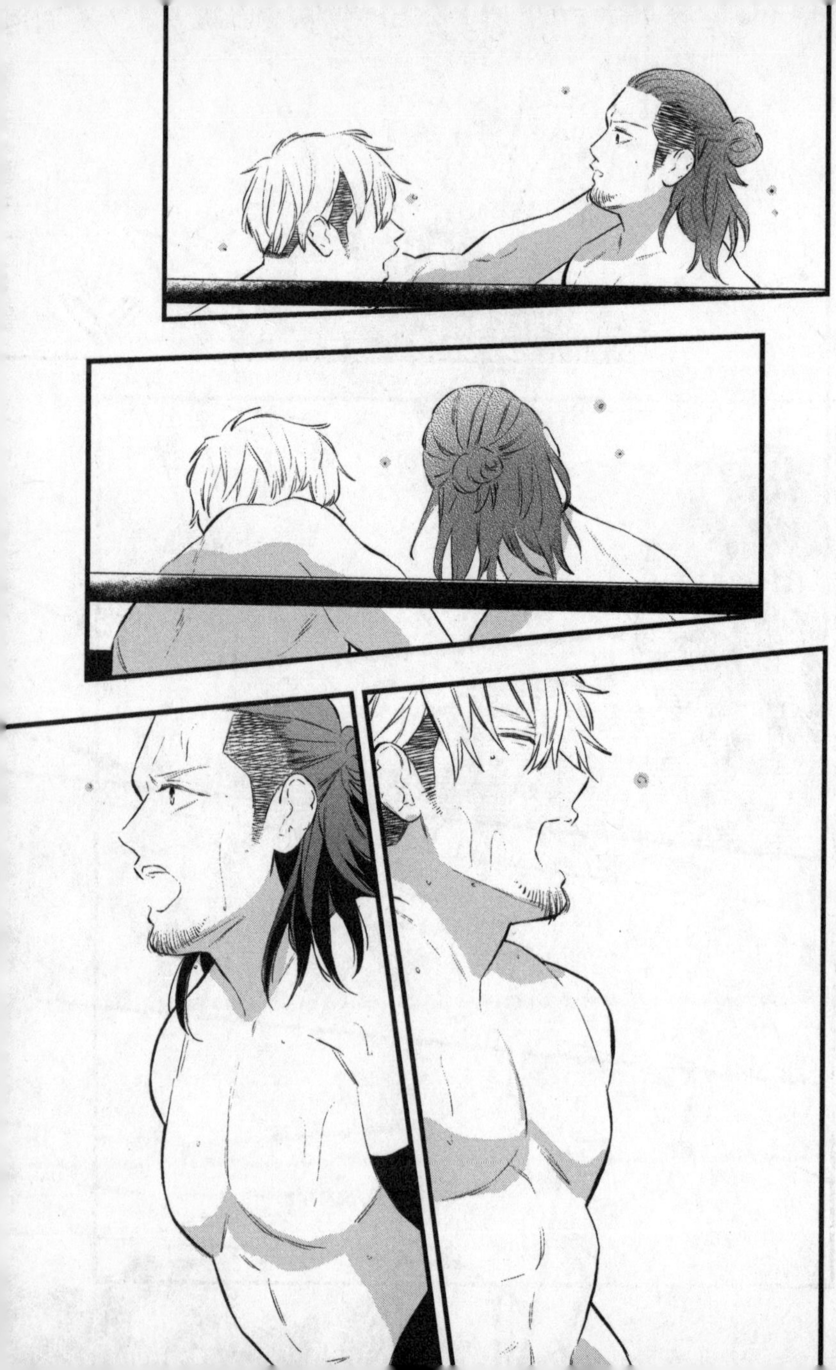

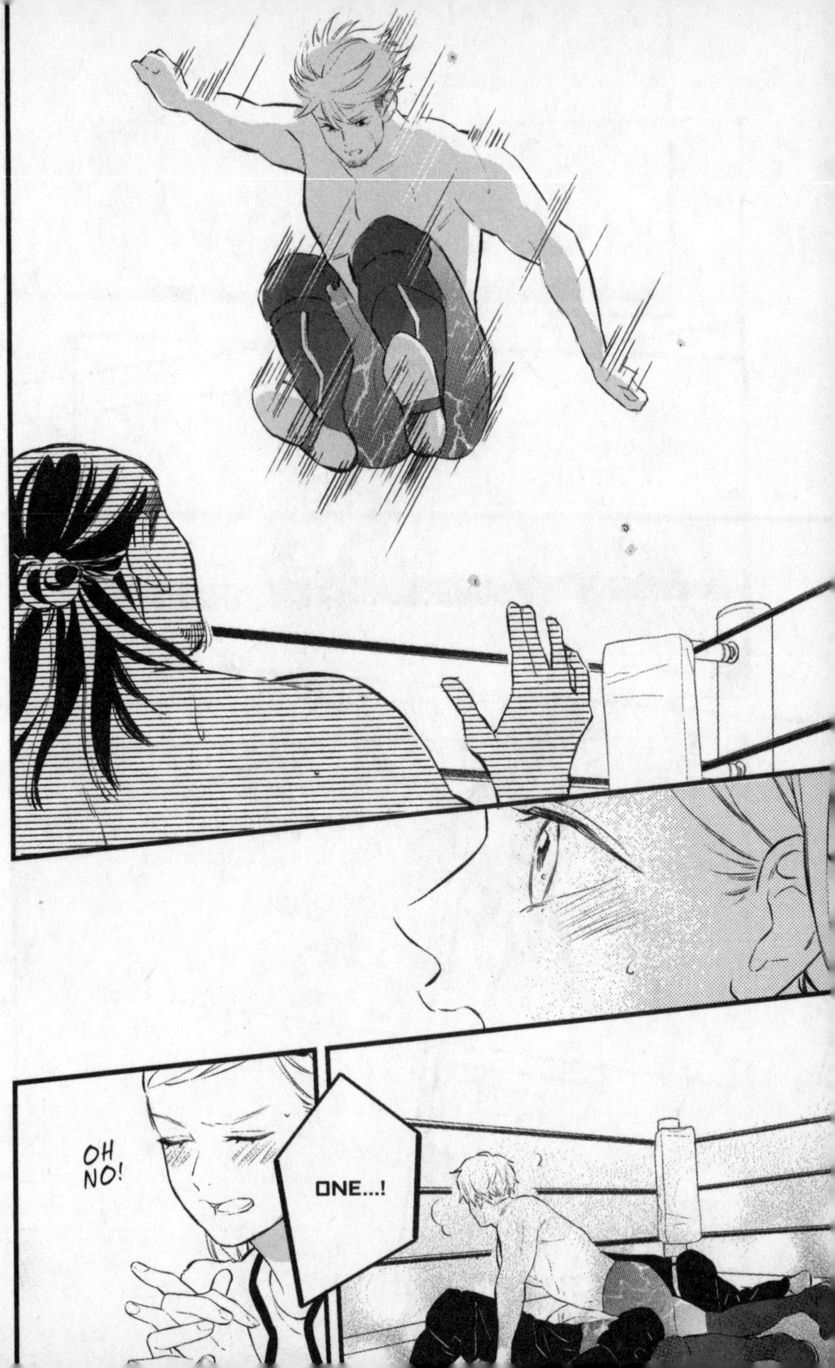
ONE...!
OH NO!

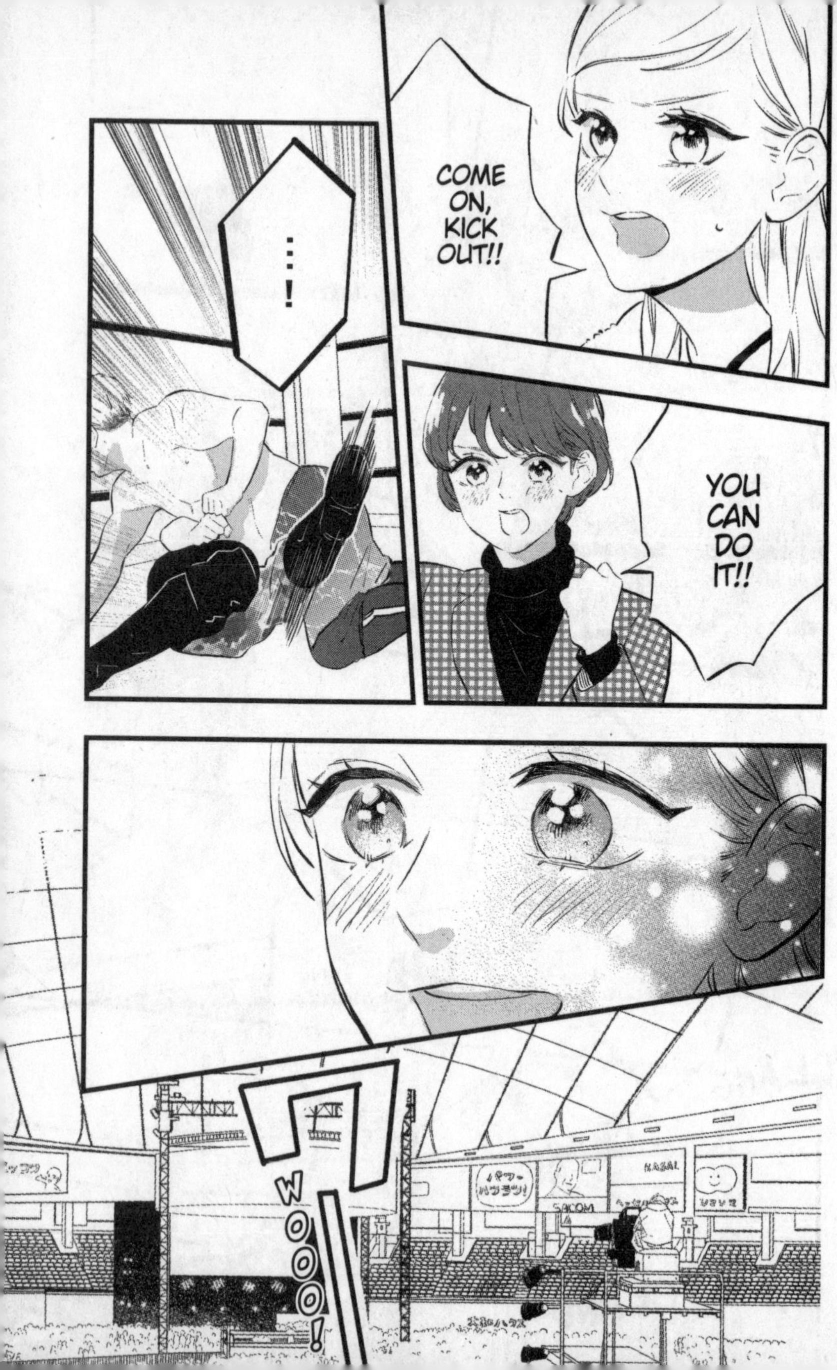
COME ON, KICK OUT!!
YOU CAN DO IT!!
...!
WOOOO!

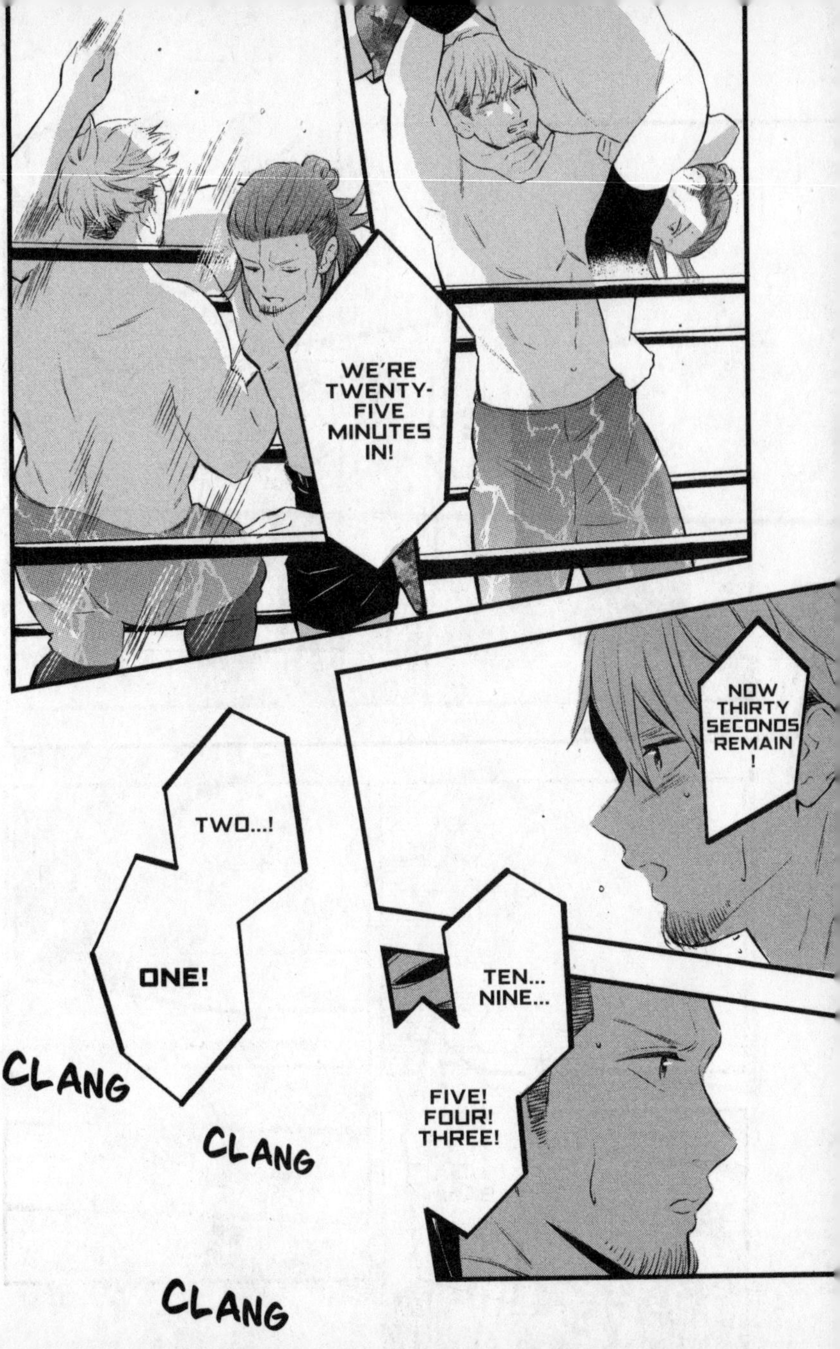
WE'RE TWENTY-FIVE MINUTES IN!
NOW THIRTY SECONDS REMAIN!
TEN... NINE...
FIVE! FOUR! THREE!
TWO...!
ONE!
CLANG
CLANG
CLANG

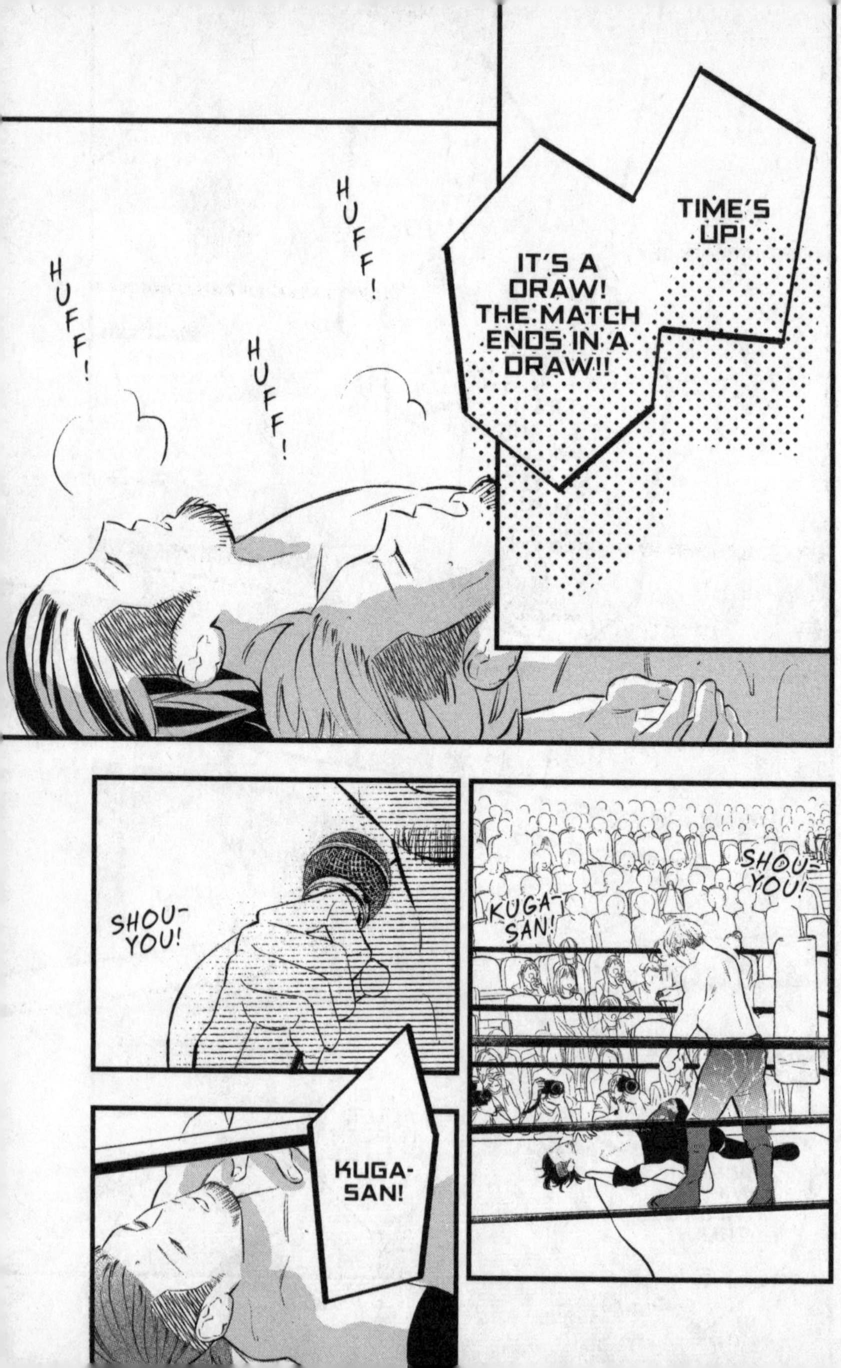
TIME'S UP!
IT'S A DRAW! THE MATCH ENDS IN A DRAW!!
HUFF!
HUFF!
HUFF!
SHOU-YOU!
KUGA-SAN!
SHOU-YOU!
KUGA-SAN!

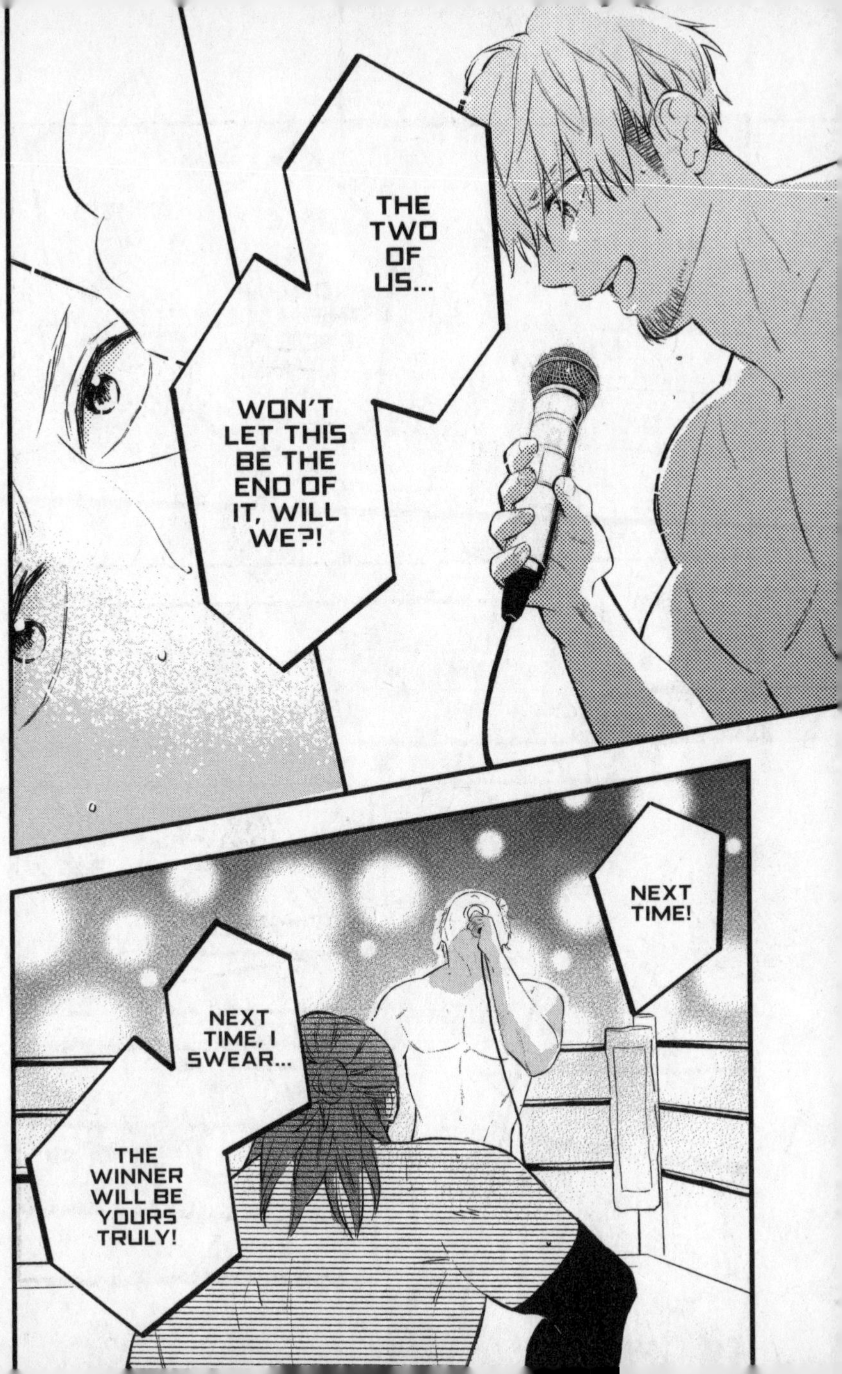
THE TWO OF US...
WON'T LET THIS BE THE END OF IT, WILL WE?!
NEXT TIME!
NEXT TIME, I SWEAR...
THE WINNER WILL BE YOURS TRULY!

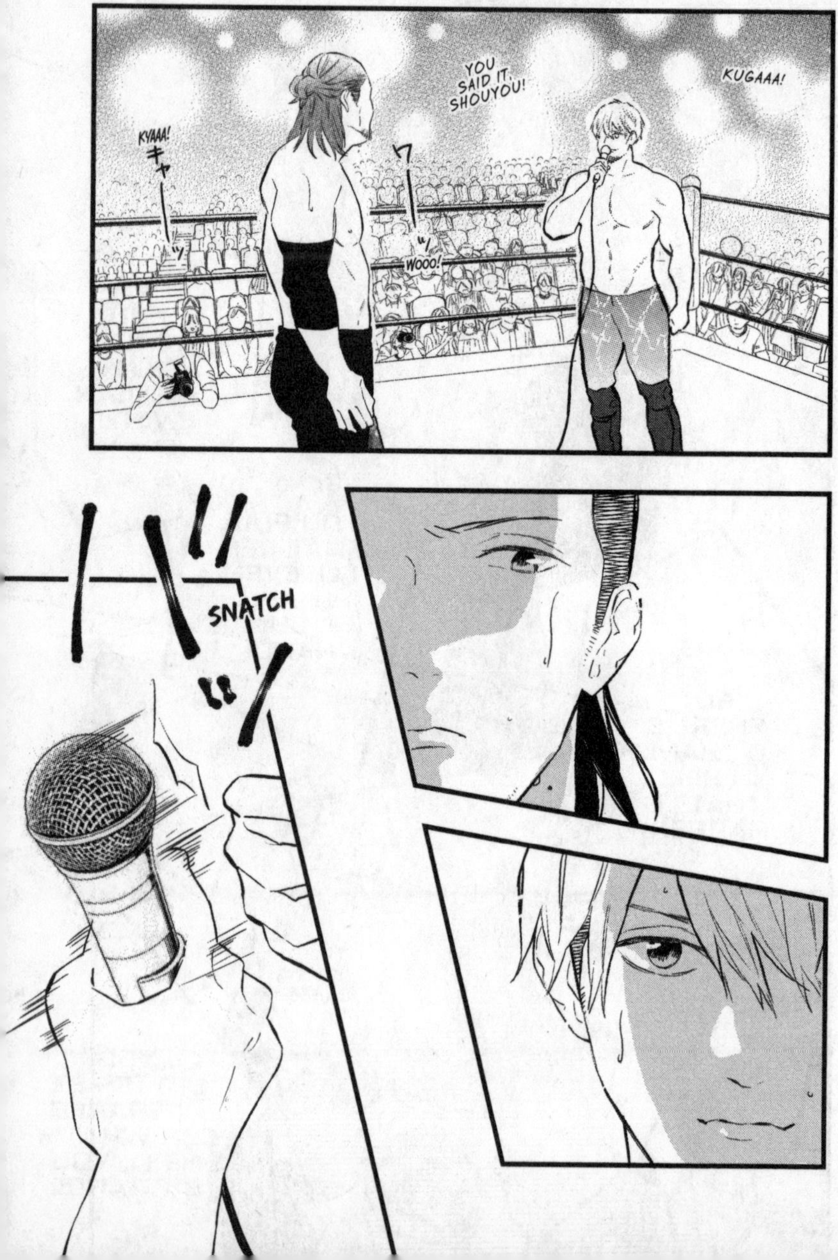
KUGAAA!
YOU SAID IT, SHOUYOU!
ワーッ
WOOO!
キャーッ
KYAAA!
SNATCH

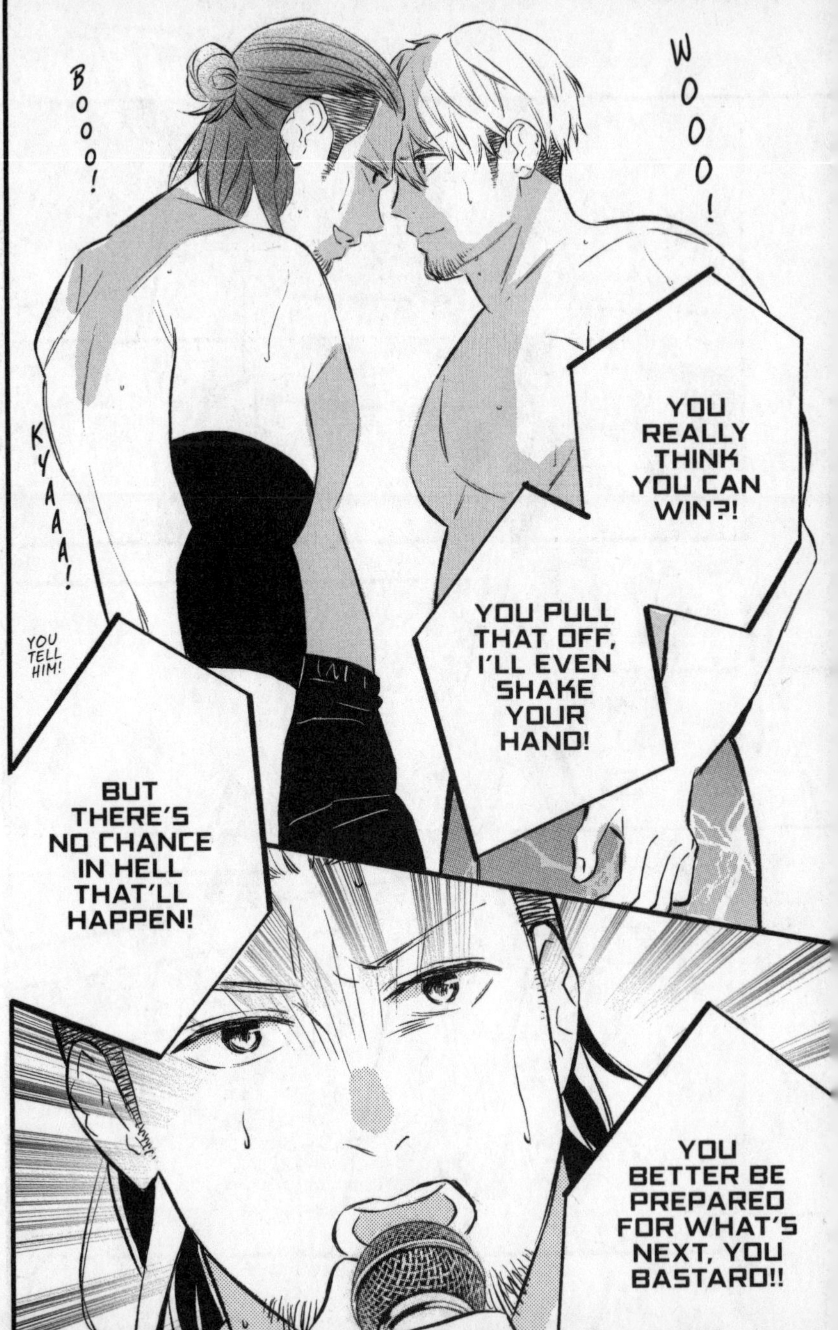
WOOOO!
YOU REALLY THINK YOU CAN WIN?!
YOU PULL THAT OFF, I'LL EVEN SHAKE YOUR HAND!
BOOO!
KYAAAA!
YOU TELL HIM!
BUT THERE'S NO CHANCE IN HELL THAT'LL HAPPEN!
YOU BETTER BE PREPARED FOR WHAT'S NEXT, YOU BASTARD!!

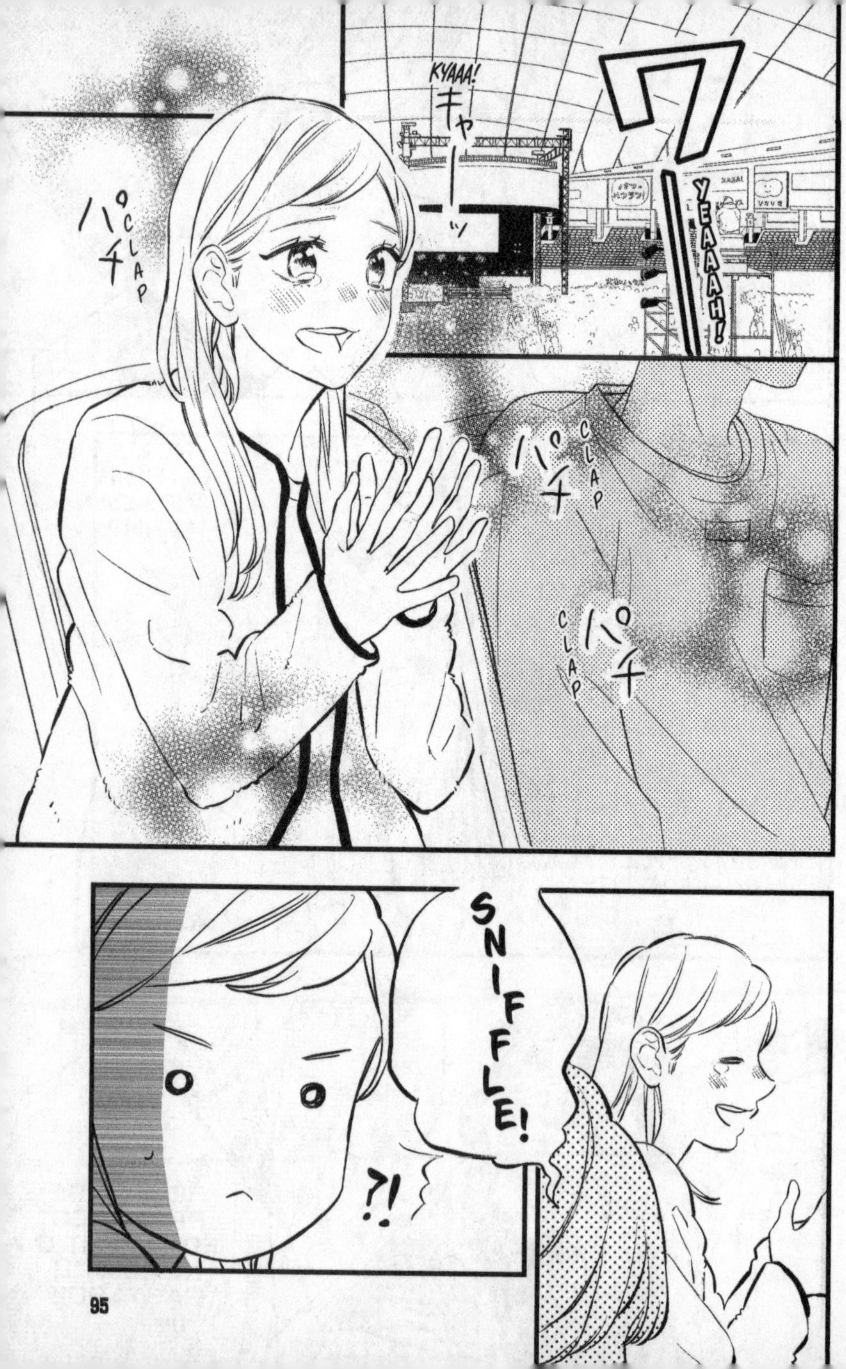
ワ
YEAAAAH!
キャーーッ
KYAAA!
パチ
CLAP
パチ
CLAP
パチ
CLAP
SNIFFLE!
?!

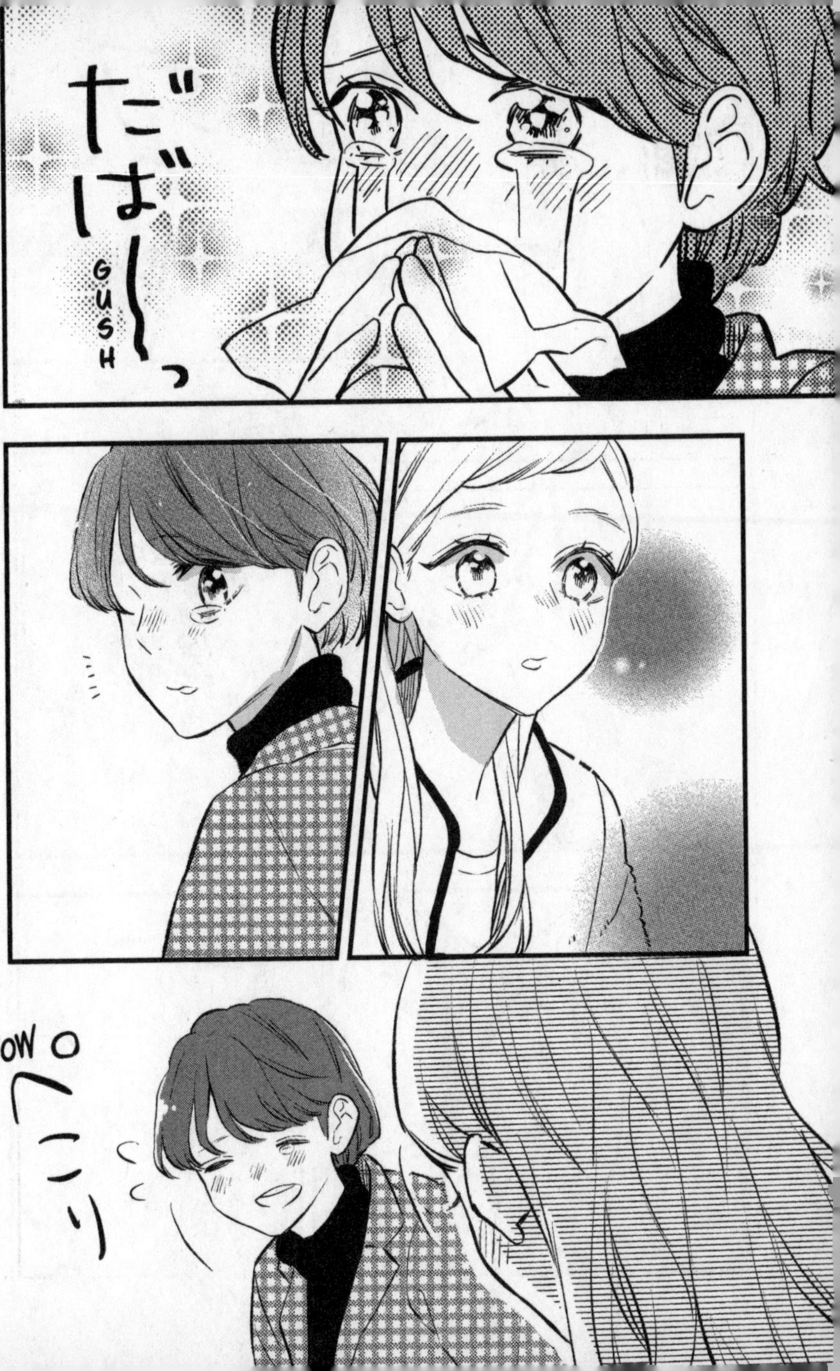
だば〜っ
GUSH
BOW
ぺこり

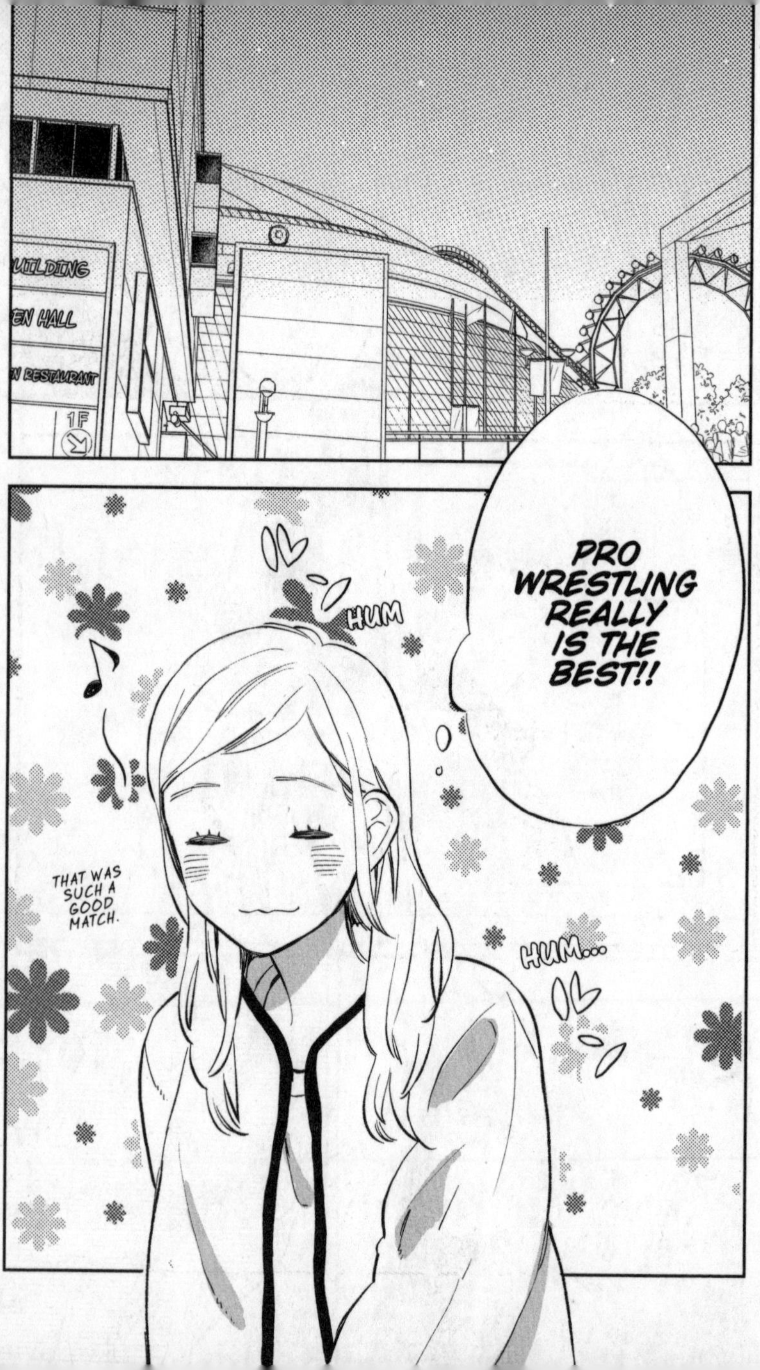
1F
PRO WRESTLING REALLY IS THE BEST!!
HUM
HUM...
THAT WAS SUCH A GOOD MATCH.

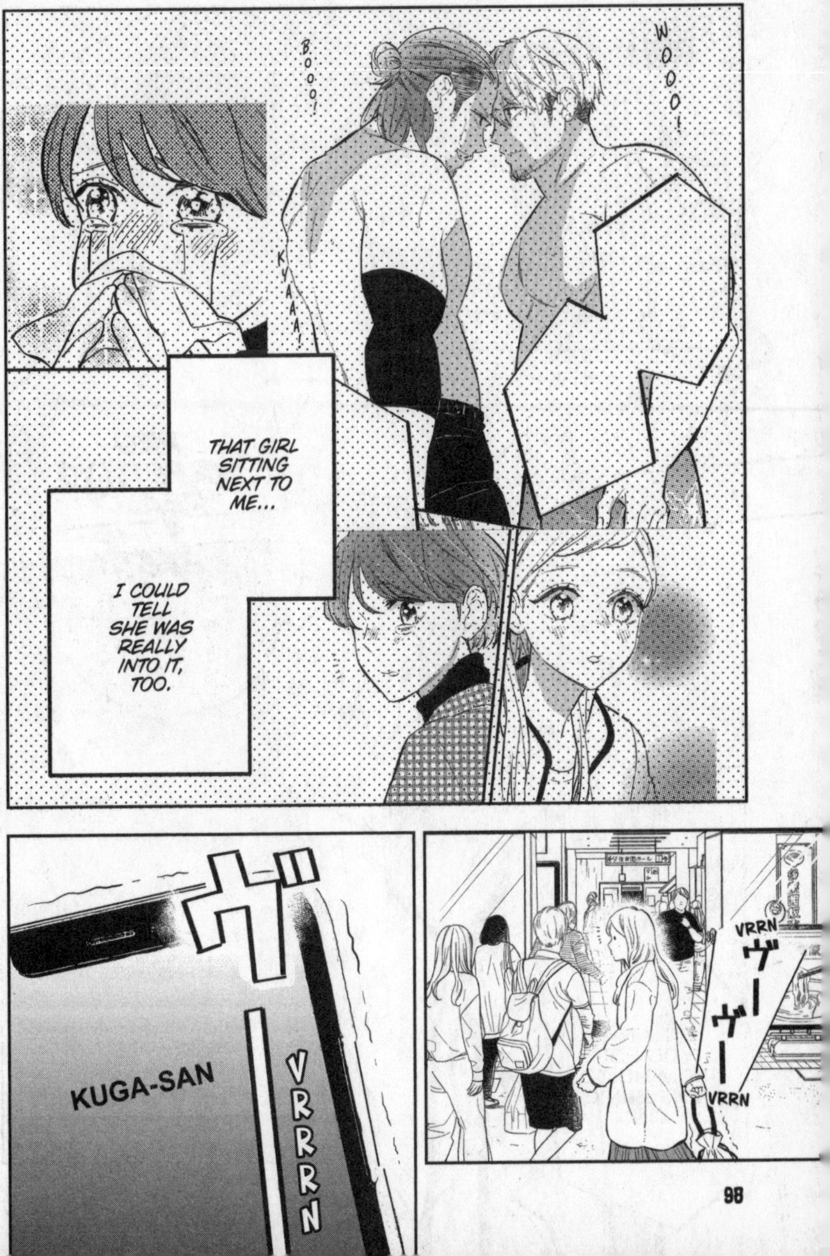
WOOO!
BOOO!
KYAAA!
THAT GIRL SITTING NEXT TO ME...
I COULD TELL SHE WAS REALLY INTO IT, TOO.
VRRN
ヴーヴー
VRRN
ヴー
KUGA-SAN
VRRRN

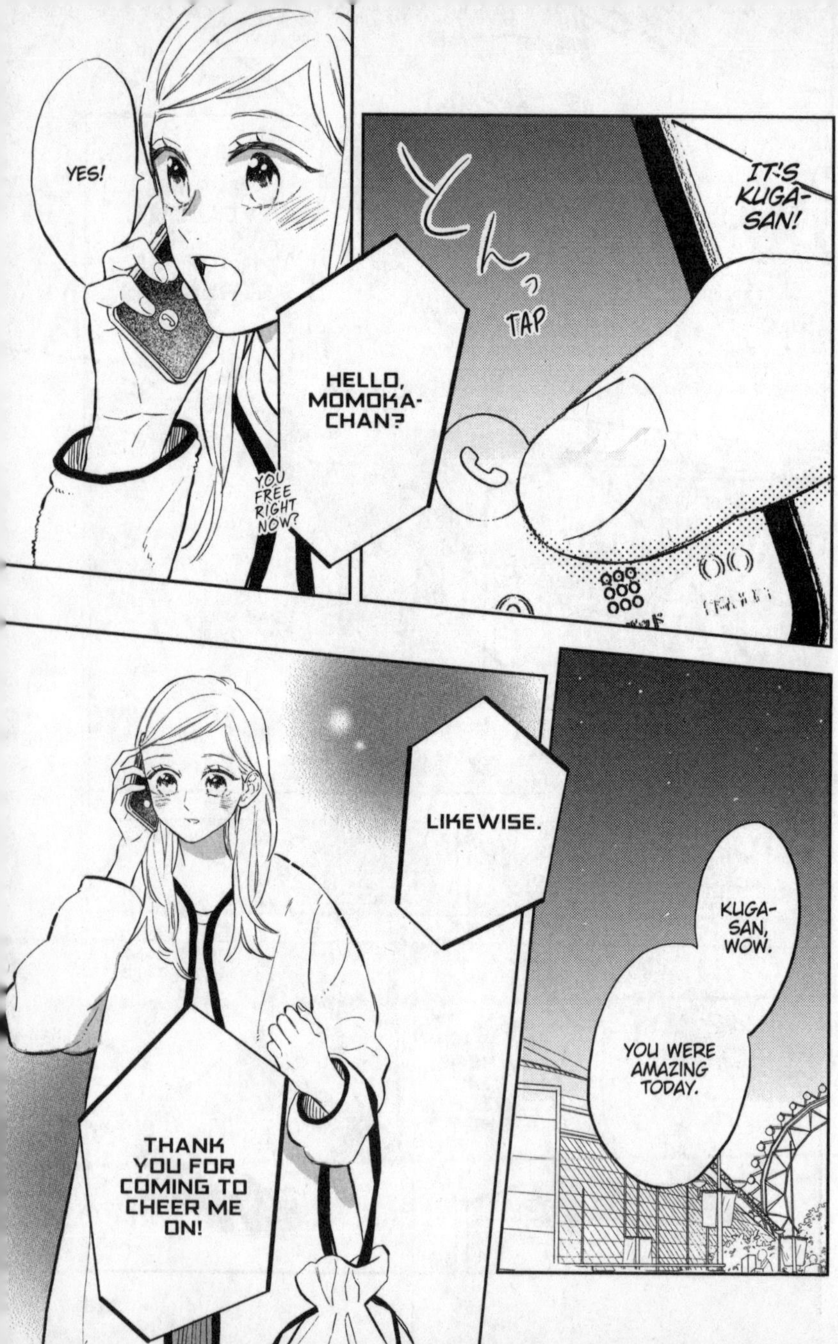
IT'S KUGA-SAN!
とんっ
TAP
HELLO, MOMOKA-CHAN?
YES!
YOU FREE RIGHT NOW?
KUGA-SAN, WOW.
YOU WERE AMAZING TODAY.
LIKEWISE.
THANK YOU FOR COMING TO CHEER ME ON!

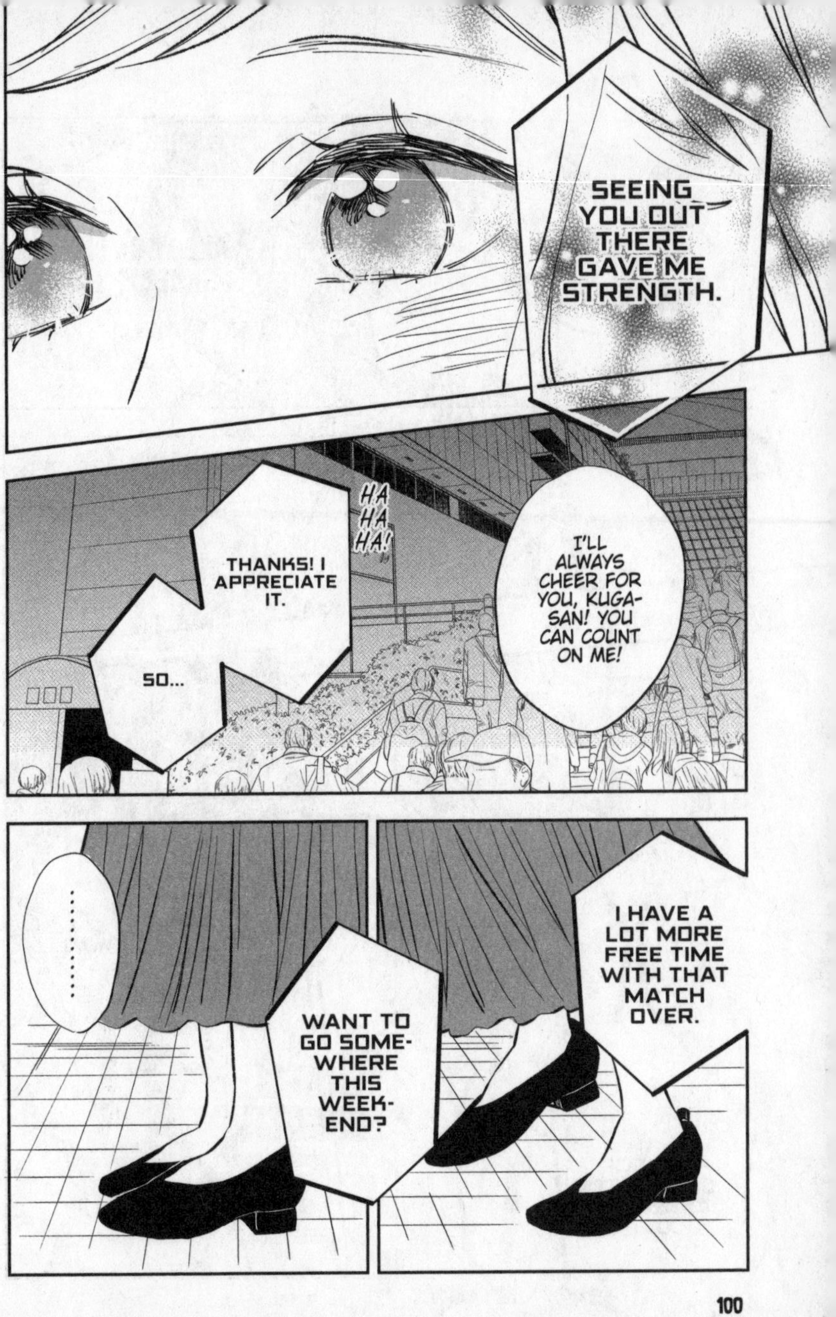
SEEING YOU OUT THERE GAVE ME STRENGTH.
I'LL ALWAYS CHEER FOR YOU, KUGA-SAN! YOU CAN COUNT ON ME!
HA HA HA!
THANKS! I APPRECIATE IT.
SO...
I HAVE A LOT MORE FREE TIME WITH THAT MATCH OVER.
WANT TO GO SOME-WHERE THIS WEEK-END?
....

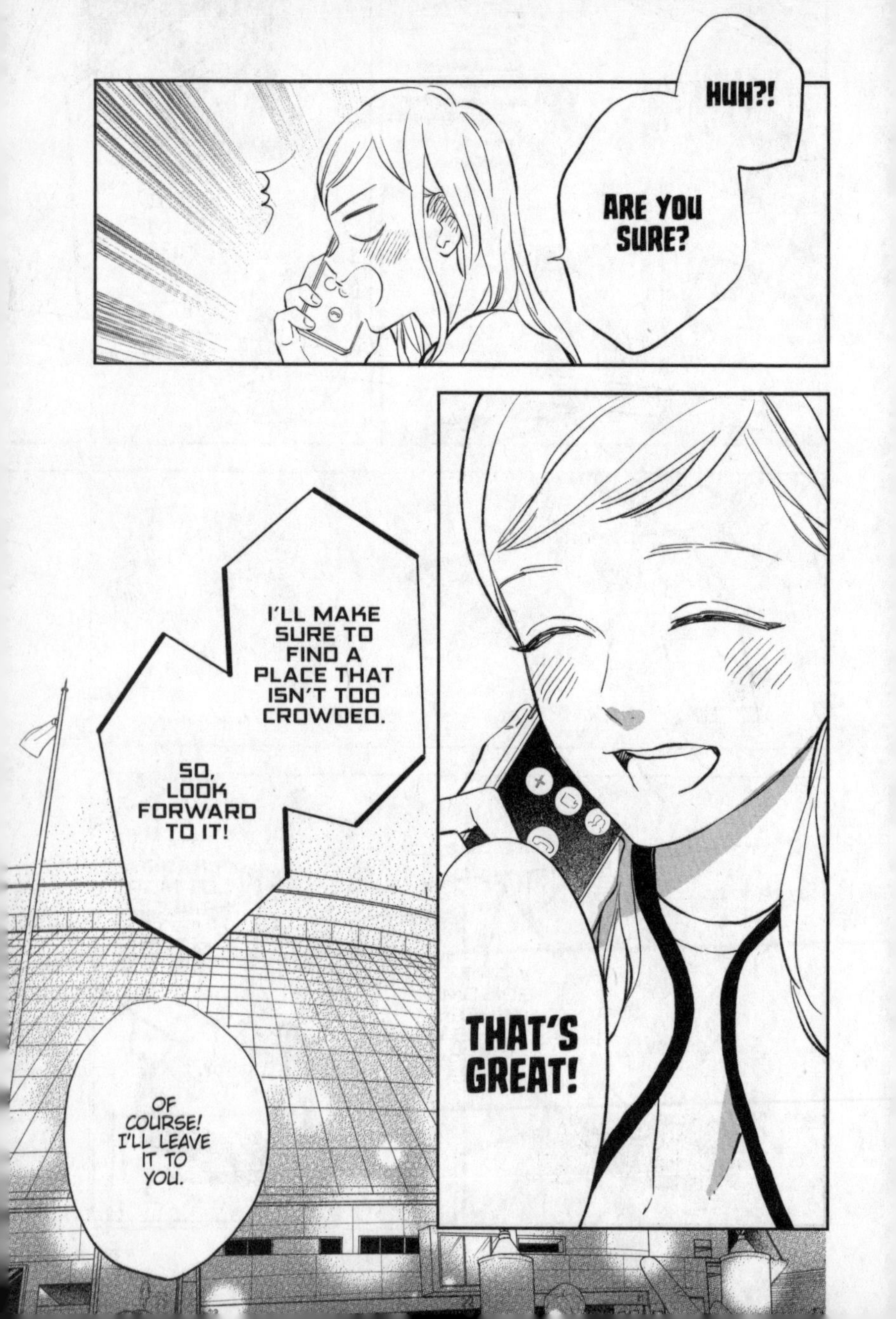
HUH?!
ARE YOU SURE?
THAT'S GREAT!
I'LL MAKE SURE TO FIND A PLACE THAT ISN'T TOO CROWDED.
SO, LOOK FORWARD TO IT!
OF COURSE! I'LL LEAVE IT TO YOU.

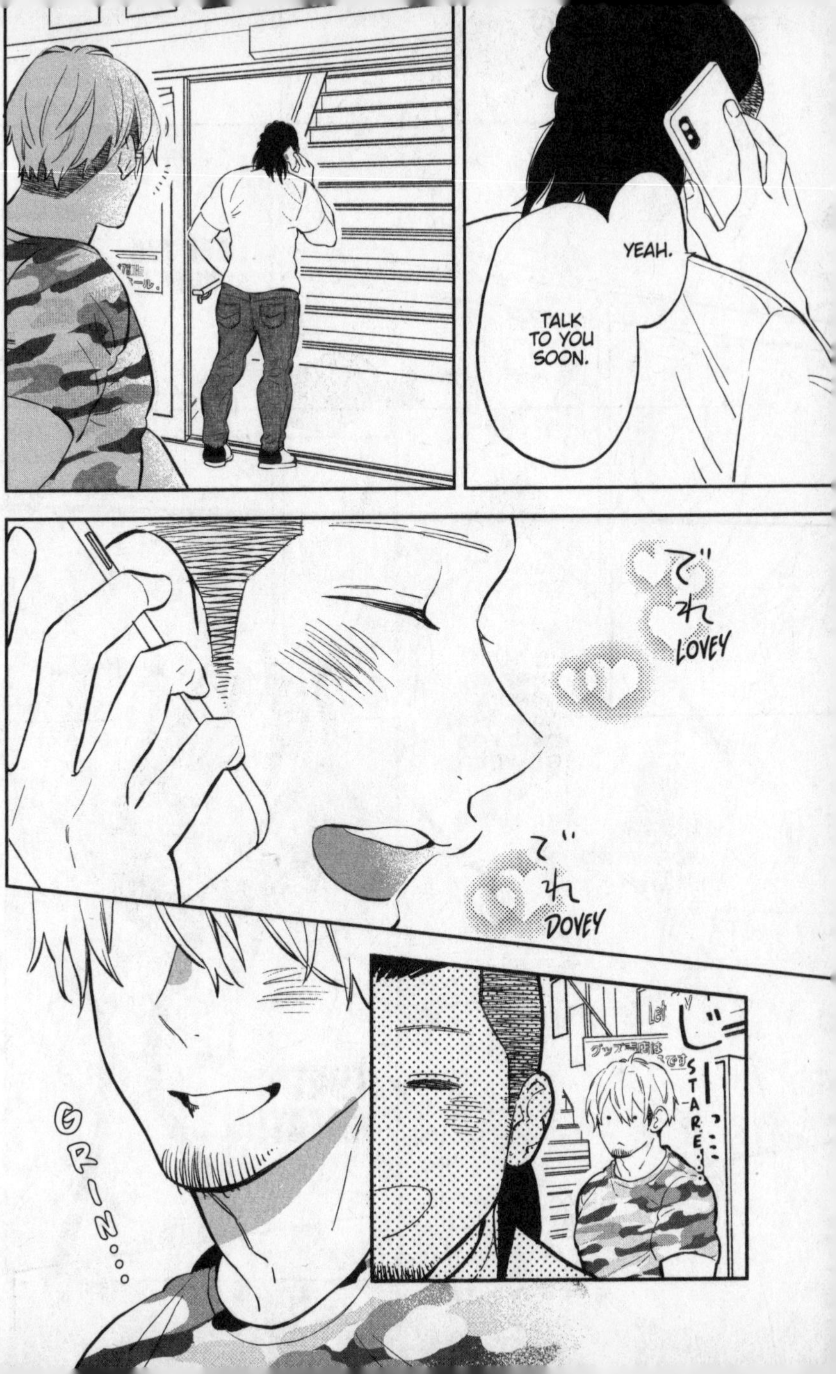
YEAH.
TALK TO YOU SOON.
でれ
LOVEY
でれ
DOVEY
STARE...
GRIN...

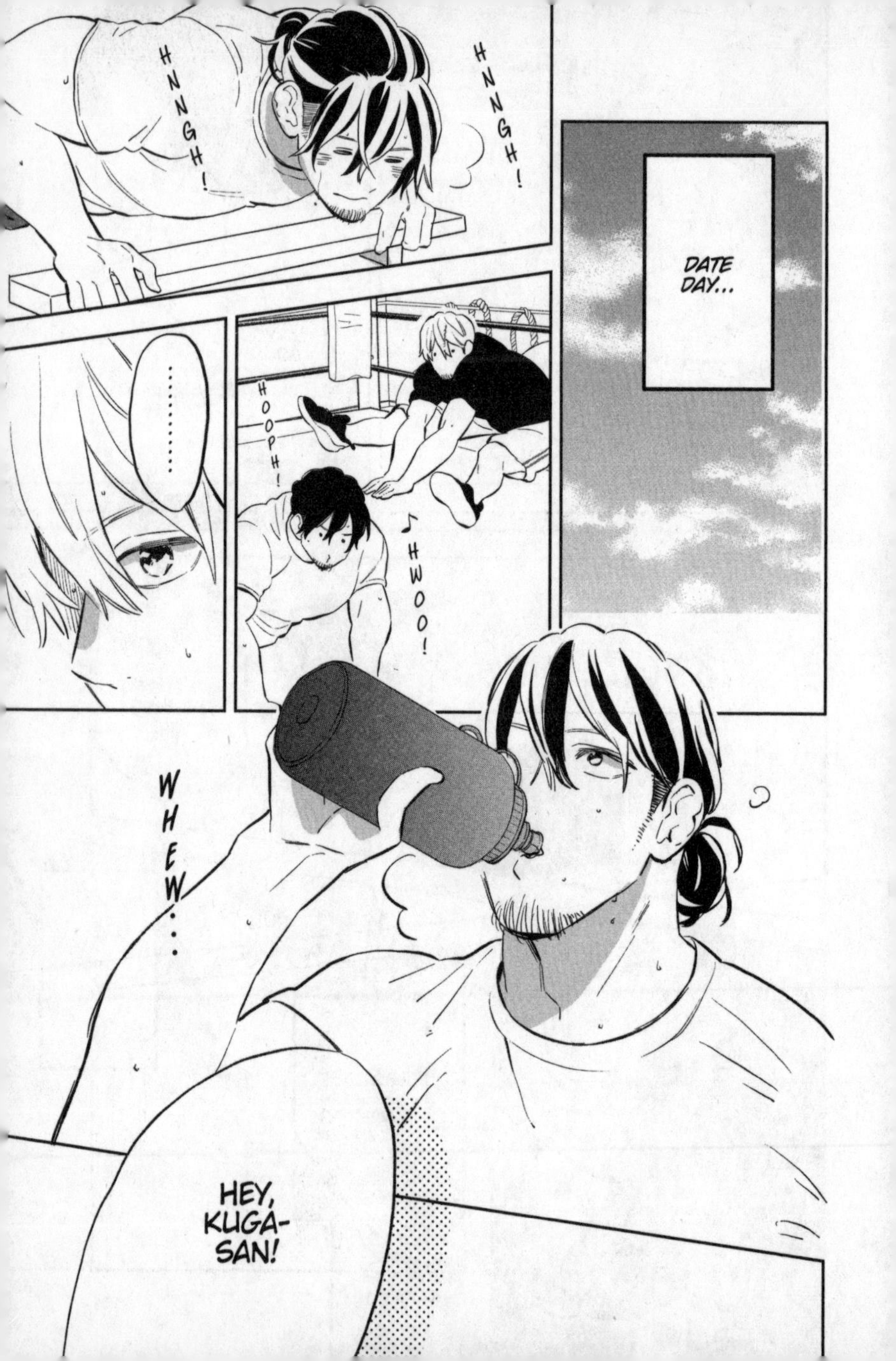
DATE DAY...
HNNGH!
HNNGH!
HOOPH!
♪ HWOOO!
....
WHEW...
HEY, KUGA-SAN!

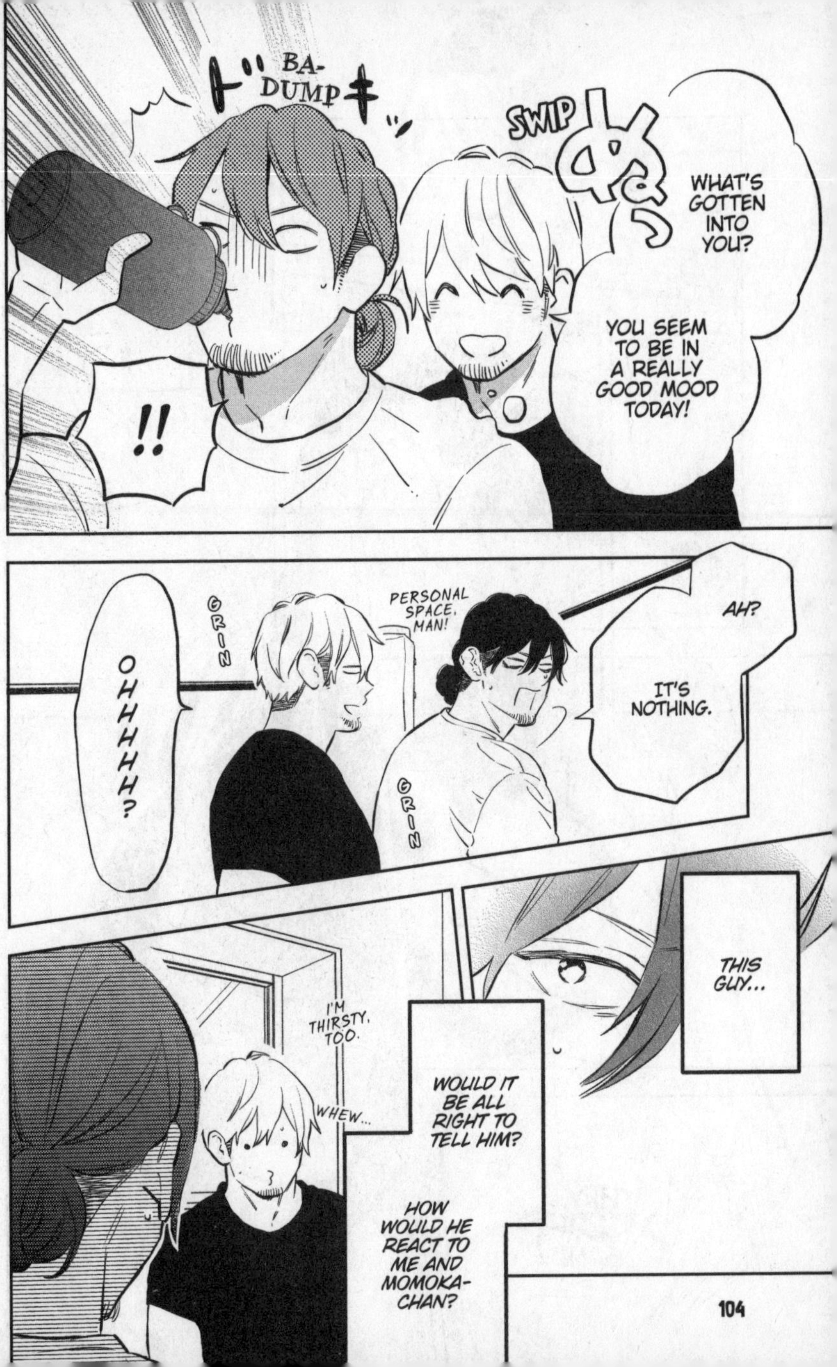
SWIP
WHAT'S GOTTEN INTO YOU?
YOU SEEM TO BE IN A REALLY GOOD MOOD TODAY!
BA-DUMP
!!
AH?
IT'S NOTHING.
PERSONAL SPACE, MAN!
GRIN
GRIN
OHHHHHH?
THIS GUY...
WOULD IT BE ALL RIGHT TO TELL HIM?
HOW WOULD HE REACT TO ME AND MOMOKA-CHAN?
I'M THIRSTY, TOO.
WHEW...

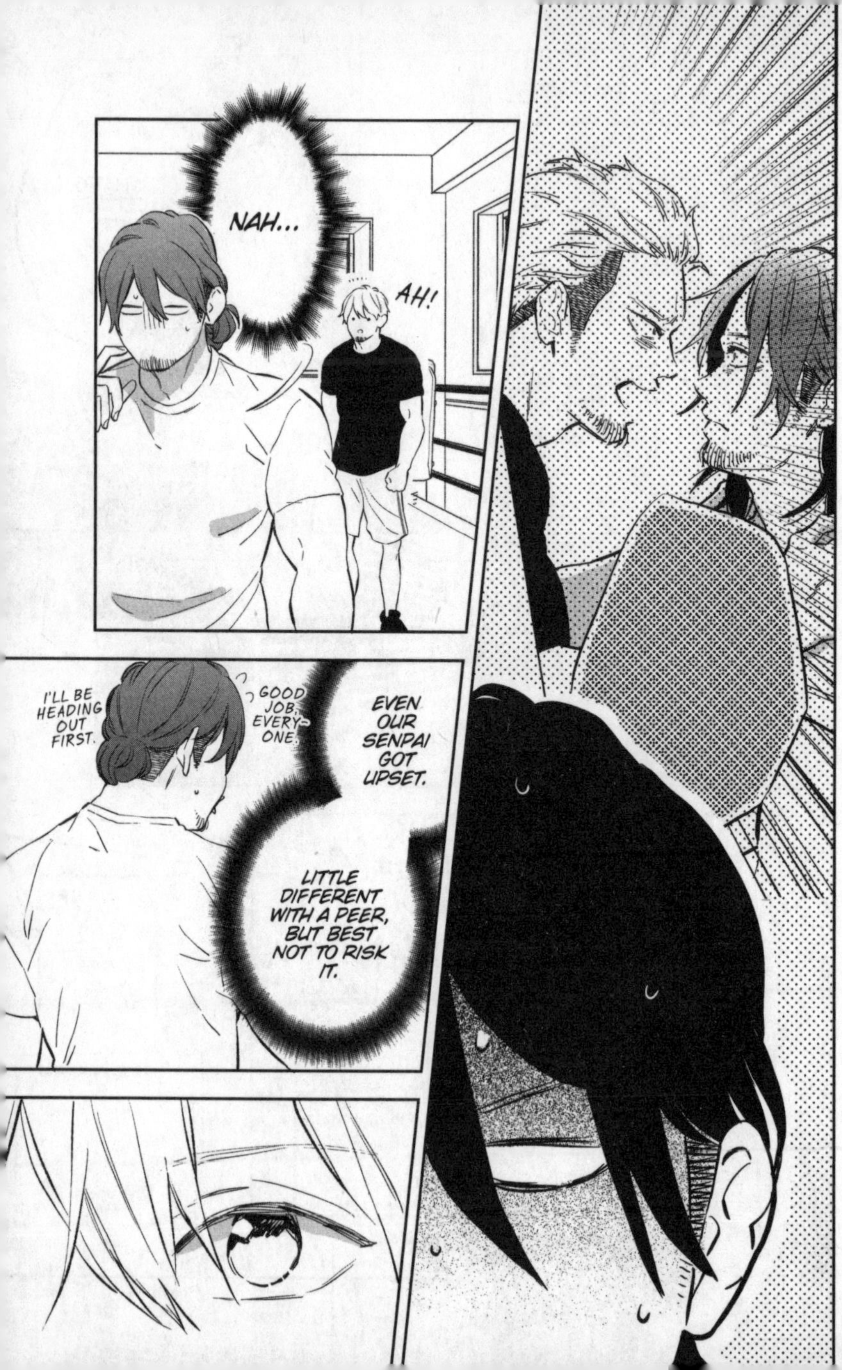
NAH...
AH!
EVEN OUR SENPAI GOT UPSET.
GOOD JOB, EVERY-ONE.
I'LL BE HEADING OUT FIRST.
LITTLE DIFFERENT WITH A PEER, BUT BEST NOT TO RISK IT.

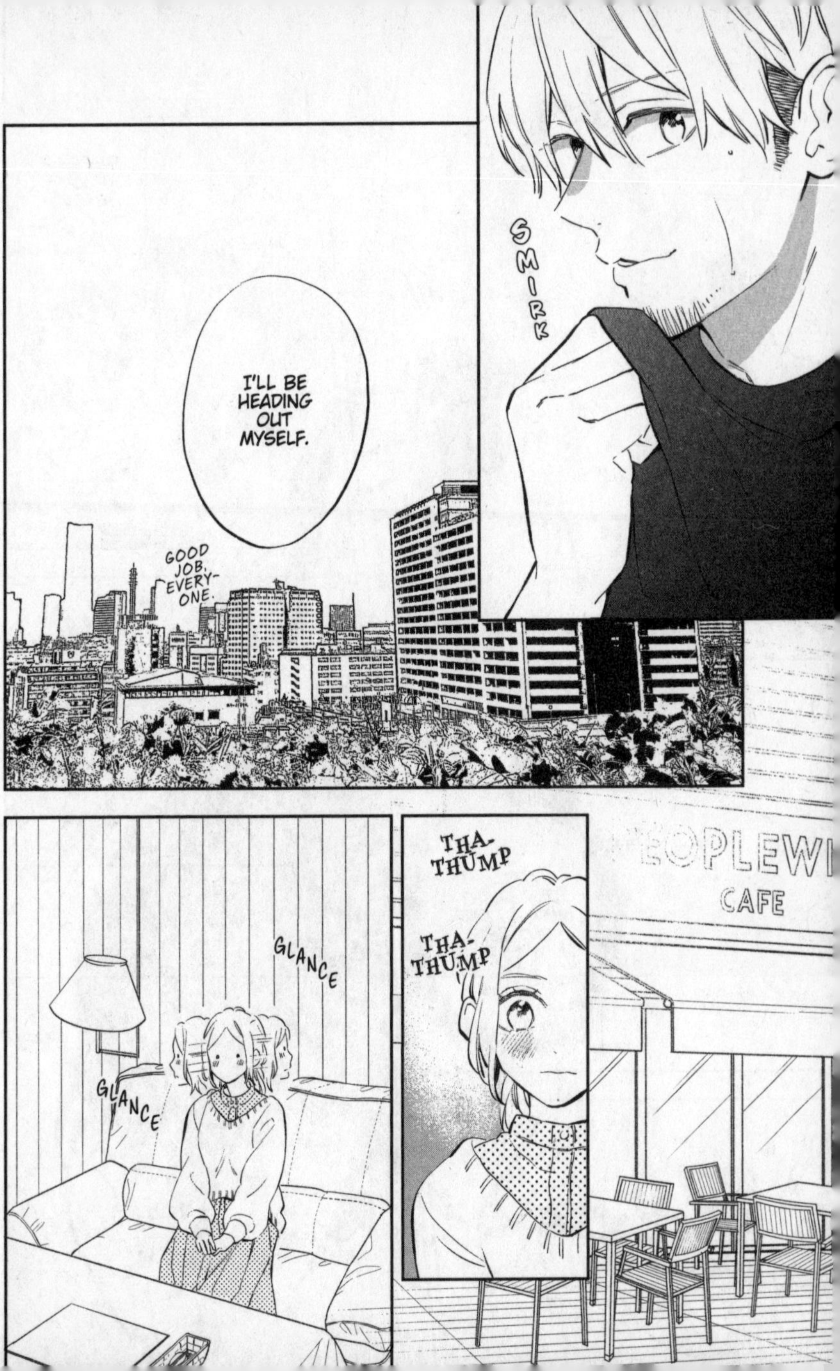
SMIRK
I'LL BE HEADING OUT MYSELF.
GOOD JOB, EVERY-ONE.
THA-THUMP
THA-THUMP
CAFE
GLANCE
GLANCE

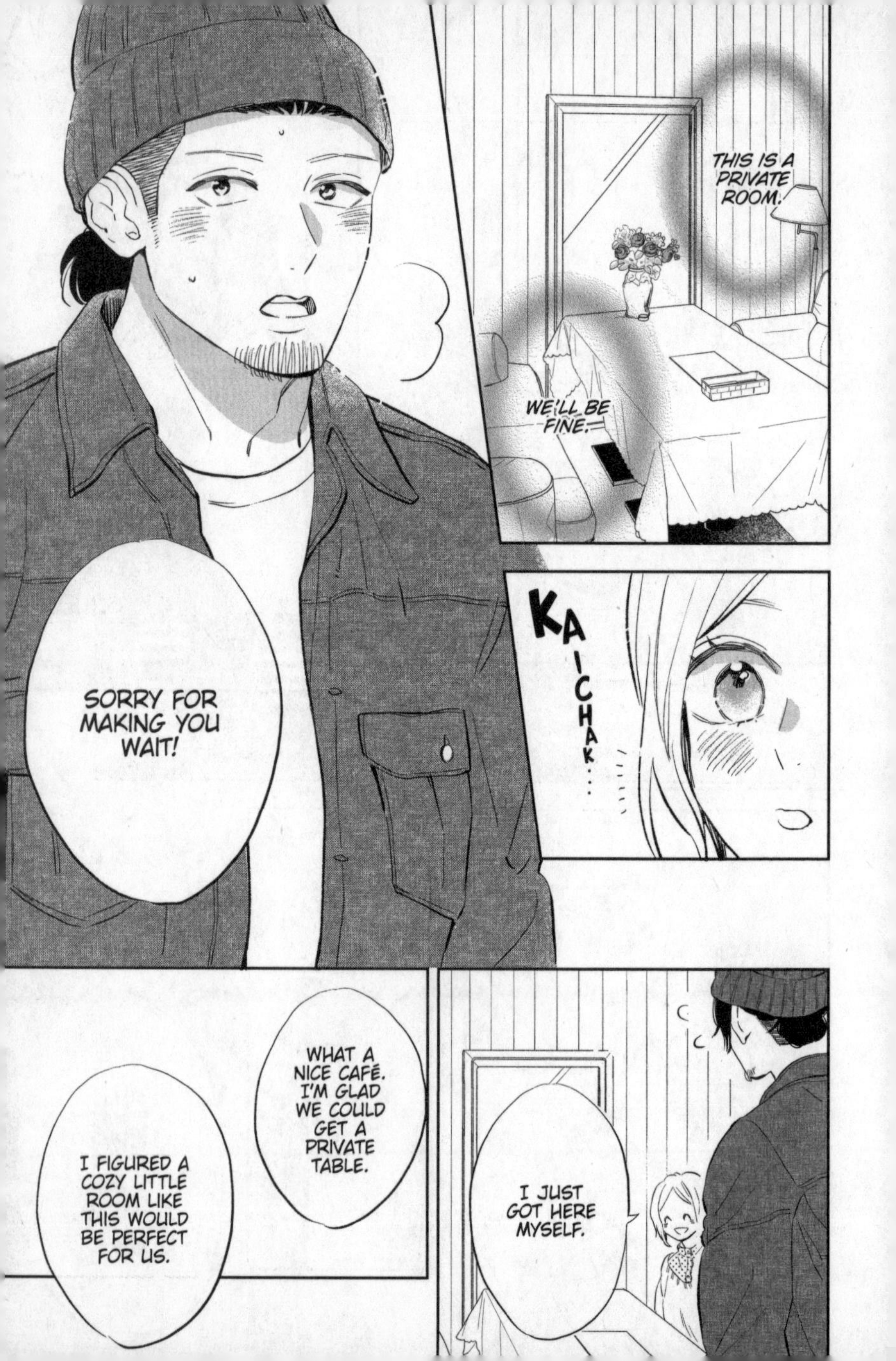
THIS IS A PRIVATE ROOM.
WE'LL BE FINE.
KAICHAK...
SORRY FOR MAKING YOU WAIT!
I JUST GOT HERE MYSELF.
WHAT A NICE CAFÉ. I'M GLAD WE COULD GET A PRIVATE TABLE.
I FIGURED A COZY LITTLE ROOM LIKE THIS WOULD BE PERFECT FOR US.

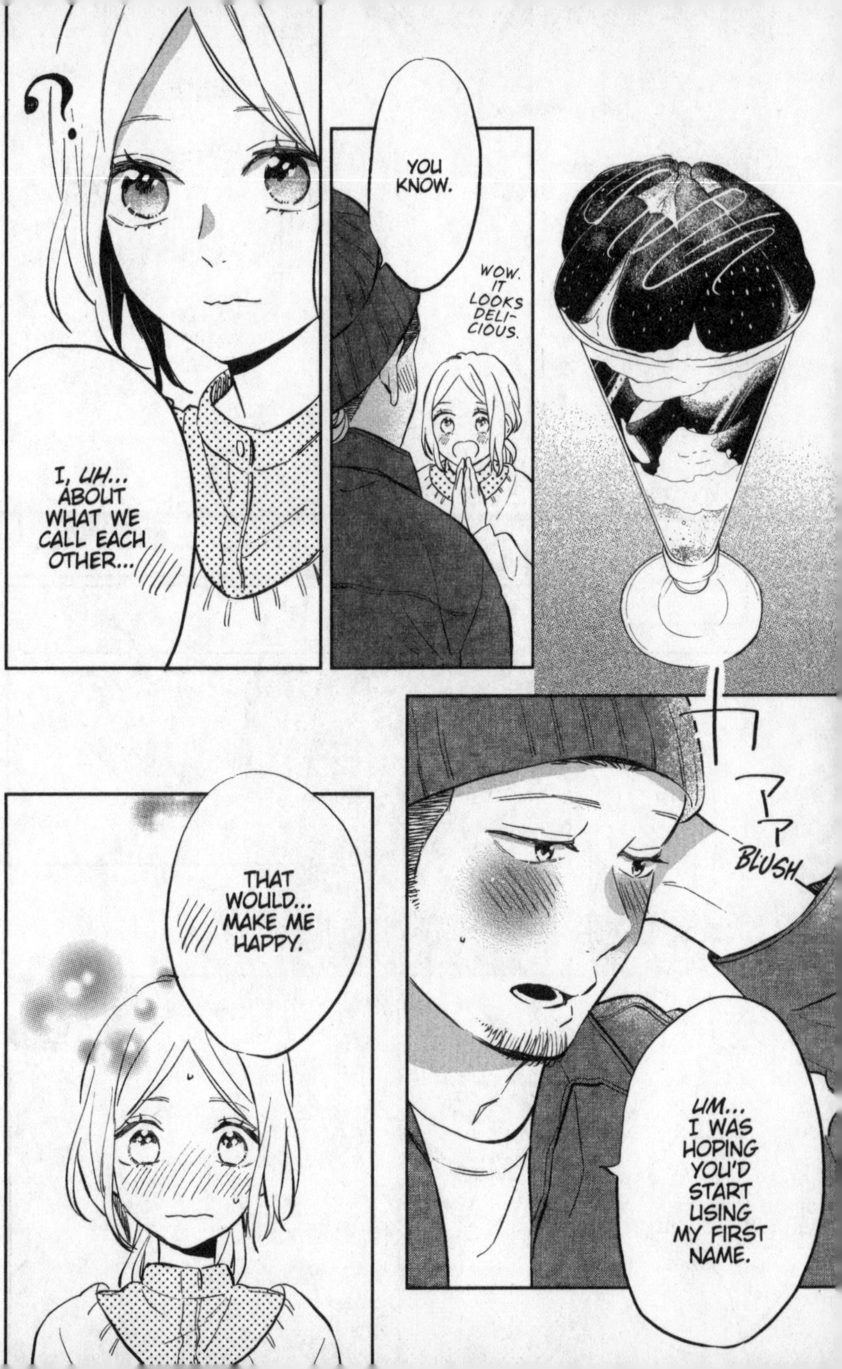
WOW. IT LOOKS DELICIOUS.
YOU KNOW.
I, UH... ABOUT WHAT WE CALL EACH OTHER...
カアア
BLUSH
UM... I WAS HOPING YOU'D START USING MY FIRST NAME.
THAT WOULD... MAKE ME HAPPY.

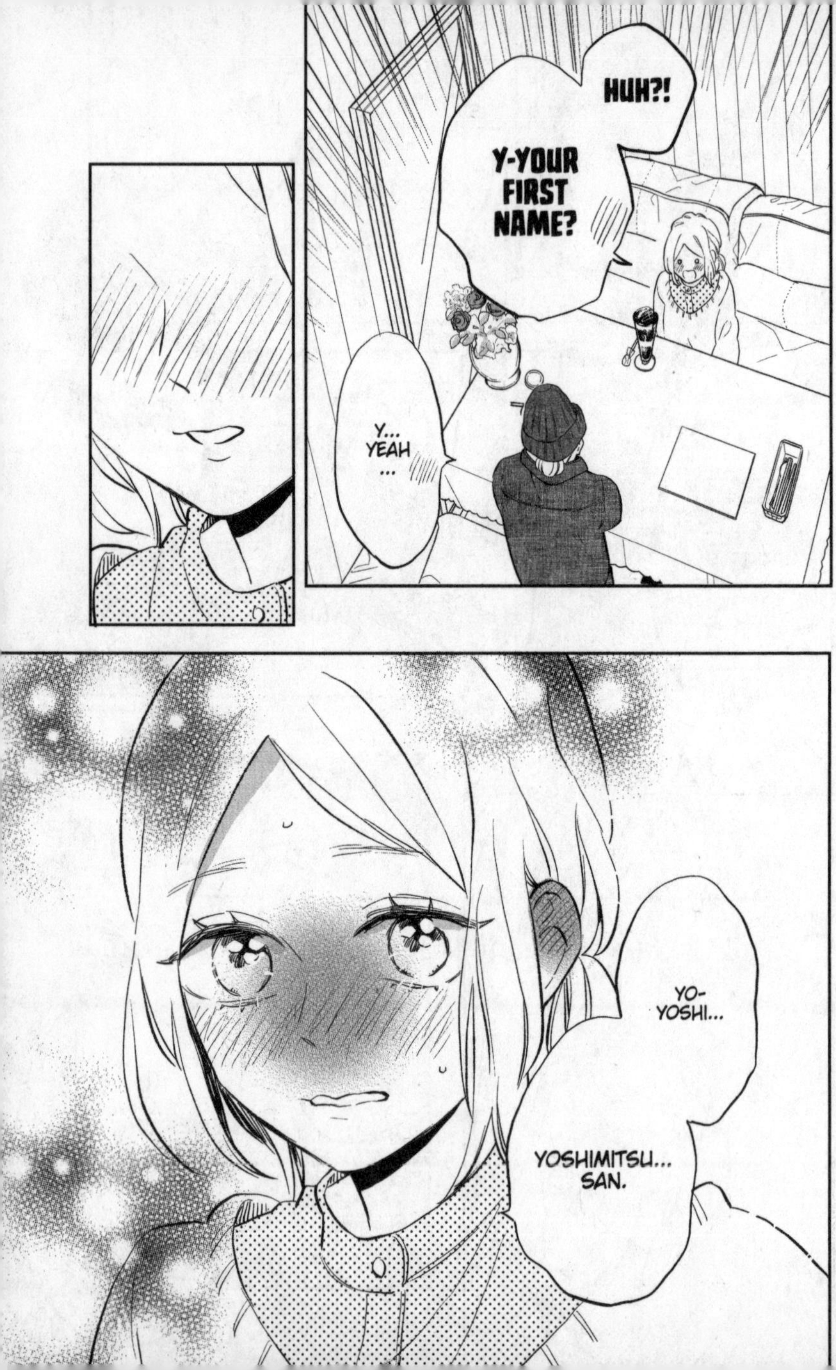
HUH?!
Y-YOUR FIRST NAME?
Y... YEAH...
YO-YOSHI...
YOSHIMITSU... SAN.

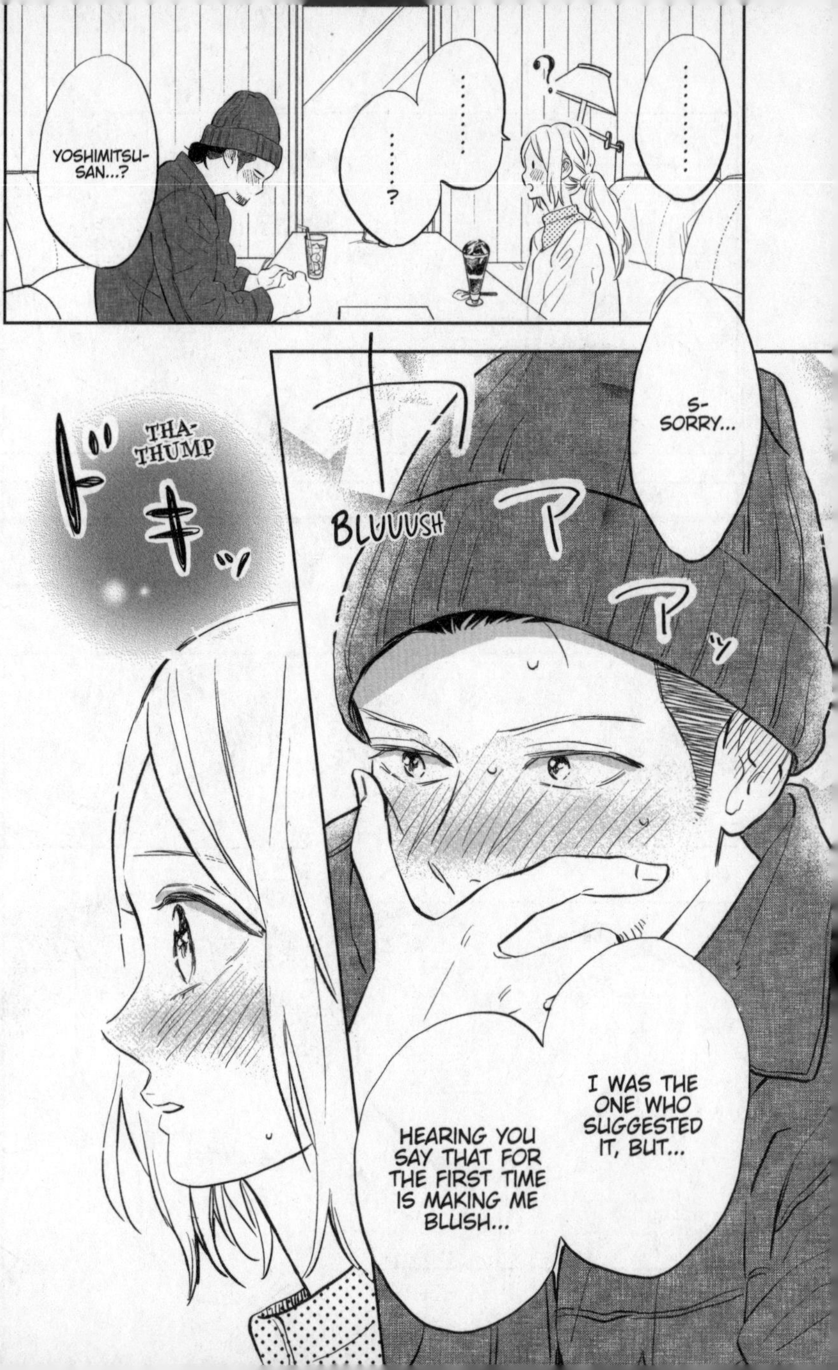
......
......
......?
YOSHIMITSU-SAN...?
S-SORRY...
カァァッ
BLUUUSH
I WAS THE ONE WHO SUGGESTED IT, BUT...
HEARING YOU SAY THAT FOR THE FIRST TIME IS MAKING ME BLUSH...
ドキッ
THA-THUMP

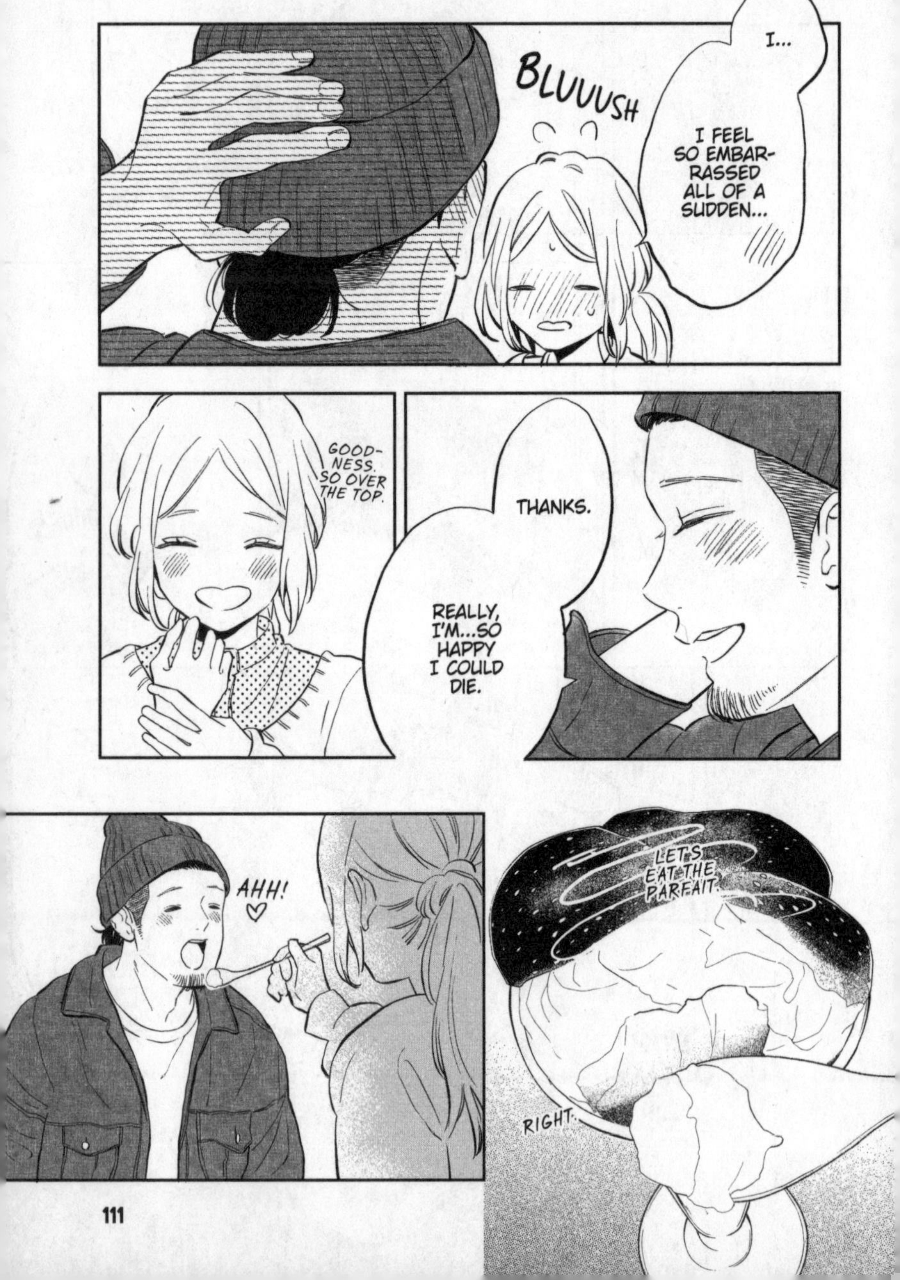
BLUUUSH
I...
I FEEL SO EMBAR-RASSED ALL OF A SUDDEN...
THANKS.
REALLY, I'M...SO HAPPY I COULD DIE.
GOOD-NESS. SO OVER THE TOP.
LET'S EAT THE PARFAIT.
RIGHT.
AHH! ♥

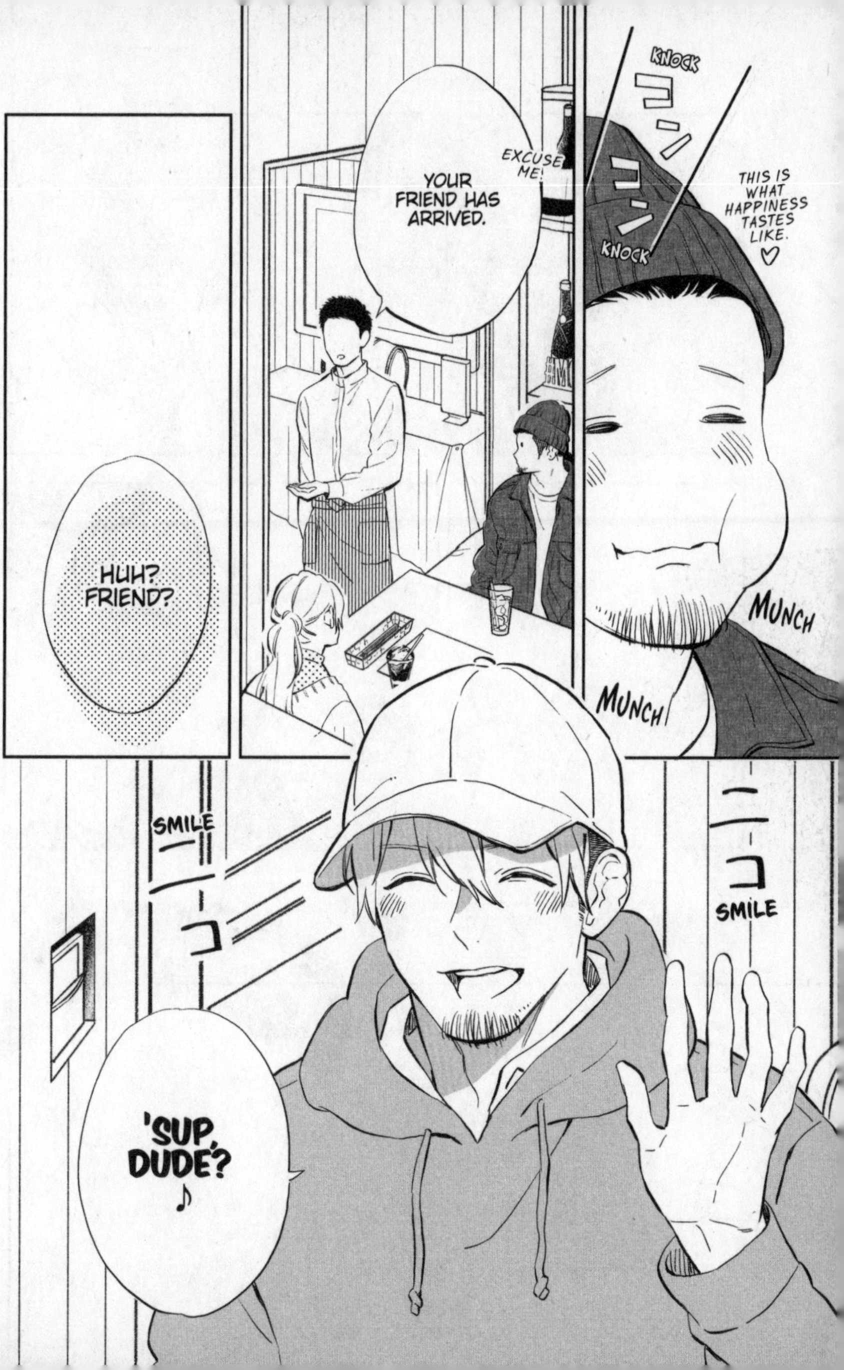
THIS IS WHAT HAPPINESS TASTES LIKE. ♡
MUNCH
MUNCH
KNOCK
KNOCK
EXCUSE ME!
YOUR FRIEND HAS ARRIVED.
HUH? FRIEND?
SMILE
SMILE
'SUP, DUDE? ♪

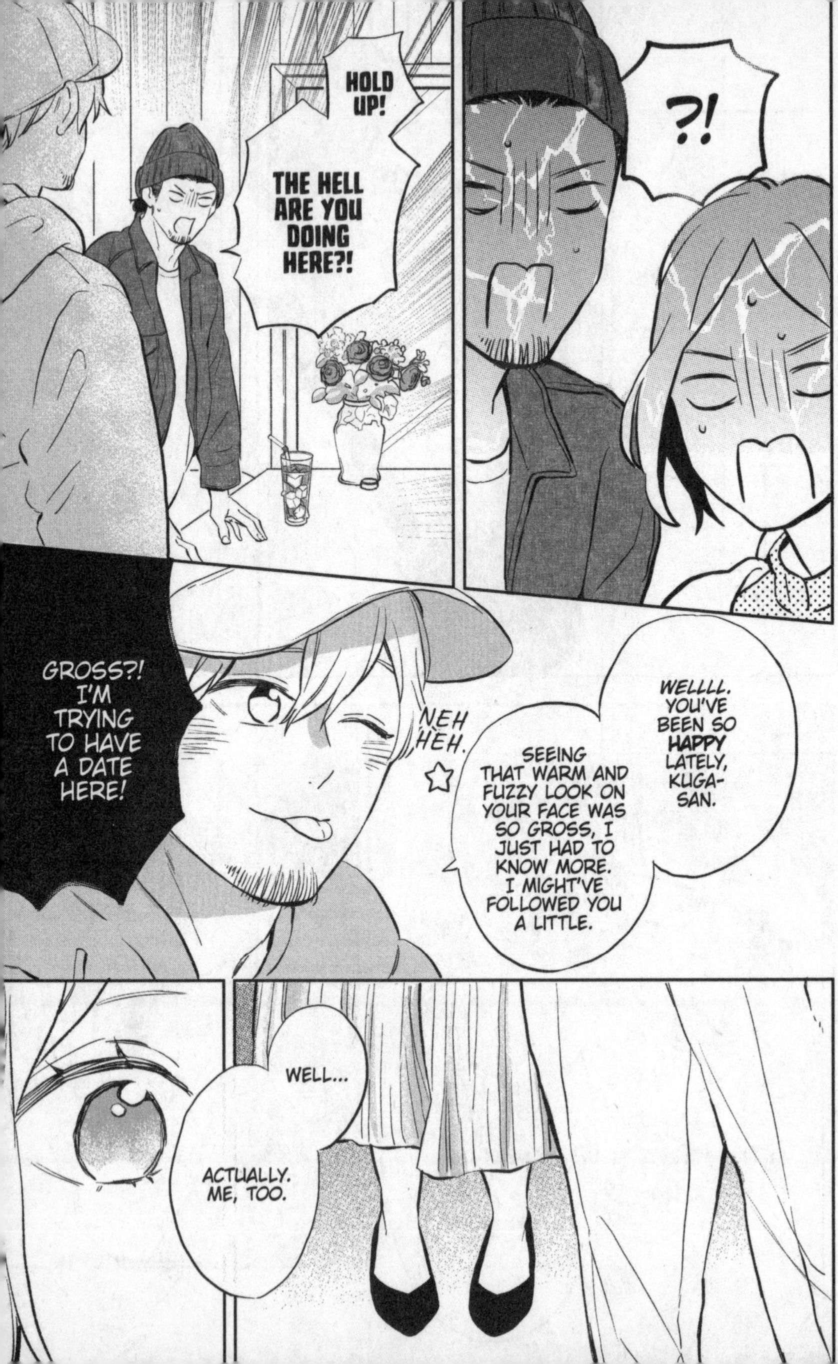
?!
HOLD UP!
THE HELL ARE YOU DOING HERE?!
WELLLL. YOU'VE BEEN SO HAPPY LATELY, KUGA-SAN.
SEEING THAT WARM AND FUZZY LOOK ON YOUR FACE WAS SO GROSS, I JUST HAD TO KNOW MORE. I MIGHT'VE FOLLOWED YOU A LITTLE.
NEH HEH.
GROSS?! I'M TRYING TO HAVE A DATE HERE!
WELL...
ACTUALLY. ME, TOO.

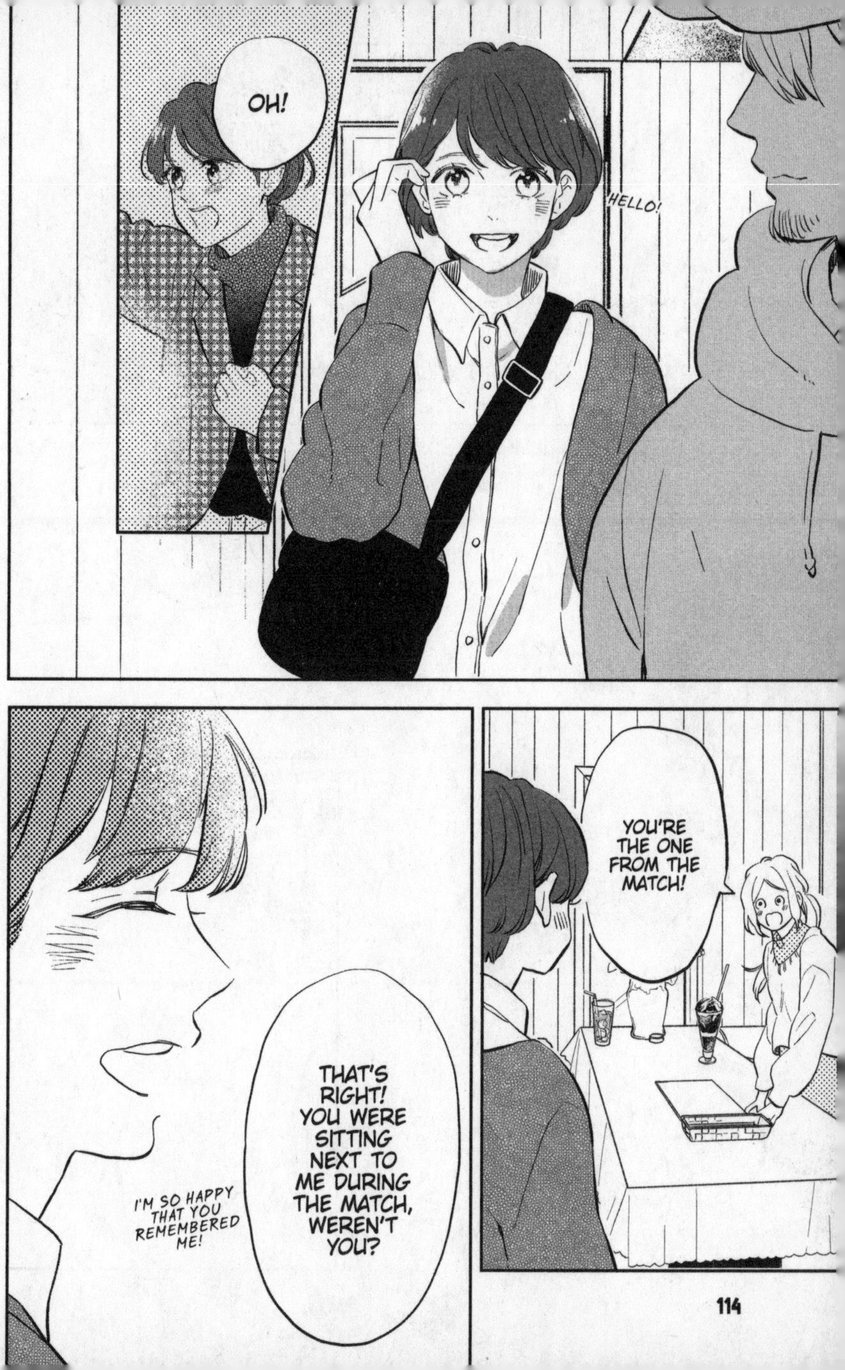
HELLO!
OH!
YOU'RE THE ONE FROM THE MATCH!
THAT'S RIGHT! YOU WERE SITTING NEXT TO ME DURING THE MATCH, WEREN'T YOU?
I'M SO HAPPY THAT YOU REMEMBERED ME!

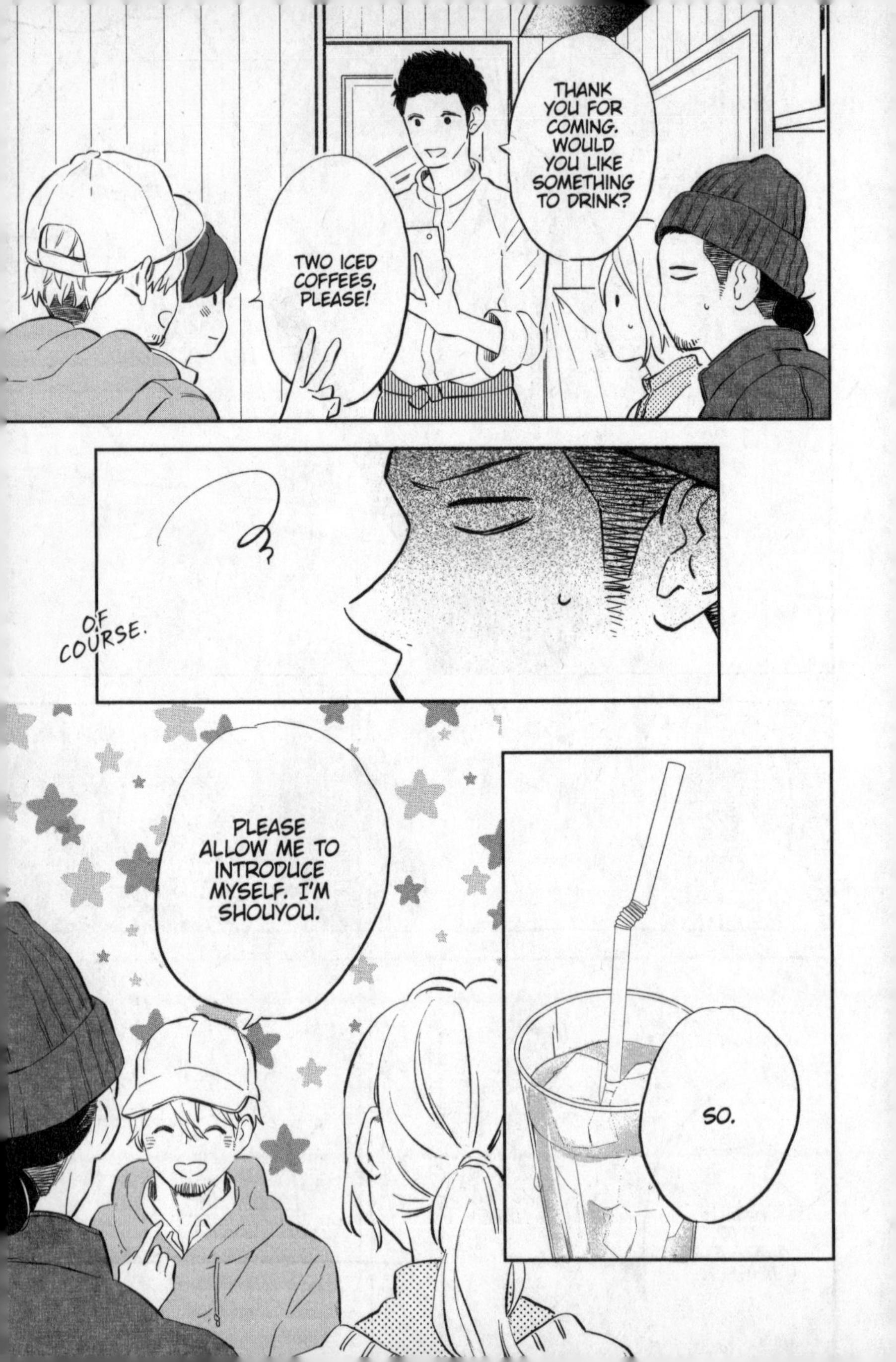
THANK YOU FOR COMING. WOULD YOU LIKE SOMETHING TO DRINK?
TWO ICED COFFEES, PLEASE!
OF COURSE.
SO.
PLEASE ALLOW ME TO INTRODUCE MYSELF. I'M SHOUYOU.

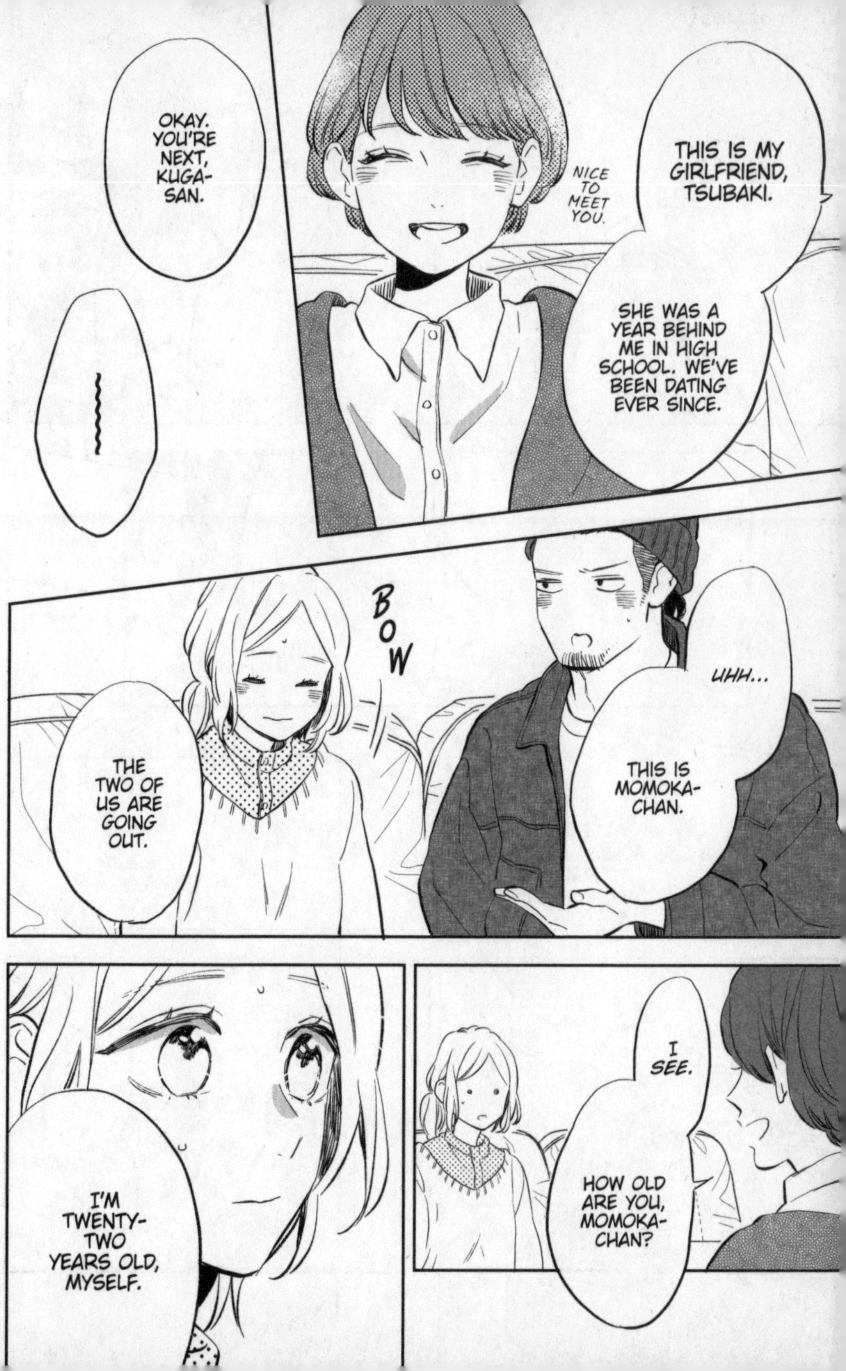
THIS IS MY GIRLFRIEND, TSUBAKI.
NICE TO MEET YOU.
SHE WAS A YEAR BEHIND ME IN HIGH SCHOOL. WE'VE BEEN DATING EVER SINCE.
OKAY. YOU'RE NEXT, KUGA-SAN.
UHH...
THIS IS MOMOKA-CHAN.
BOW
THE TWO OF US ARE GOING OUT.
I SEE.
HOW OLD ARE YOU, MOMOKA-CHAN?
I'M TWENTY-TWO YEARS OLD, MYSELF.

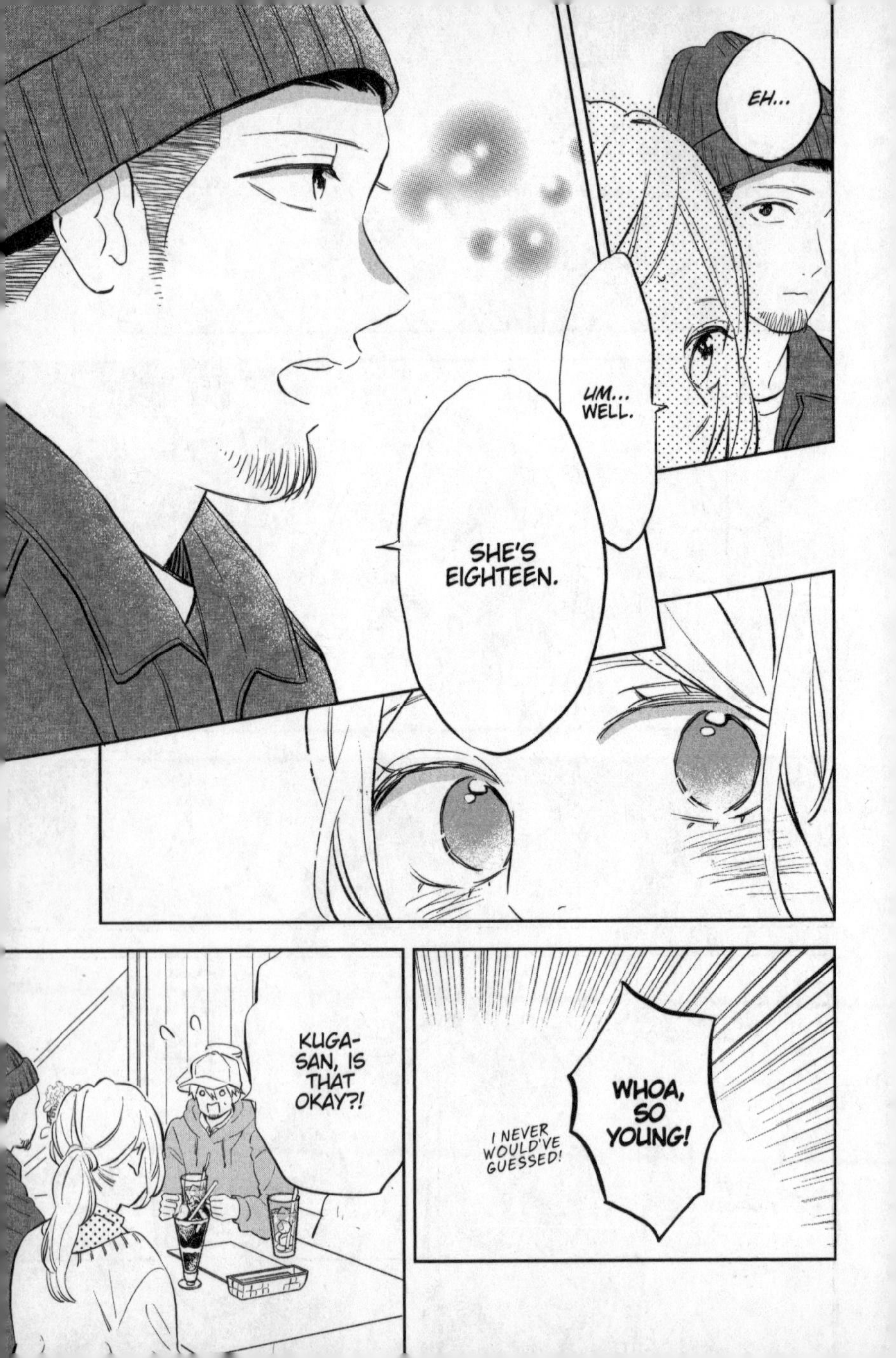
EH...
UM... WELL.
SHE'S EIGHTEEN.
WHOA, SO YOUNG!
I NEVER WOULD'VE GUESSED!
KUGA-SAN, IS THAT OKAY?!

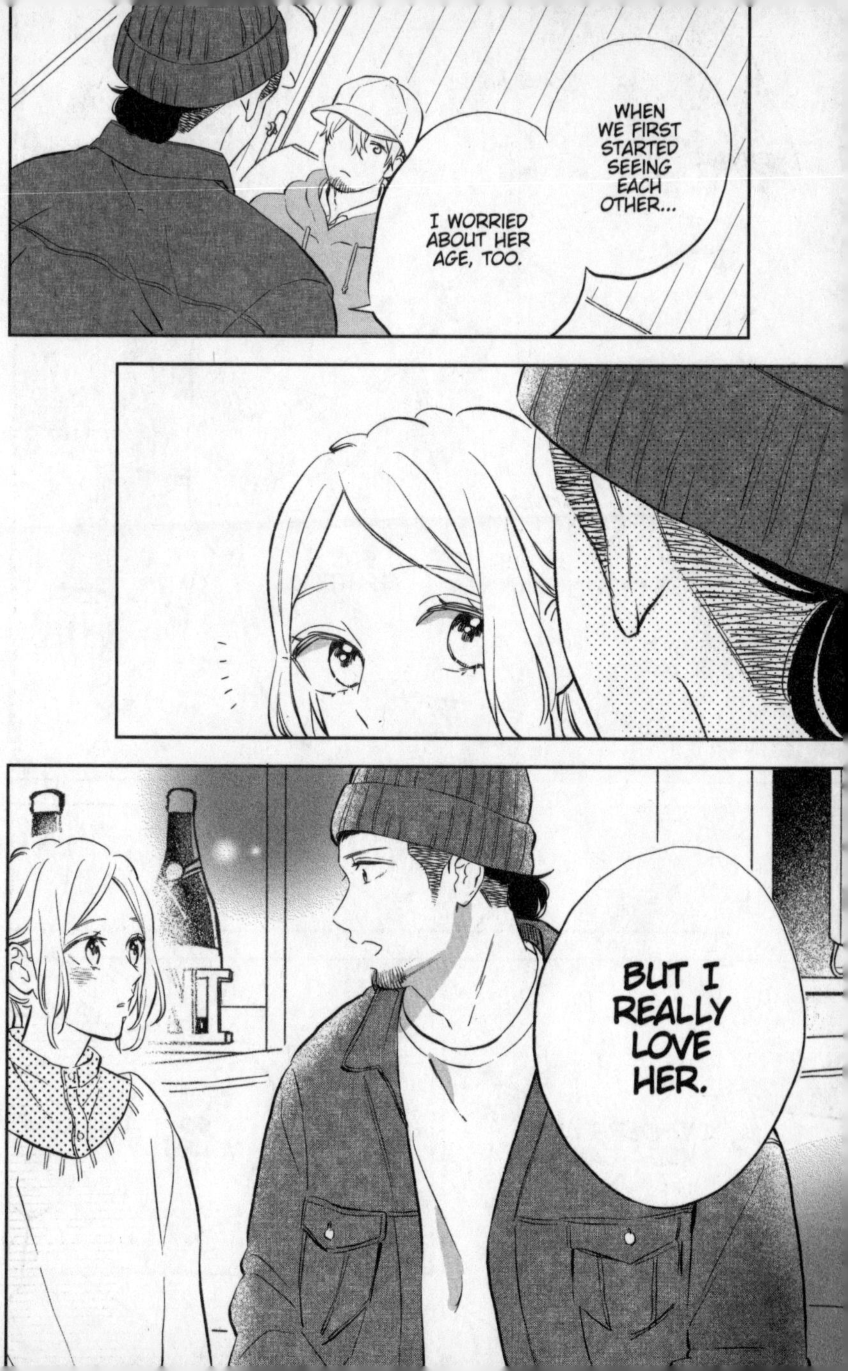
WHEN WE FIRST STARTED SEEING EACH OTHER...
I WORRIED ABOUT HER AGE, TOO.
BUT I REALLY LOVE HER.

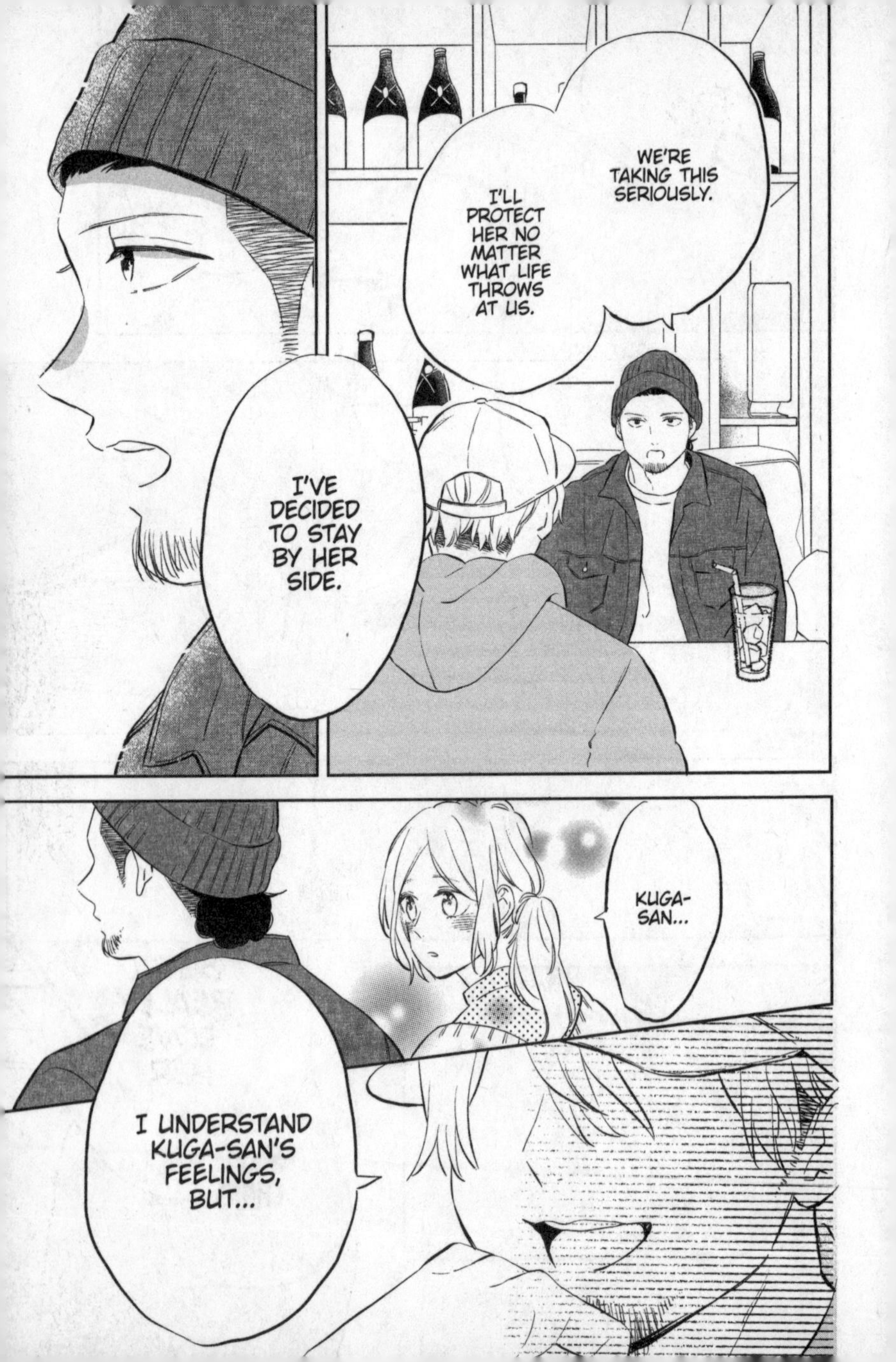
WE'RE TAKING THIS SERIOUSLY.
I'LL PROTECT HER NO MATTER WHAT LIFE THROWS AT US.
I'VE DECIDED TO STAY BY HER SIDE.
KUGA-SAN...
I UNDERSTAND KUGA-SAN'S FEELINGS, BUT...

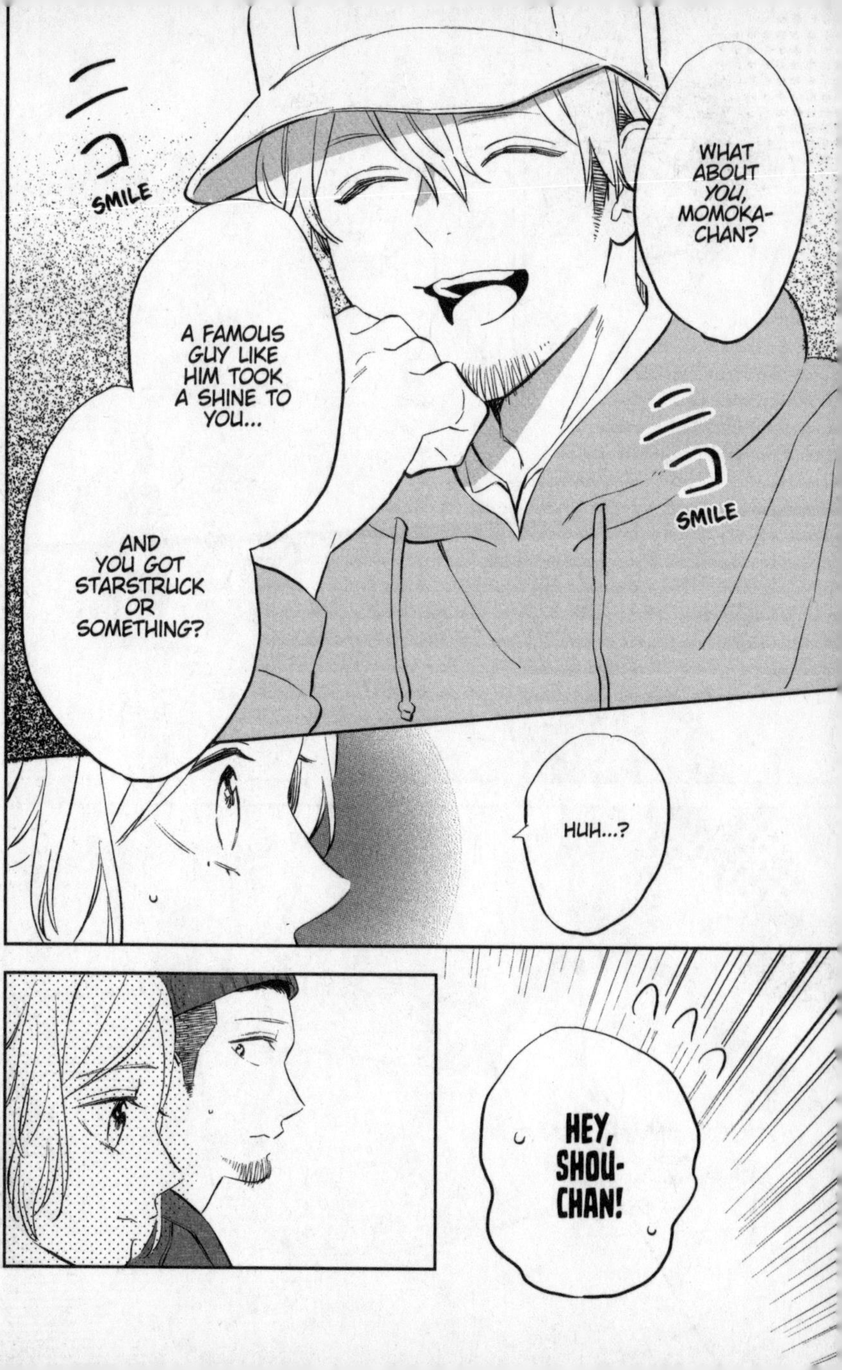
WHAT ABOUT YOU, MOMOKA-CHAN?
SMILE
A FAMOUS GUY LIKE HIM TOOK A SHINE TO YOU...
AND YOU GOT STARSTRUCK OR SOMETHING?
SMILE
HUH...?
HEY, SHOU-CHAN!

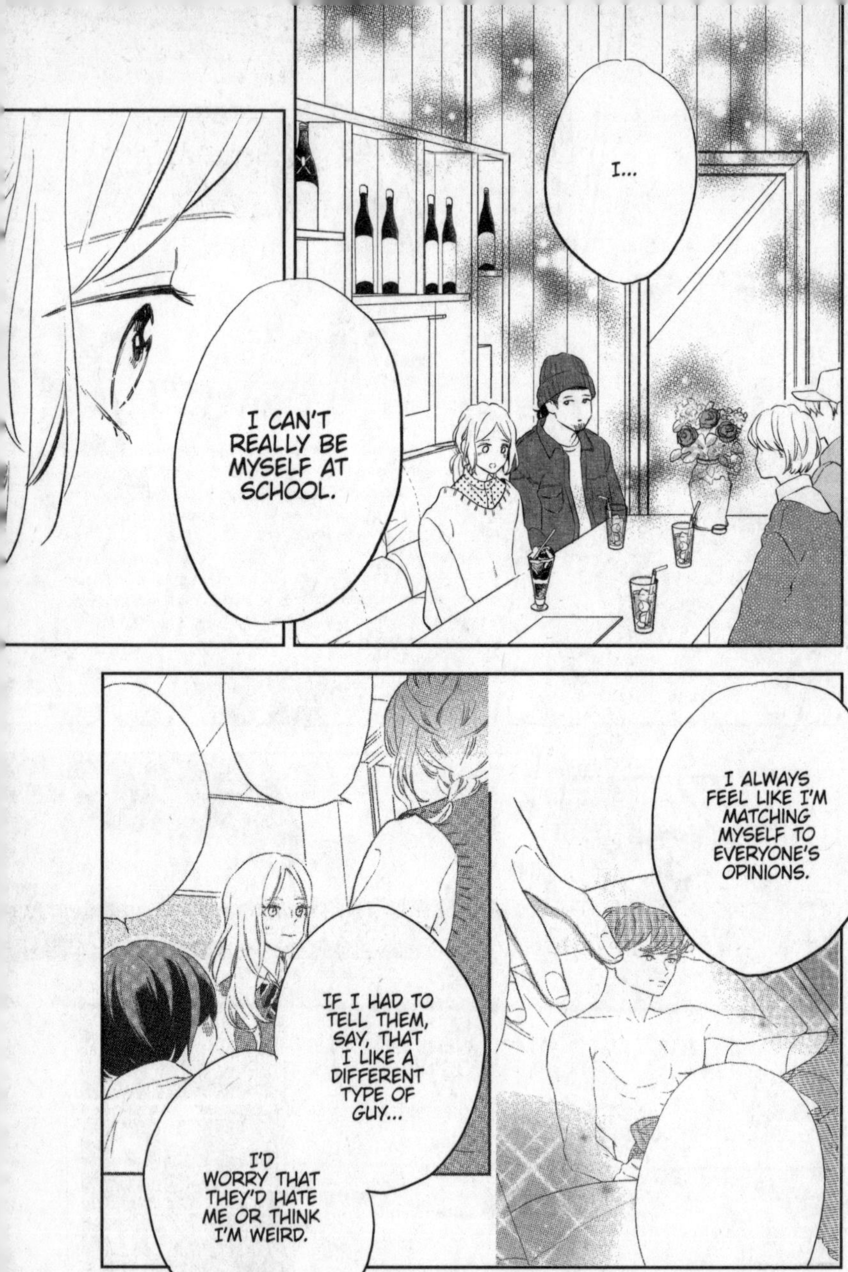
I...
I CAN'T REALLY BE MYSELF AT SCHOOL.
I ALWAYS FEEL LIKE I'M MATCHING MYSELF TO EVERYONE'S OPINIONS.
IF I HAD TO TELL THEM, SAY, THAT I LIKE A DIFFERENT TYPE OF GUY...
I'D WORRY THAT THEY'D HATE ME OR THINK I'M WEIRD.

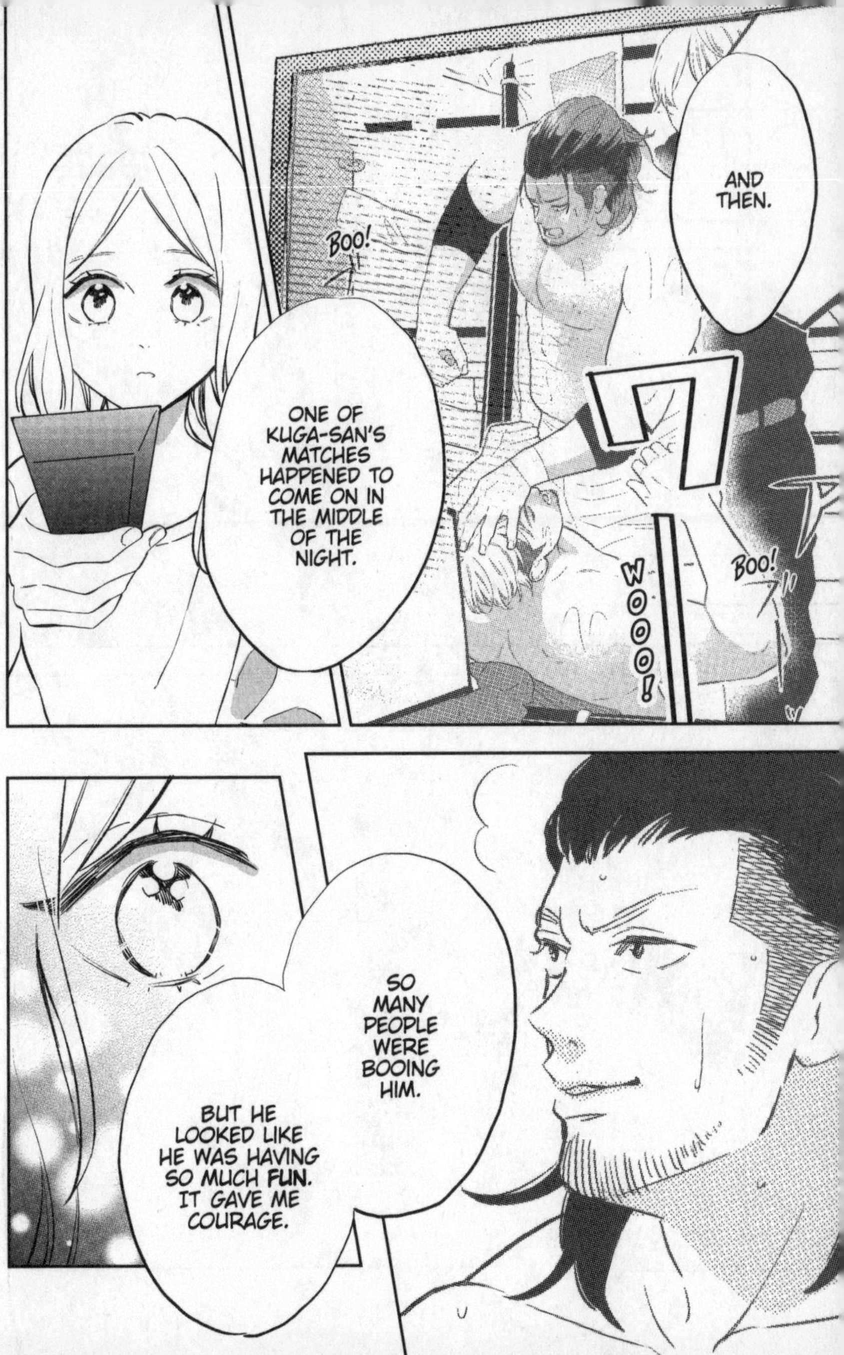
AND THEN.
BOO!
WOOOO!
BOO!
ONE OF KUGA-SAN'S MATCHES HAPPENED TO COME ON IN THE MIDDLE OF THE NIGHT.
SO MANY PEOPLE WERE BOOING HIM.
BUT HE LOOKED LIKE HE WAS HAVING SO MUCH FUN. IT GAVE ME COURAGE.

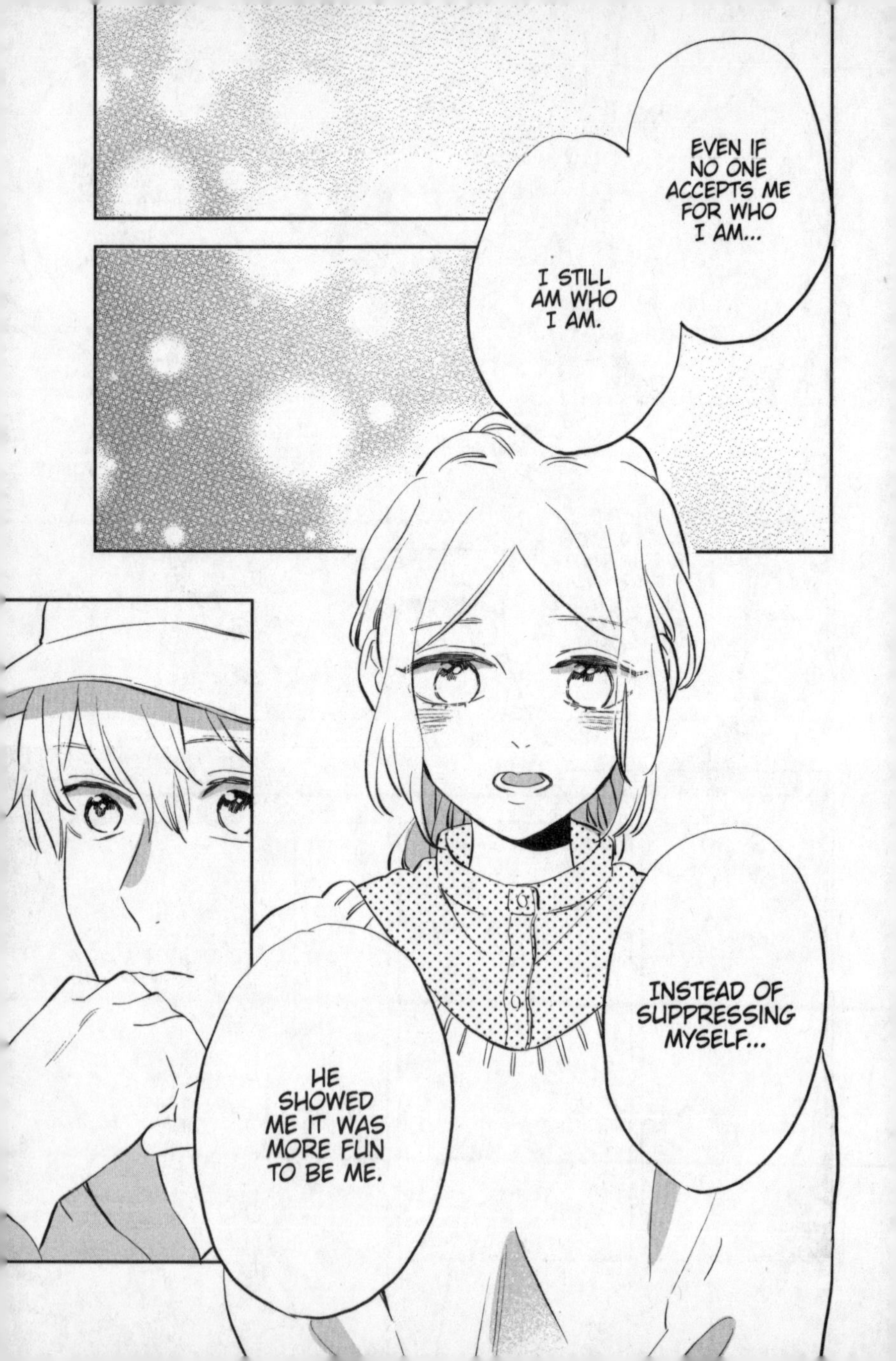
EVEN IF NO ONE ACCEPTS ME FOR WHO I AM...
I STILL AM WHO I AM.
INSTEAD OF SUPPRESSING MYSELF...
HE SHOWED ME IT WAS MORE FUN TO BE ME.

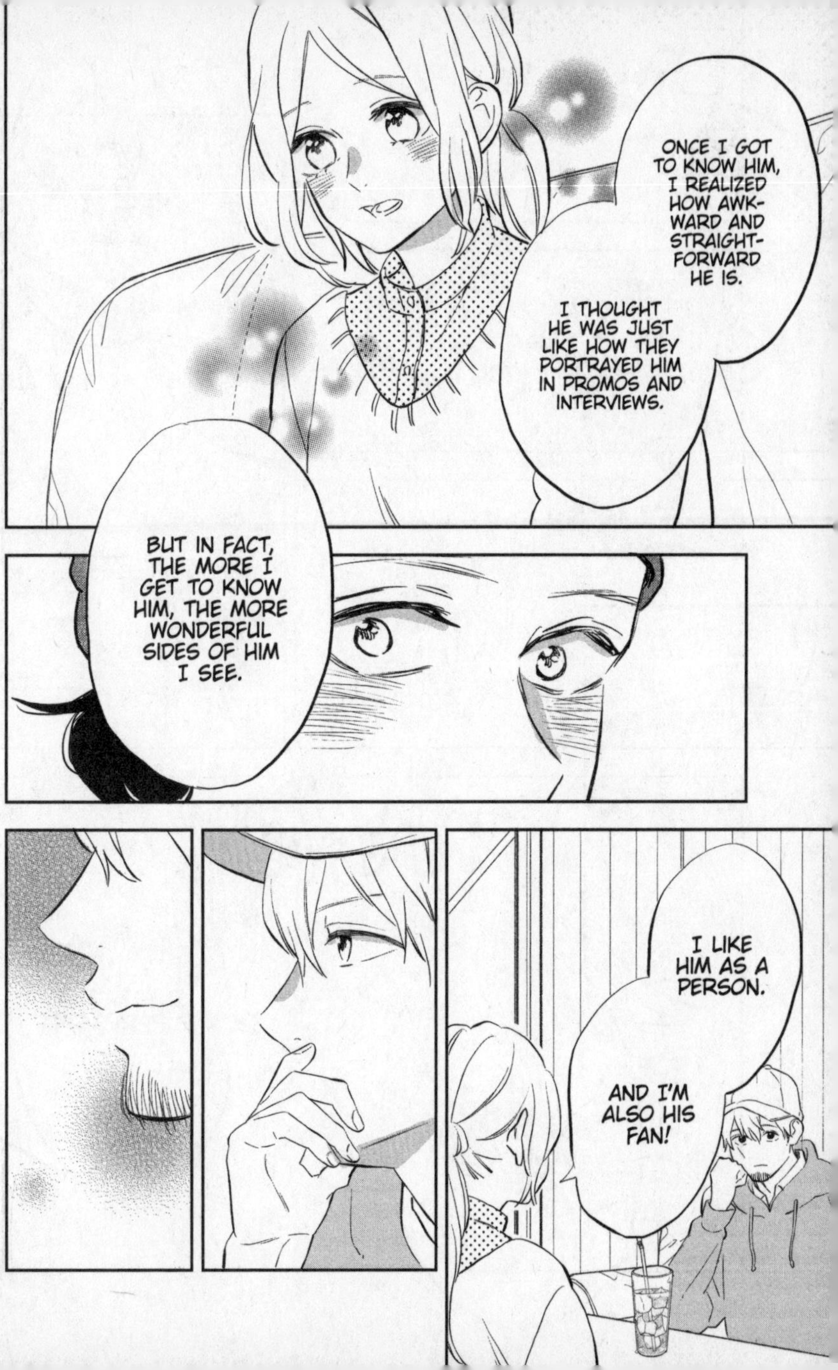
ONCE I GOT TO KNOW HIM, I REALIZED HOW AWK-WARD AND STRAIGHT-FORWARD HE IS.
I THOUGHT HE WAS JUST LIKE HOW THEY PORTRAYED HIM IN PROMOS AND INTERVIEWS.
BUT IN FACT, THE MORE I GET TO KNOW HIM, THE MORE WONDERFUL SIDES OF HIM I SEE.
I LIKE HIM AS A PERSON.
AND I'M ALSO HIS FAN!

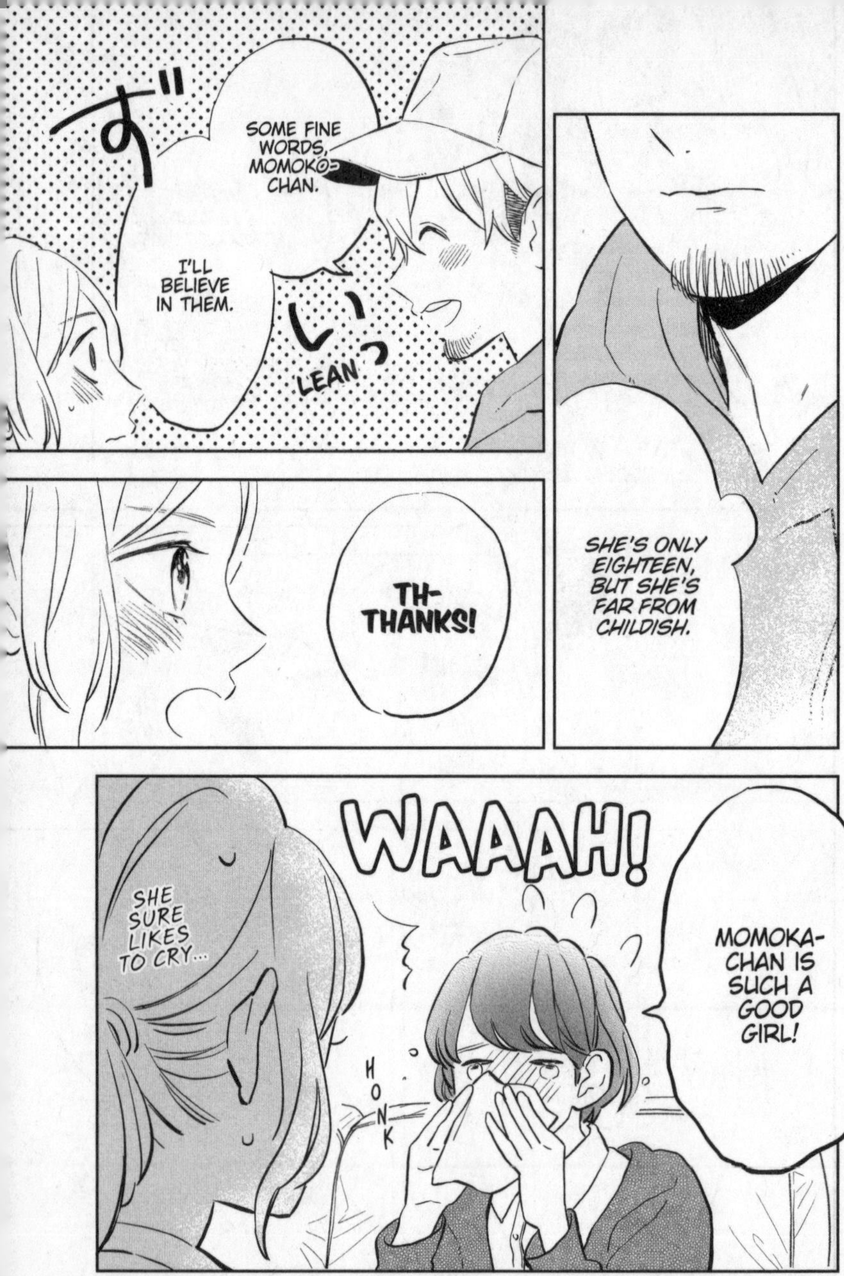
SHE'S ONLY EIGHTEEN, BUT SHE'S FAR FROM CHILDISH.
SOME FINE WORDS, MOMOKO-CHAN.
I'LL BELIEVE IN THEM.
ず
しっ
LEAN
TH-THANKS!
MOMOKA-CHAN IS SUCH A GOOD GIRL!
WAAAH!
HONK
SHE SURE LIKES TO CRY...

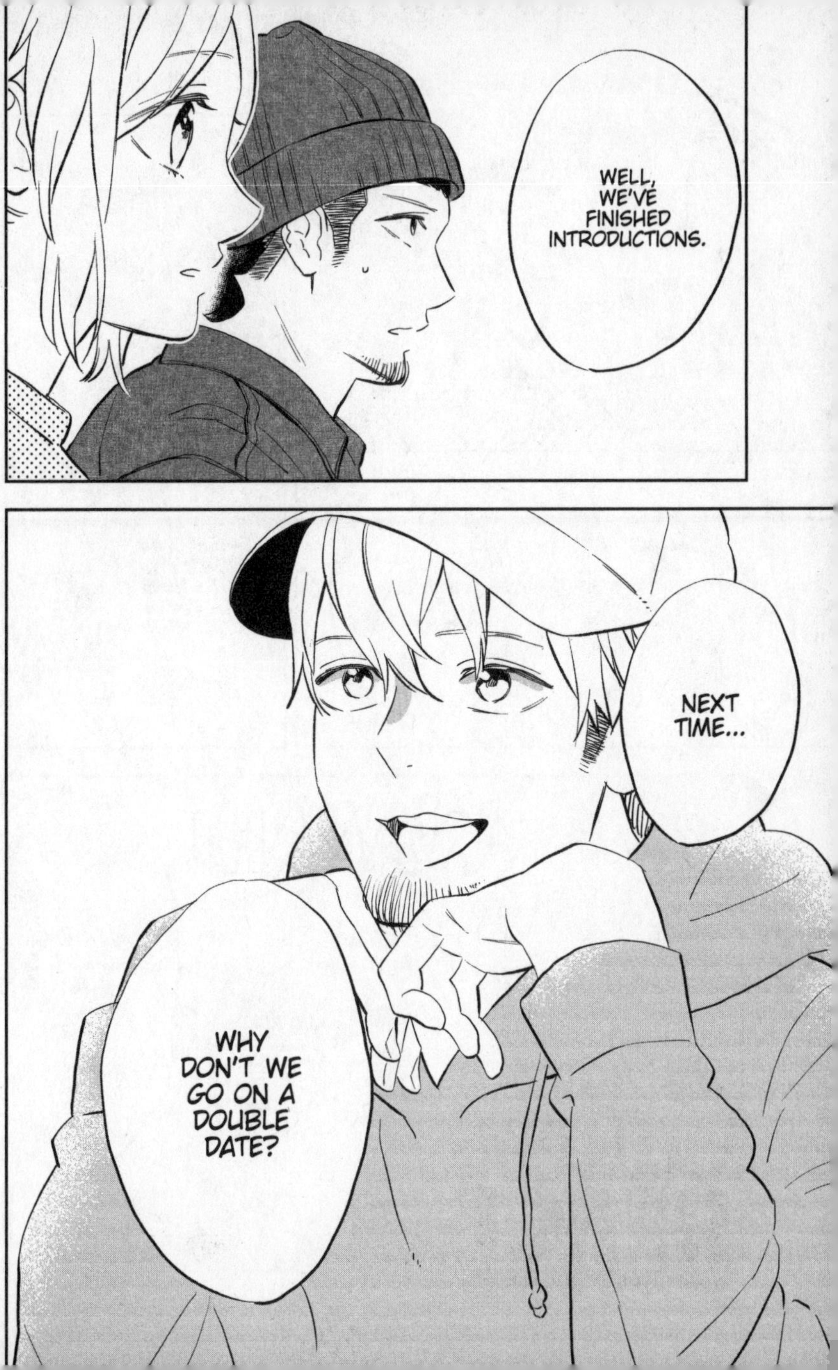
WELL, WE'VE FINISHED INTRODUCTIONS.
NEXT TIME...
WHY DON'T WE GO ON A DOUBLE DATE?

Cutie and the BEAST

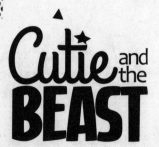

Cutie and the
BEAST

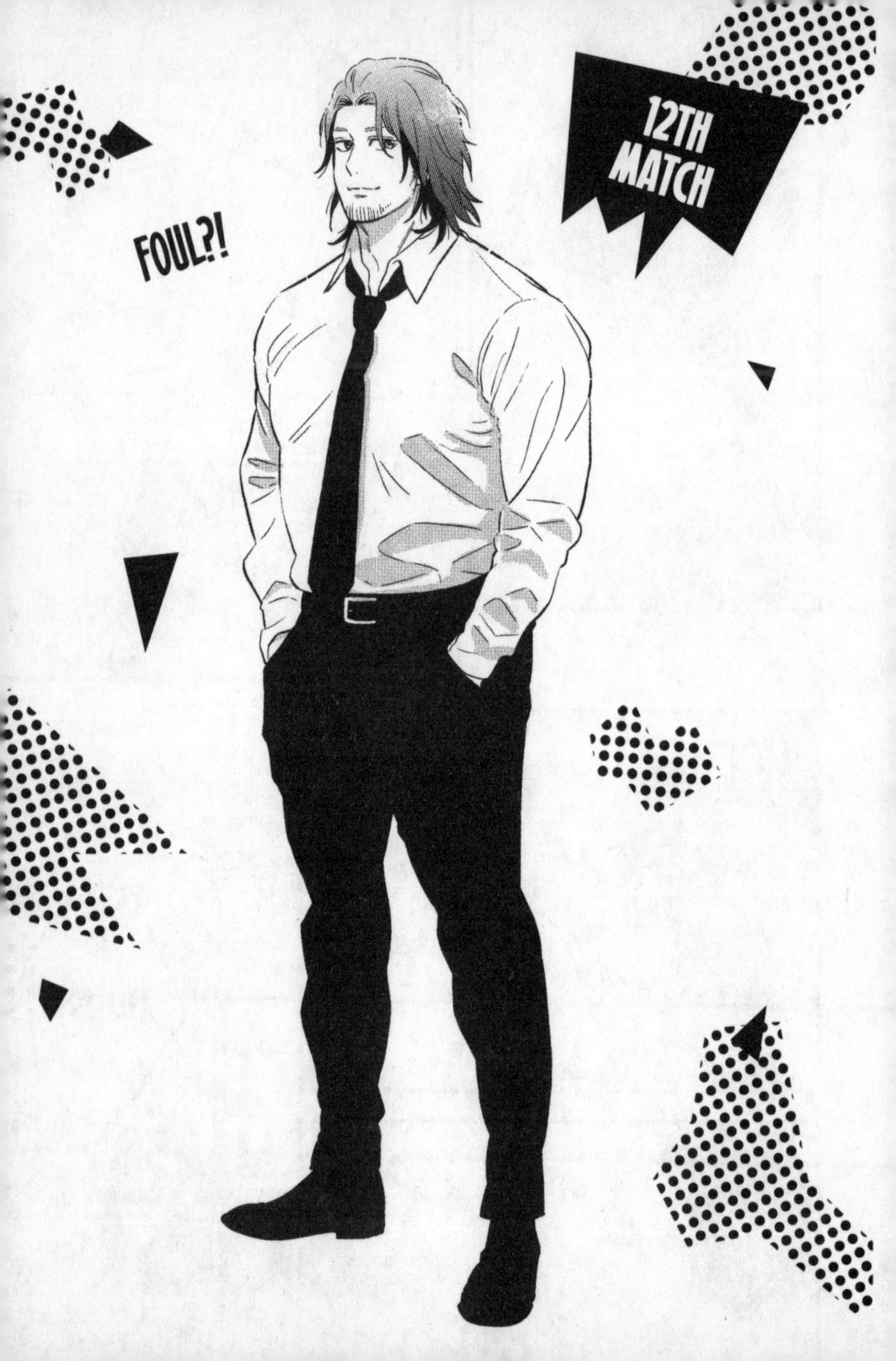
12TH MATCH
FOUL?!

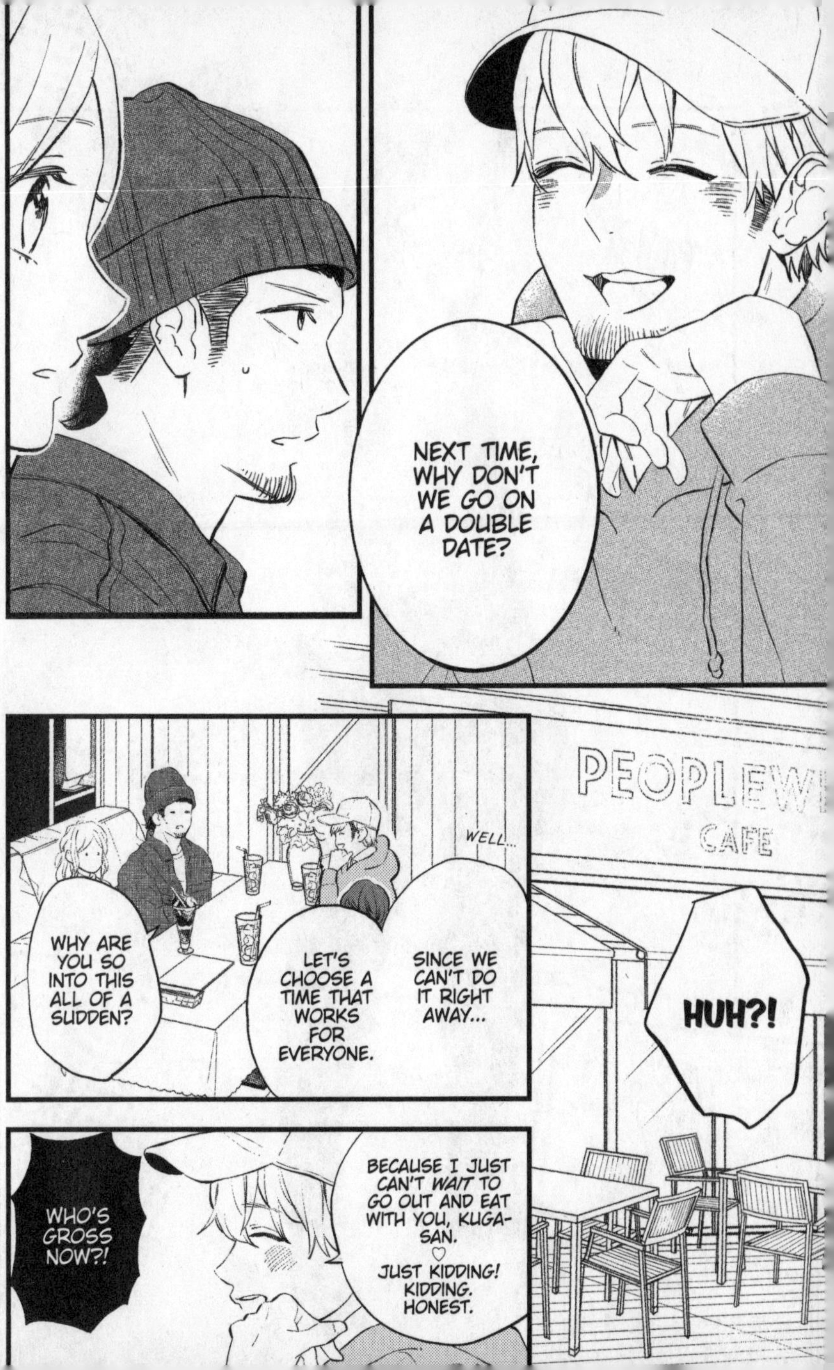
NEXT TIME, WHY DON'T WE GO ON A DOUBLE DATE?
PEOPLEW
CAFE
HUH?!
WELL...
SINCE WE CAN'T DO IT RIGHT AWAY...
LET'S CHOOSE A TIME THAT WORKS FOR EVERYONE.
WHY ARE YOU SO INTO THIS ALL OF A SUDDEN?
BECAUSE I JUST CAN'T *WAIT* TO GO OUT AND EAT WITH YOU, KUGA-SAN. ♡
JUST KIDDING! KIDDING. HONEST.
WHO'S GROSS NOW?!

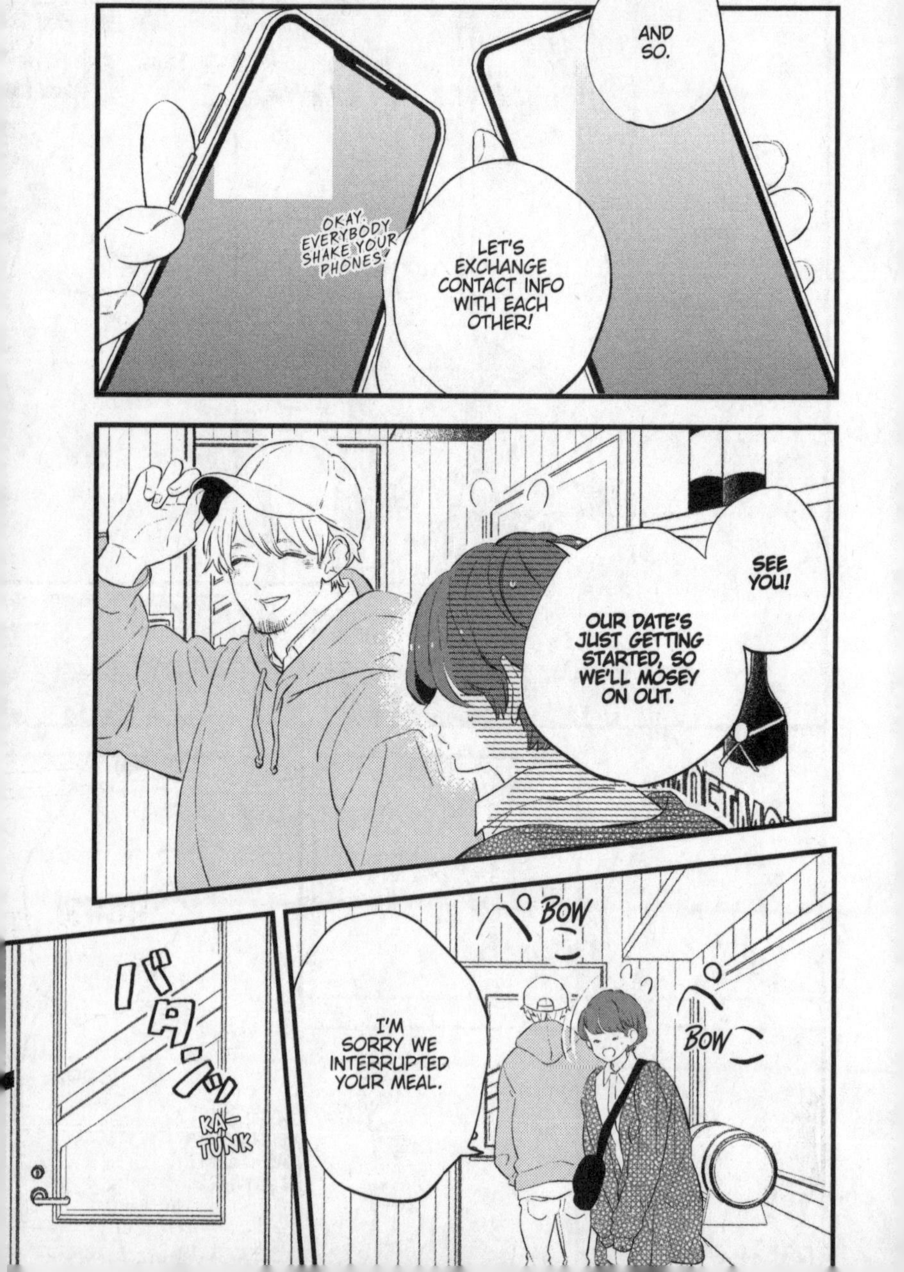
AND SO.
LET'S EXCHANGE CONTACT INFO WITH EACH OTHER!
OKAY, EVERYBODY SHAKE YOUR PHONES.
SEE YOU!
OUR DATE'S JUST GETTING STARTED, SO WE'LL MOSEY ON OUT.
BOW
BOW
I'M SORRY WE INTERRUPTED YOUR MEAL.
パタンッ
KA-TUNK

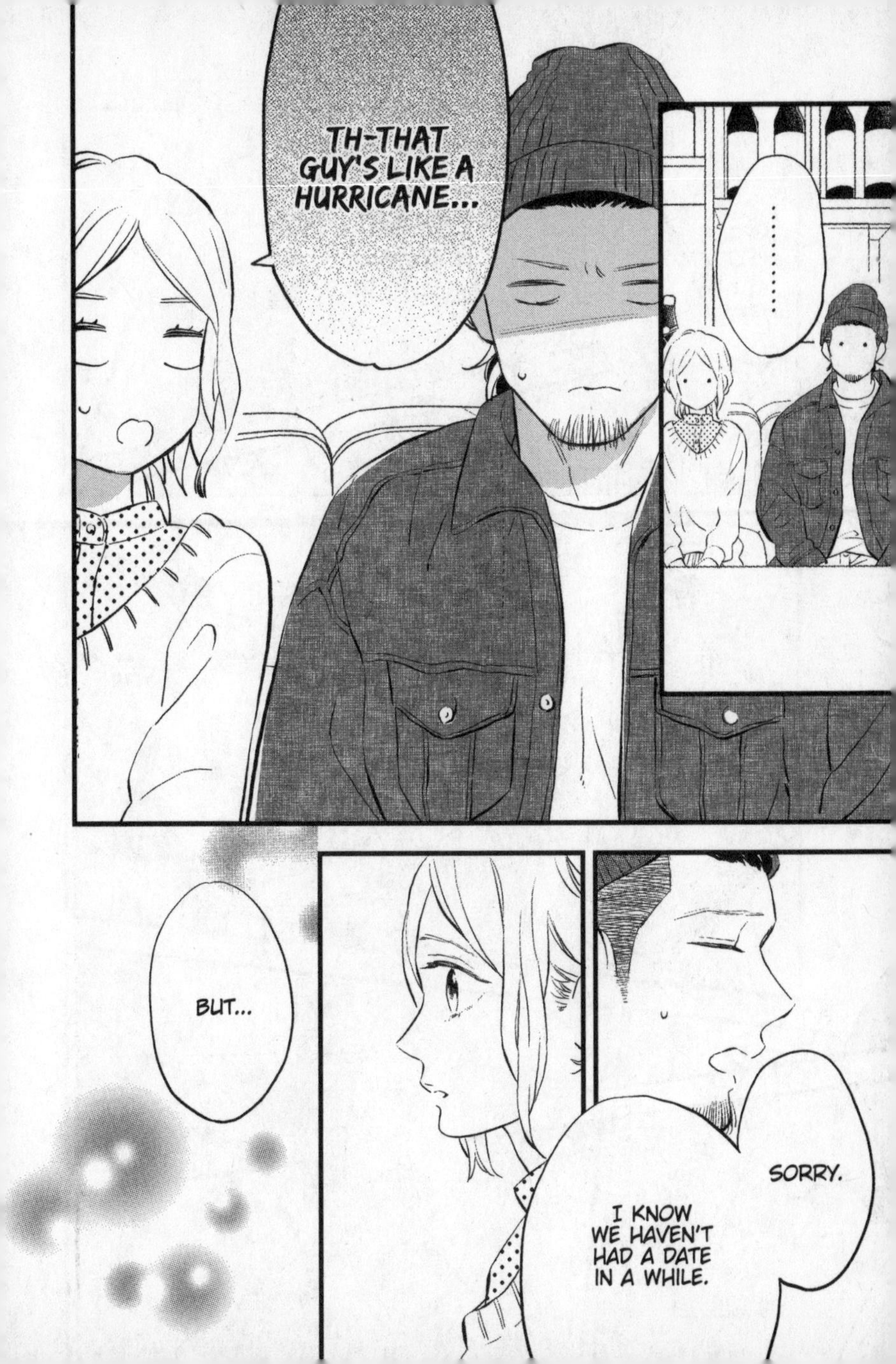
......
TH-THAT GUY'S LIKE A HURRICANE...
SORRY.
I KNOW WE HAVEN'T HAD A DATE IN A WHILE.
BUT...

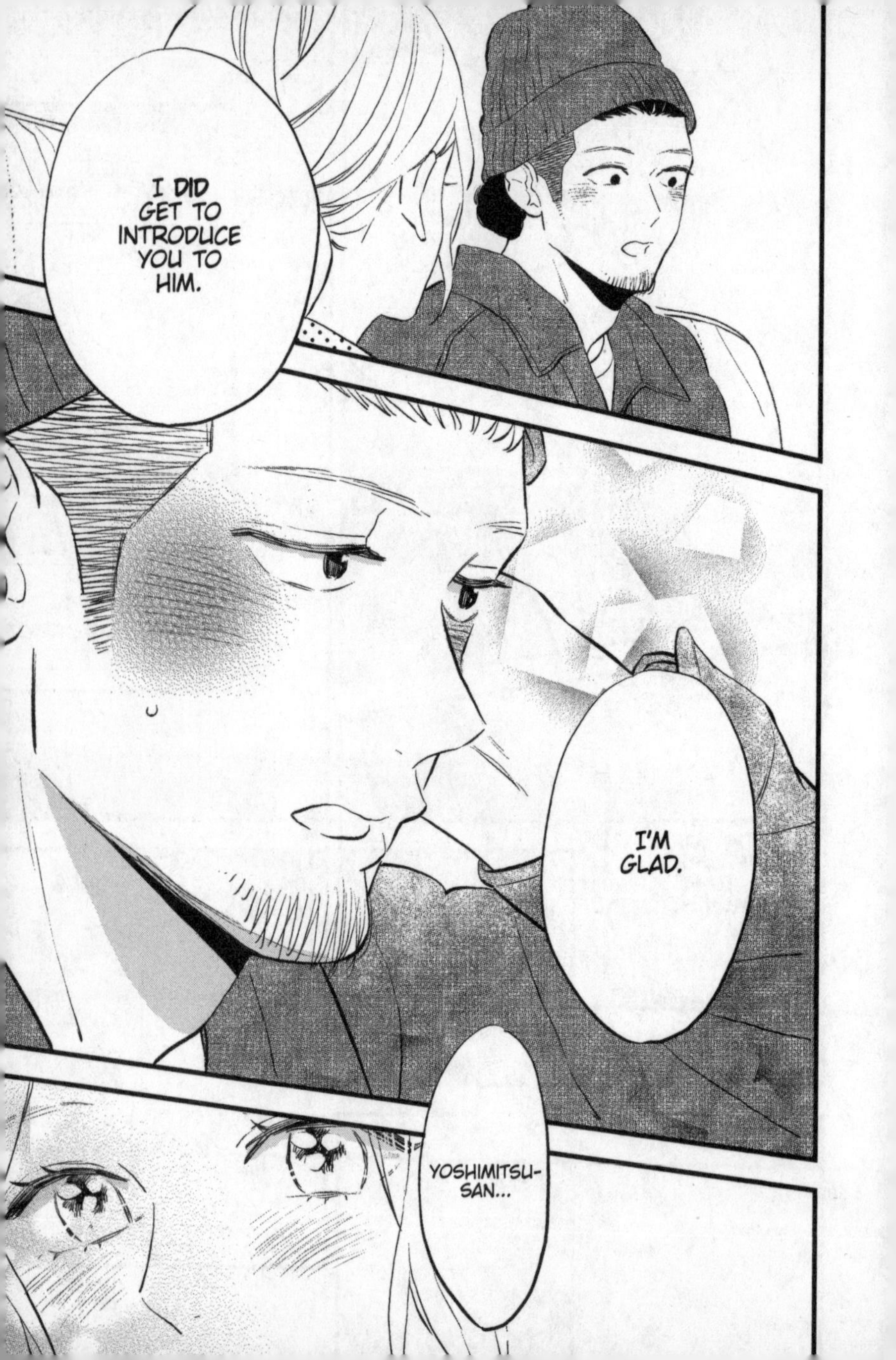
I DID GET TO INTRODUCE YOU TO HIM.
I'M GLAD.
YOSHIMITSU-SAN...

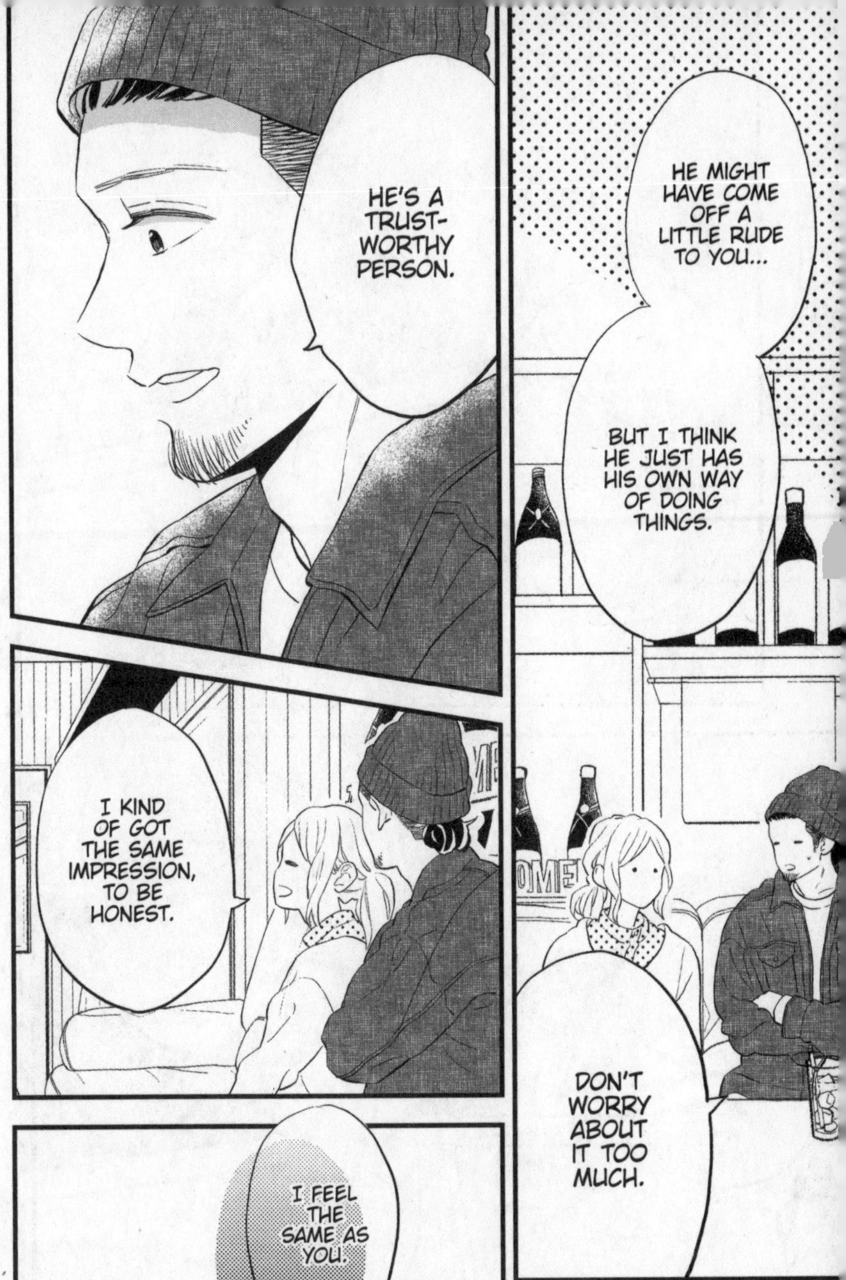
HE MIGHT HAVE COME OFF A LITTLE RUDE TO YOU...
BUT I THINK HE JUST HAS HIS OWN WAY OF DOING THINGS.
DON'T WORRY ABOUT IT TOO MUCH.
HE'S A TRUST-WORTHY PERSON.
I KIND OF GOT THE SAME IMPRESSION, TO BE HONEST.
I FEEL THE SAME AS YOU.

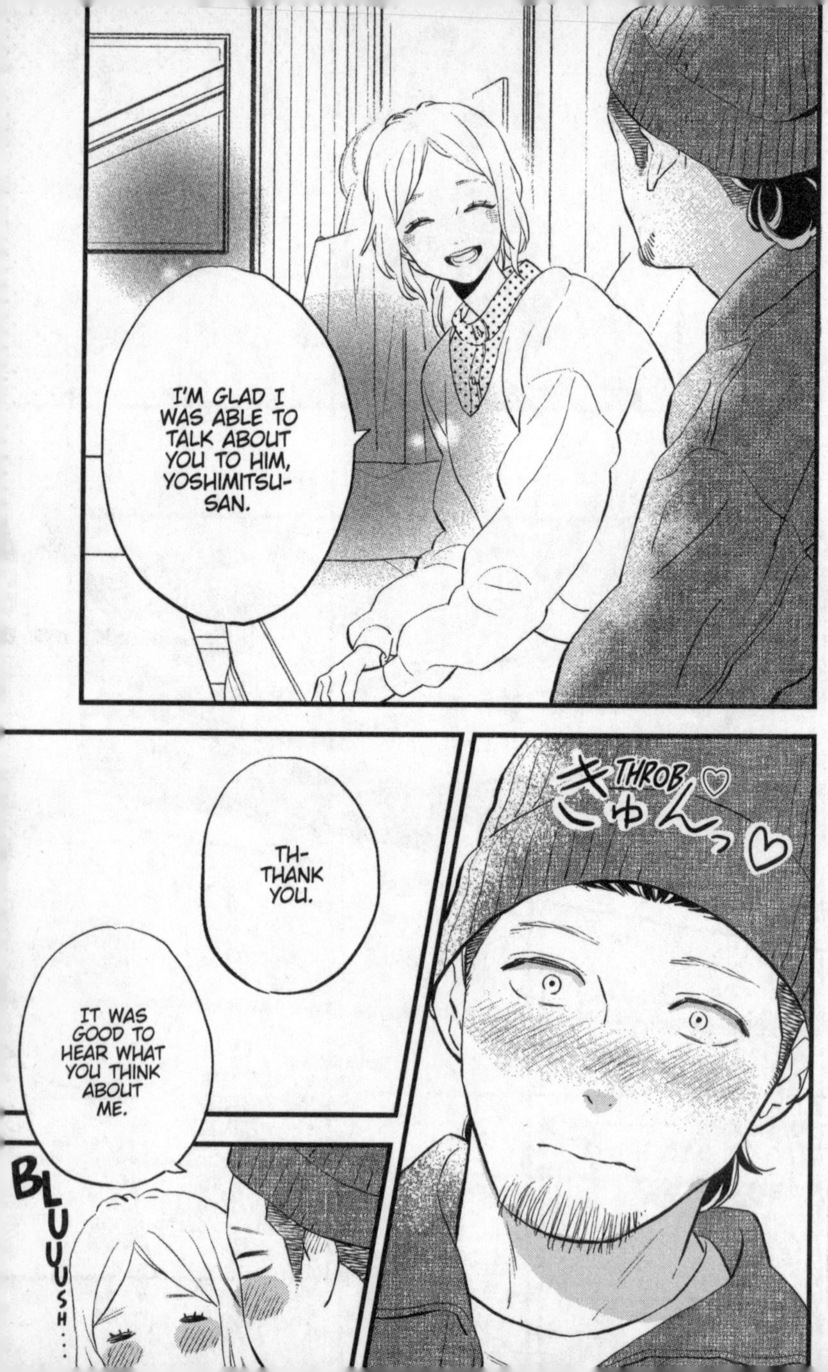
I'M GLAD I WAS ABLE TO TALK ABOUT YOU TO HIM, YOSHIMITSU-SAN.
きゅんっ
THROB
TH-THANK YOU.
IT WAS GOOD TO HEAR WHAT YOU THINK ABOUT ME.
BLUUUSH...

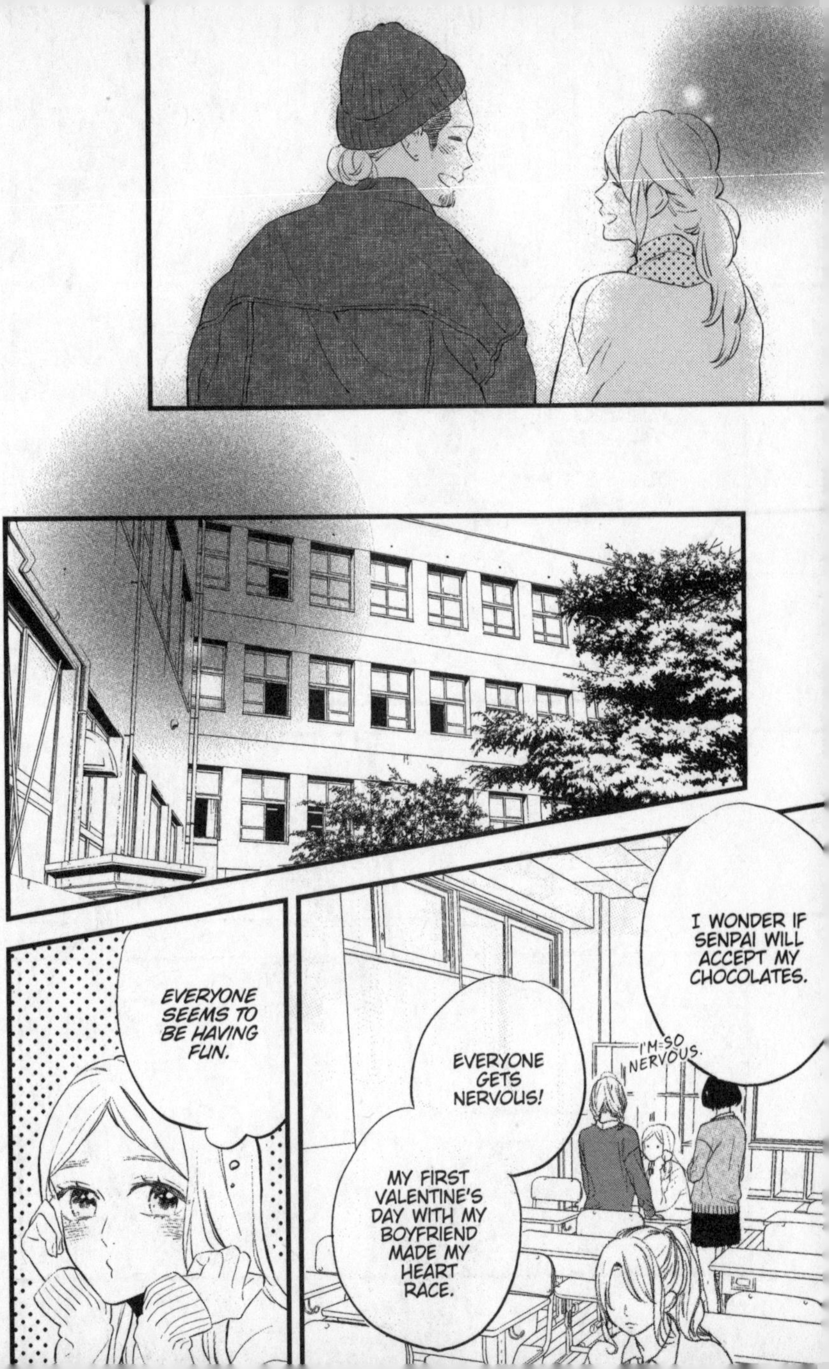
I WONDER IF SENPAI WILL ACCEPT MY CHOCOLATES.
I'M SO NERVOUS.
EVERYONE GETS NERVOUS!
MY FIRST VALENTINE'S DAY WITH MY BOYFRIEND MADE MY HEART RACE.
EVERYONE SEEMS TO BE HAVING FUN.

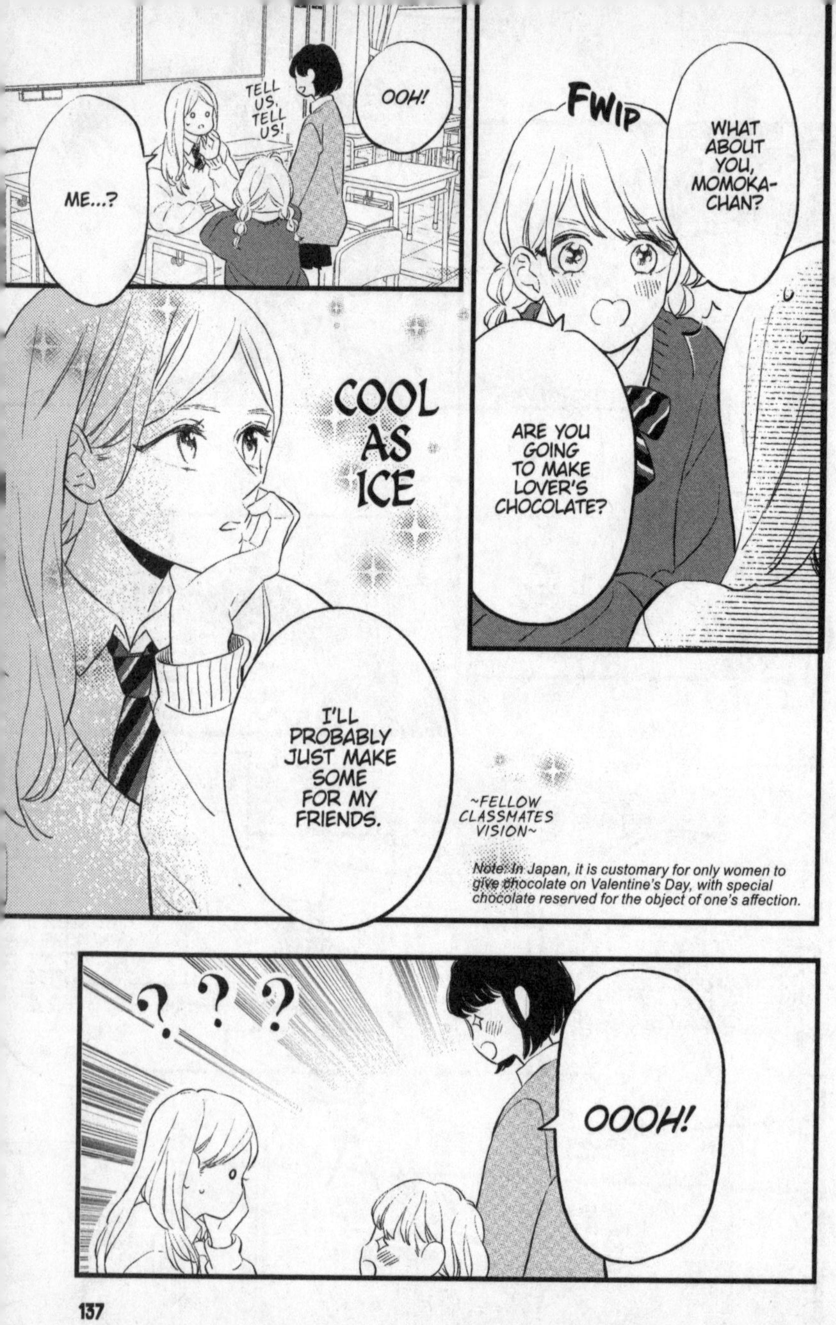
FWIP
WHAT ABOUT YOU, MOMOKA-CHAN?
ARE YOU GOING TO MAKE LOVER'S CHOCOLATE?
OOH!
TELL US, TELL US!
ME...?
COOL AS ICE
I'LL PROBABLY JUST MAKE SOME FOR MY FRIENDS.
~FELLOW CLASSMATES VISION~
Note: In Japan, it is customary for only women to give chocolate on Valentine's Day, with special chocolate reserved for the object of one's affection.
? ? ?
OOOH!

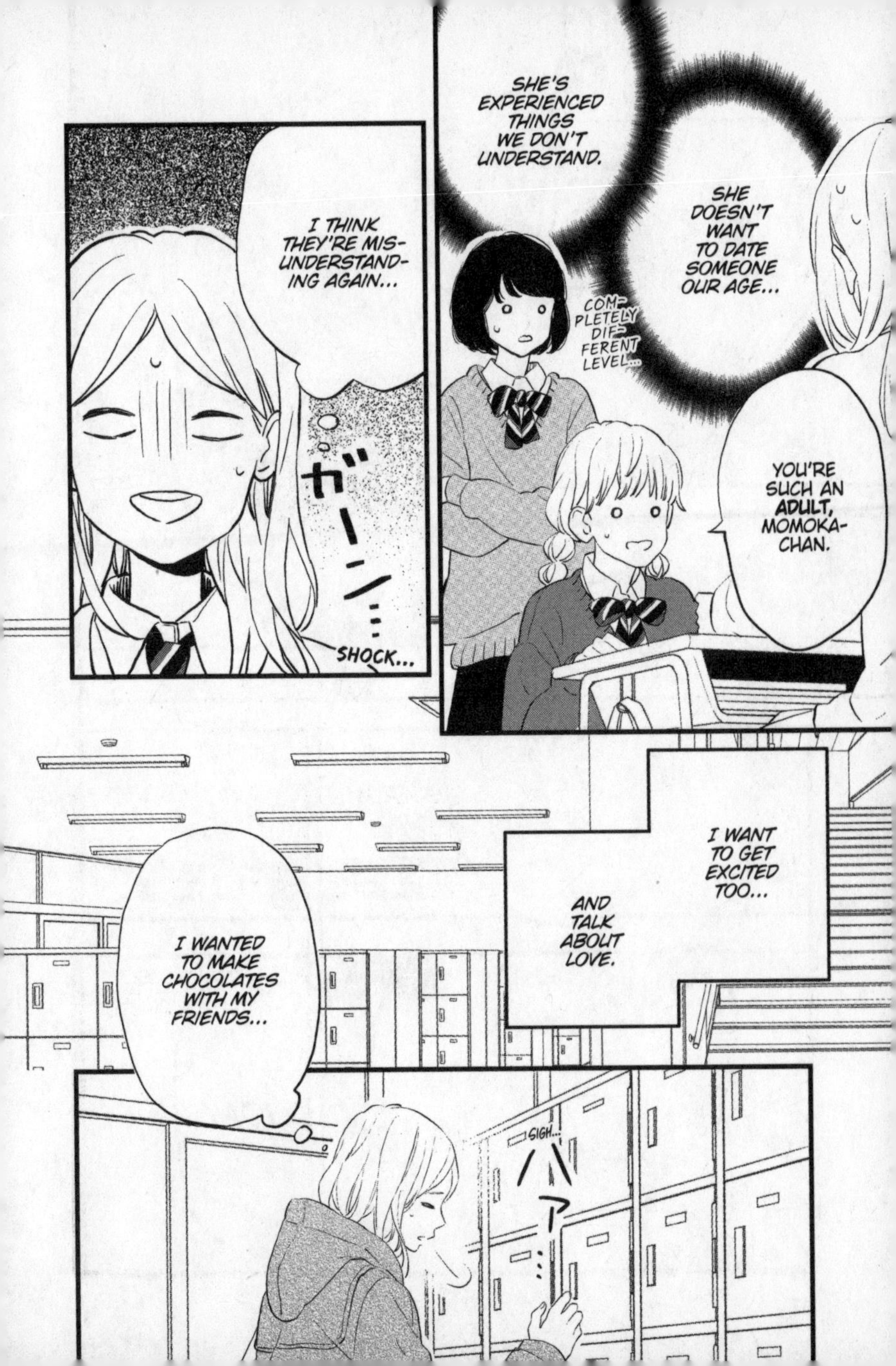
SHE'S EXPERIENCED THINGS WE DON'T UNDERSTAND.
SHE DOESN'T WANT TO DATE SOMEONE OUR AGE...
COM-PLETELY DIF-FERENT LEVEL...
YOU'RE SUCH AN **ADULT**, MOMOKA-CHAN.
I THINK THEY'RE MIS-UNDERSTAND-ING AGAIN...
ガーン…
SHOCK...
I WANT TO GET EXCITED TOO...
AND TALK ABOUT LOVE.
I WANTED TO MAKE CHOCOLATES WITH MY FRIENDS...
ハァ…
SIGH...

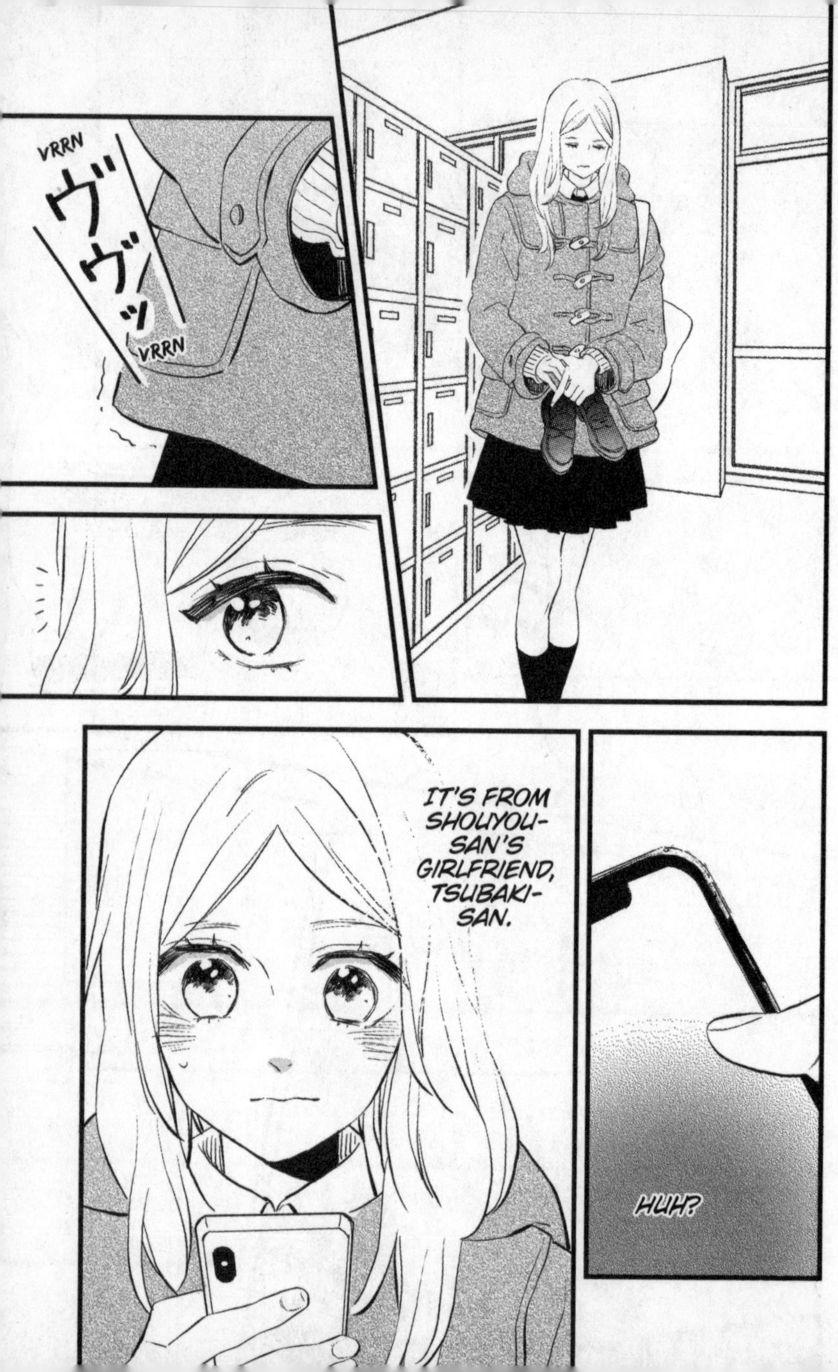
VRRN
ヴヴッ
VRRN
HUH?
IT'S FROM SHOUYOU-SAN'S GIRLFRIEND, TSUBAKI-SAN.

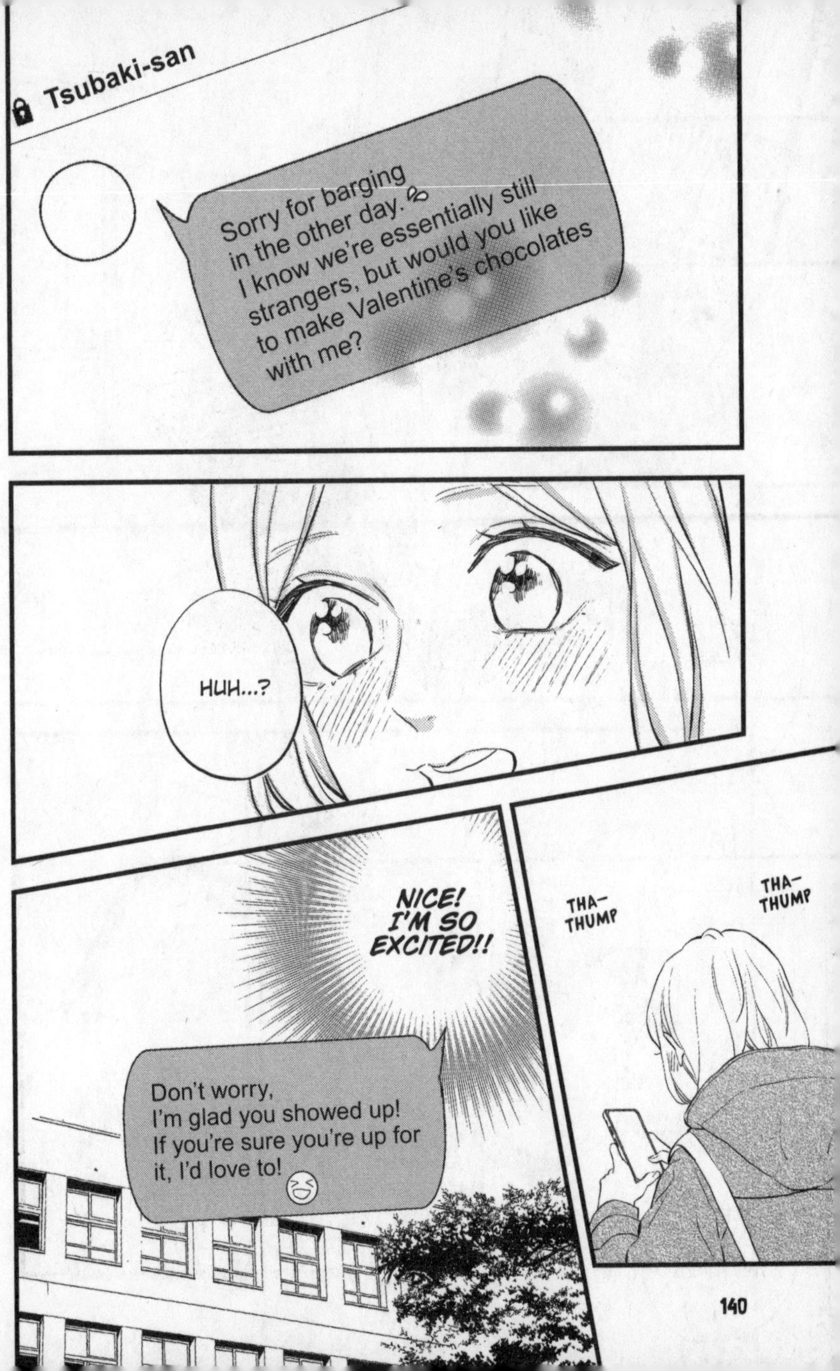
Tsubaki-san
Sorry for barging in the other day. I know we're essentially still strangers, but would you like to make Valentine's chocolates with me?
HUH...?
THA-THUMP
THA-THUMP
NICE! I'M SO EXCITED!!
Don't worry, I'm glad you showed up! If you're sure you're up for it, I'd love to!

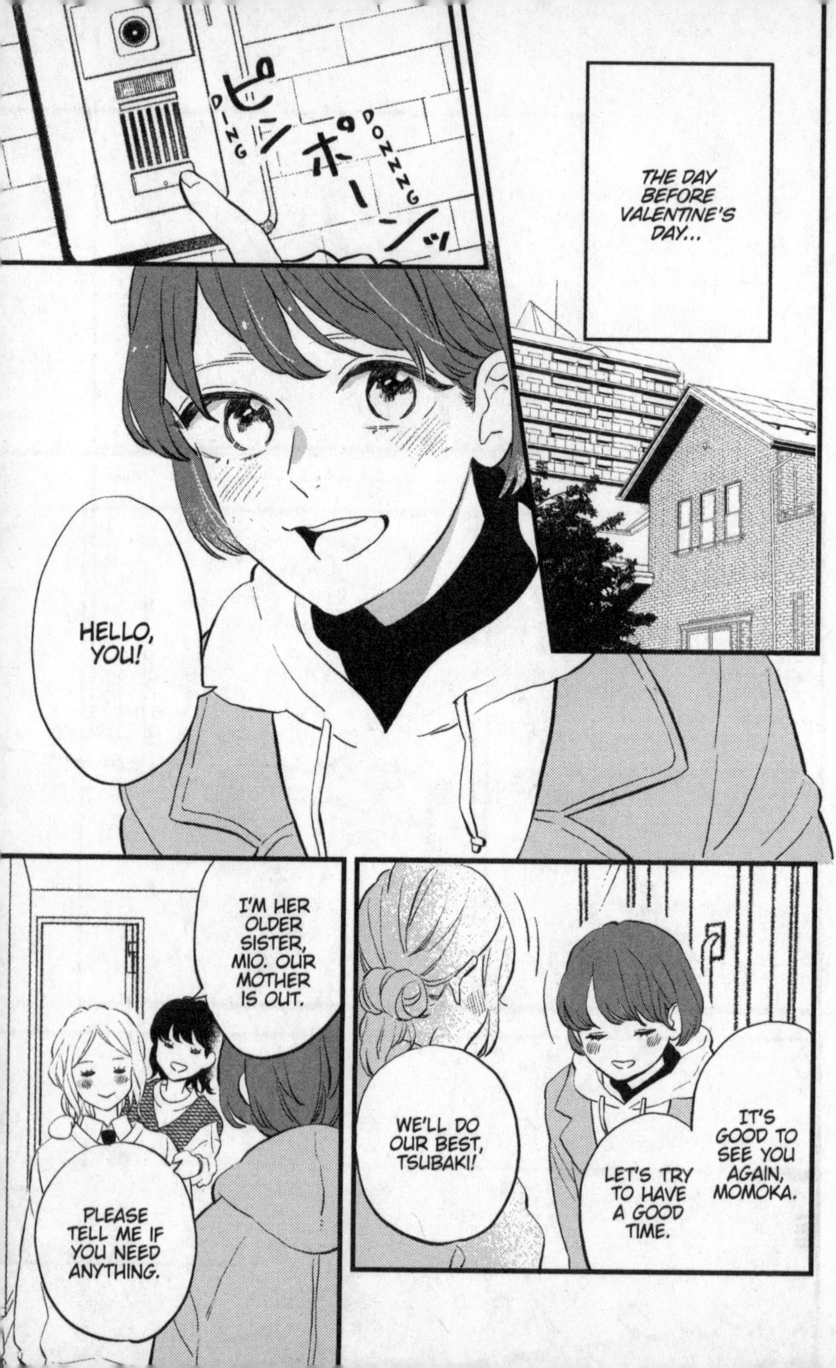
THE DAY BEFORE VALENTINE'S DAY...
ピンポーンッ
DING DONNNG
HELLO, YOU!
IT'S GOOD TO SEE YOU AGAIN, MOMOKA.
LET'S TRY TO HAVE A GOOD TIME.
WE'LL DO OUR BEST, TSUBAKI!
I'M HER OLDER SISTER, MIO. OUR MOTHER IS OUT.
PLEASE TELL ME IF YOU NEED ANYTHING.

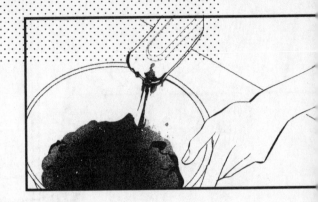

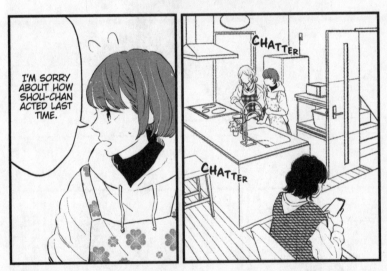

I'M SORRY ABOUT HOW SHOU-CHAN ACTED LAST TIME.

CHATTER

CHATTER

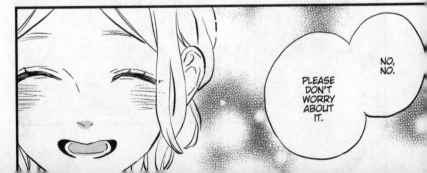

NO, NO.

PLEASE DON'T WORRY ABOUT IT.

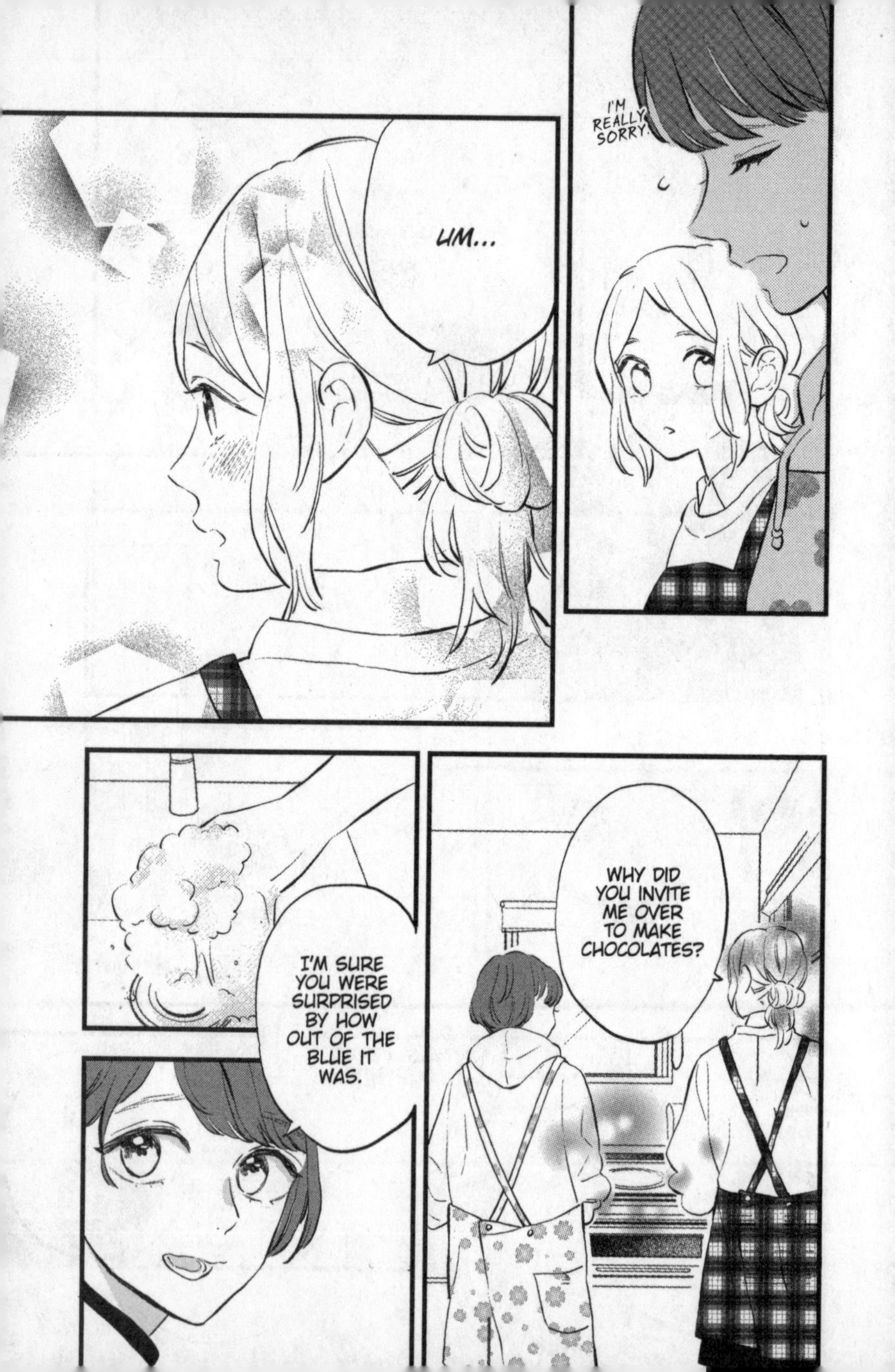
I'M REALLY SORRY.
UM...
WHY DID YOU INVITE ME OVER TO MAKE CHOCOLATES?
I'M SURE YOU WERE SURPRISED BY HOW OUT OF THE BLUE IT WAS.

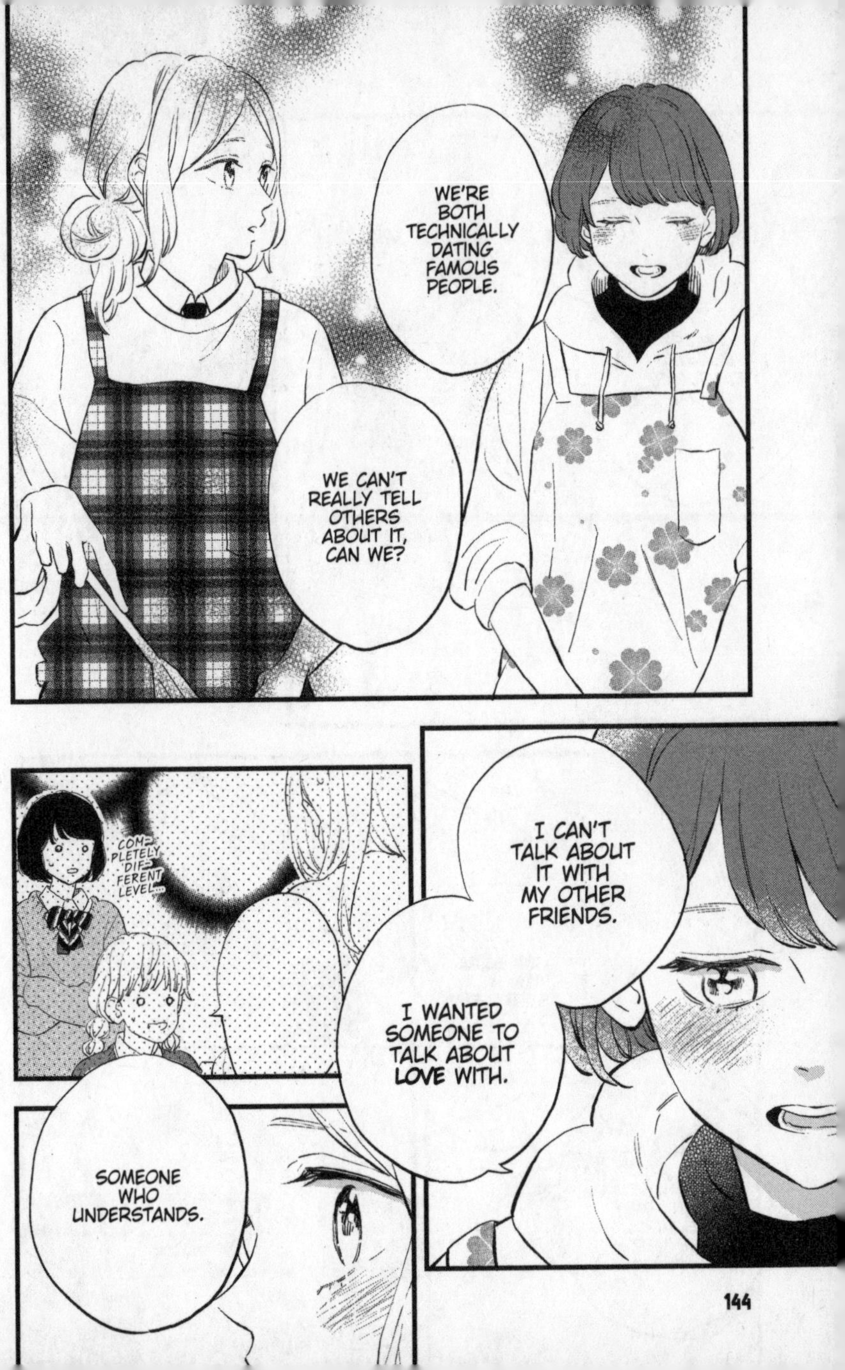
WE'RE BOTH TECHNICALLY DATING FAMOUS PEOPLE.
WE CAN'T REALLY TELL OTHERS ABOUT IT, CAN WE?
I CAN'T TALK ABOUT IT WITH MY OTHER FRIENDS.
I WANTED SOMEONE TO TALK ABOUT **LOVE** WITH.
COMPLETELY DIFFERENT LEVEL...
SOMEONE WHO UNDERSTANDS.

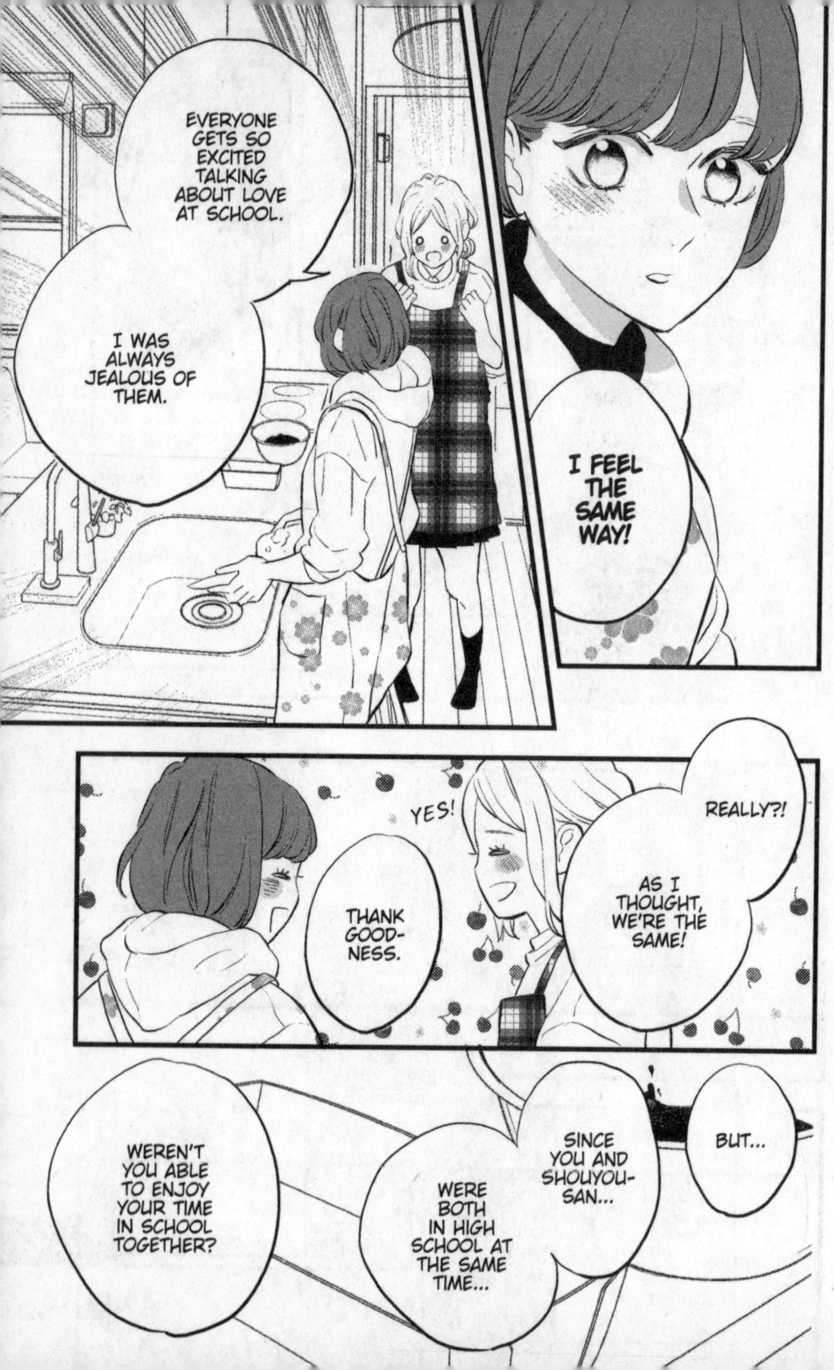
I FEEL THE SAME WAY!
EVERYONE GETS SO EXCITED TALKING ABOUT LOVE AT SCHOOL.
I WAS ALWAYS JEALOUS OF THEM.
REALLY?!
AS I THOUGHT, WE'RE THE SAME!
YES!
THANK GOODNESS.
BUT...
SINCE YOU AND SHOUYOU-SAN...
WERE BOTH IN HIGH SCHOOL AT THE SAME TIME...
WEREN'T YOU ABLE TO ENJOY YOUR TIME IN SCHOOL TOGETHER?

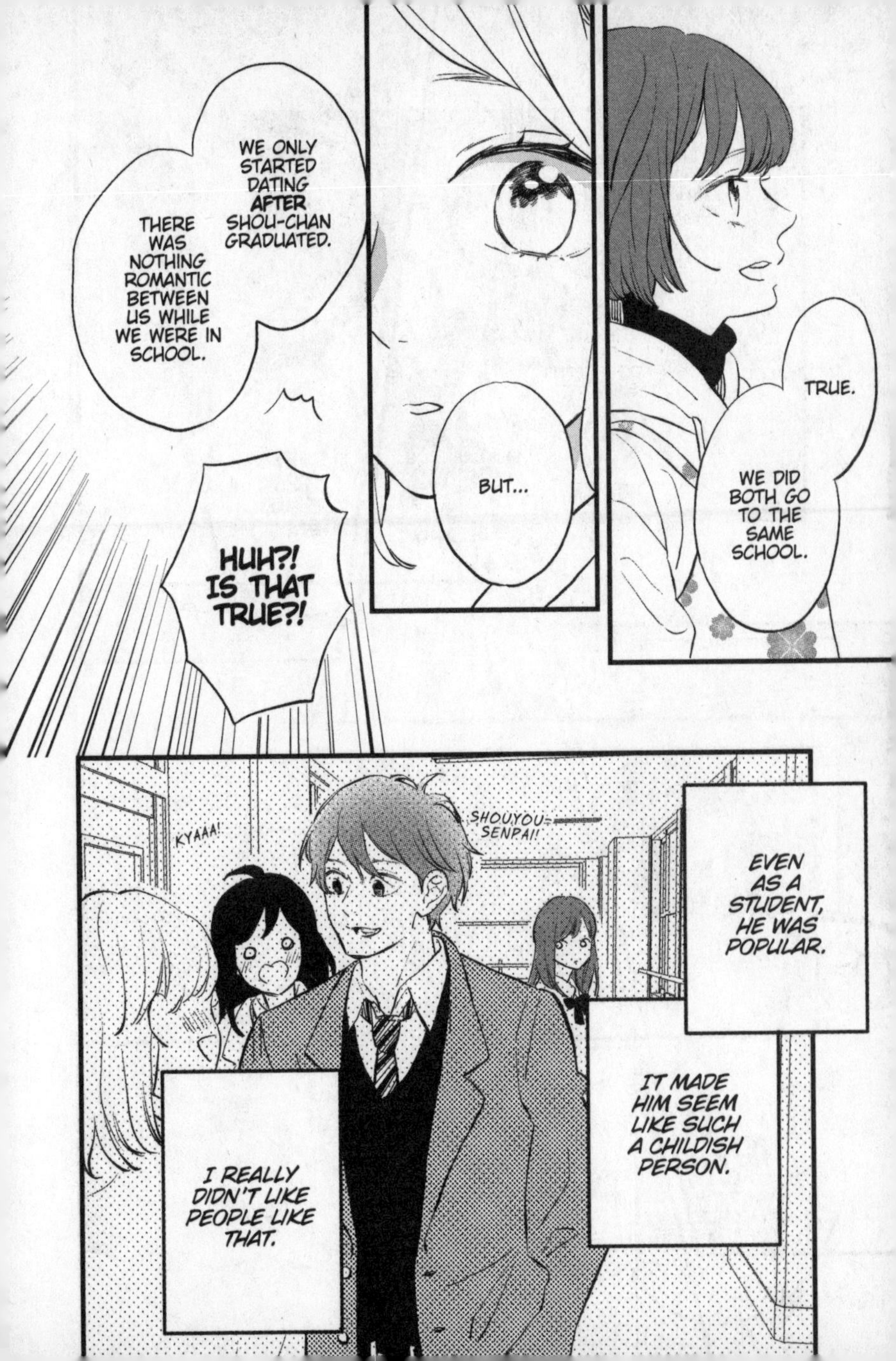
TRUE.
WE DID BOTH GO TO THE SAME SCHOOL.
BUT...
WE ONLY STARTED DATING AFTER SHOU-CHAN GRADUATED. THERE WAS NOTHING ROMANTIC BETWEEN US WHILE WE WERE IN SCHOOL.
HUH?! IS THAT TRUE?!
EVEN AS A STUDENT, HE WAS POPULAR.
SHOUYOU-SENPAI!
KYAAA!
IT MADE HIM SEEM LIKE SUCH A CHILDISH PERSON.
I REALLY DIDN'T LIKE PEOPLE LIKE THAT.

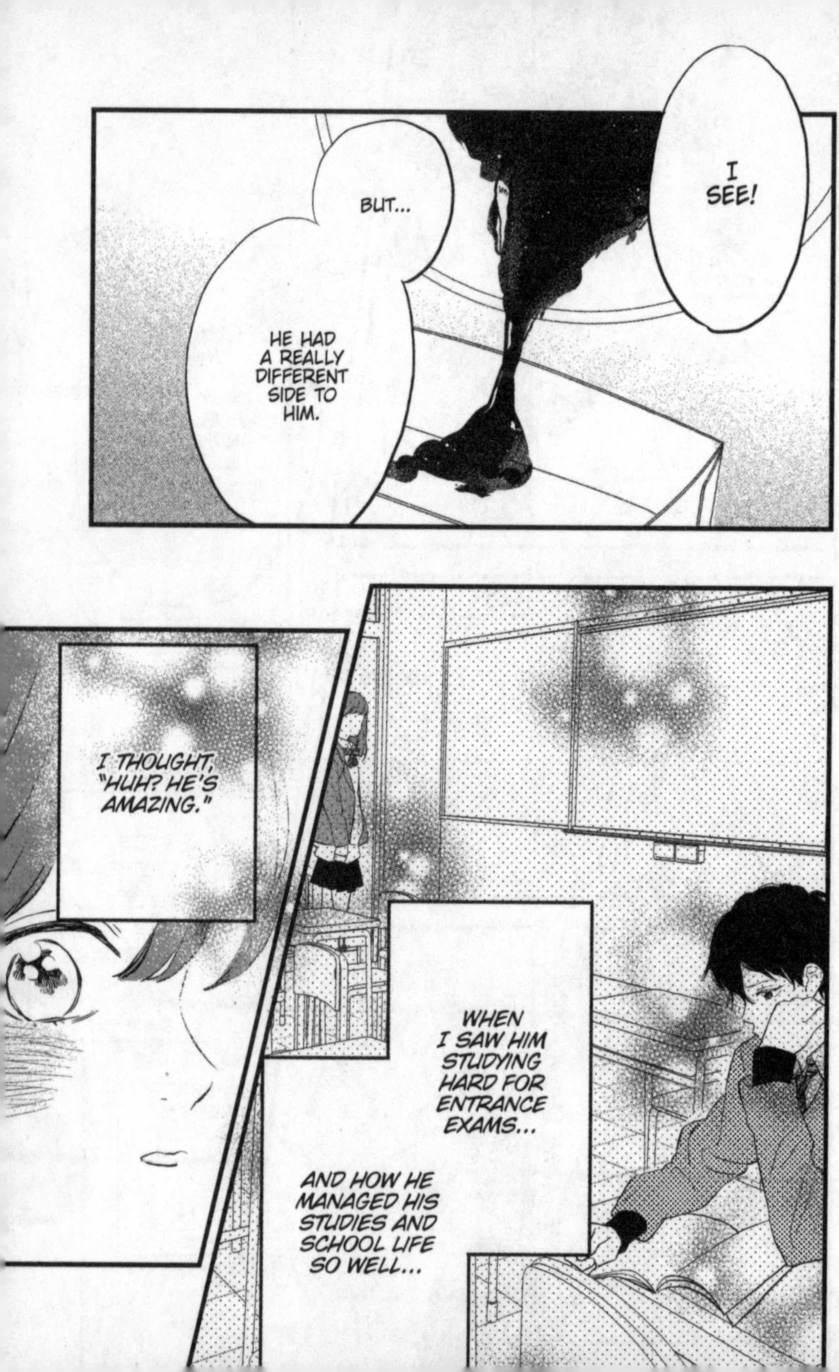
I SEE!
BUT...
HE HAD A REALLY DIFFERENT SIDE TO HIM.
WHEN I SAW HIM STUDYING HARD FOR ENTRANCE EXAMS...
AND HOW HE MANAGED HIS STUDIES AND SCHOOL LIFE SO WELL...
I THOUGHT, "HUH? HE'S AMAZING."

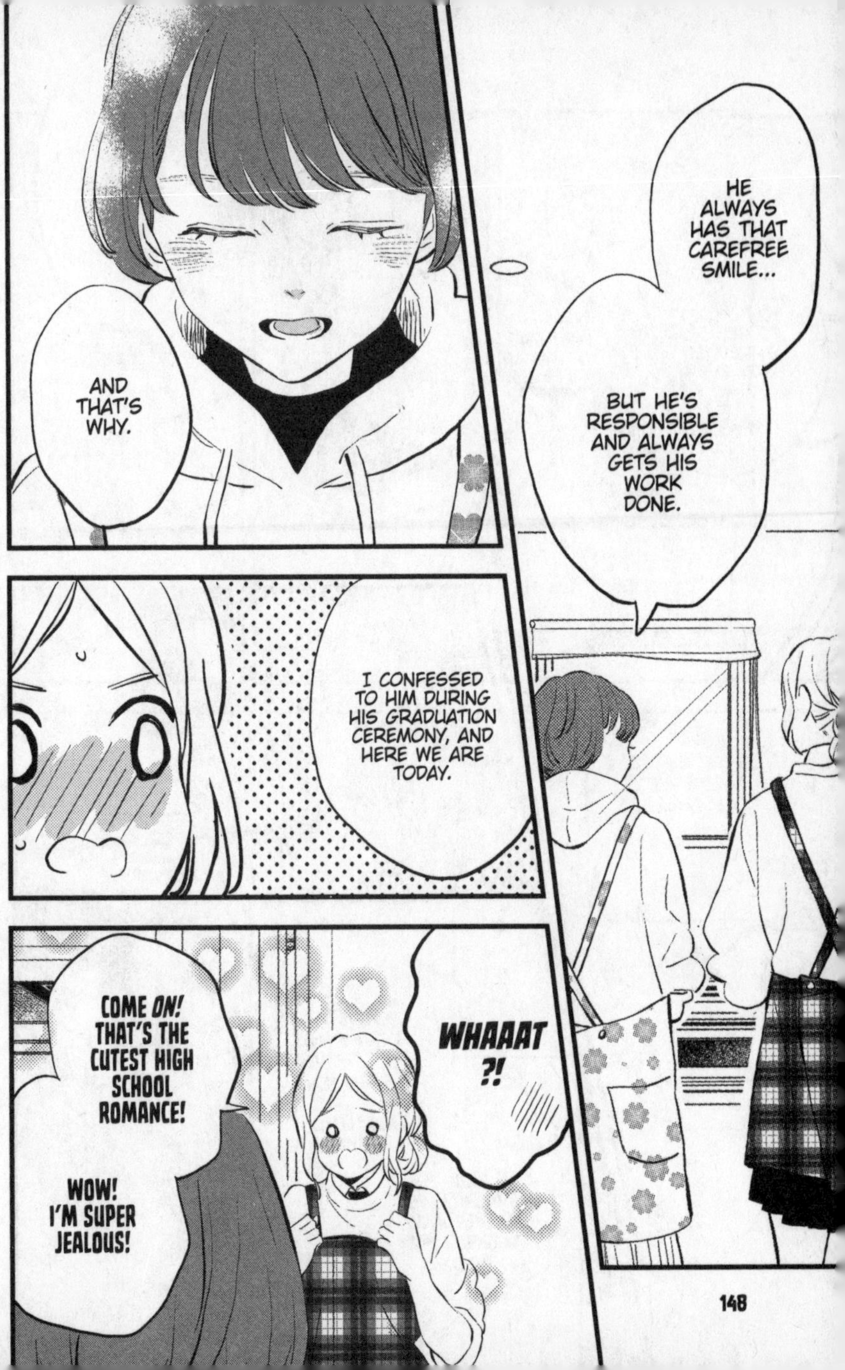
HE ALWAYS HAS THAT CAREFREE SMILE...
BUT HE'S RESPONSIBLE AND ALWAYS GETS HIS WORK DONE.
AND THAT'S WHY.
I CONFESSED TO HIM DURING HIS GRADUATION CEREMONY, AND HERE WE ARE TODAY.
WHAAAT ?!
COME ON! THAT'S THE CUTEST HIGH SCHOOL ROMANCE!
WOW! I'M SUPER JEALOUS!

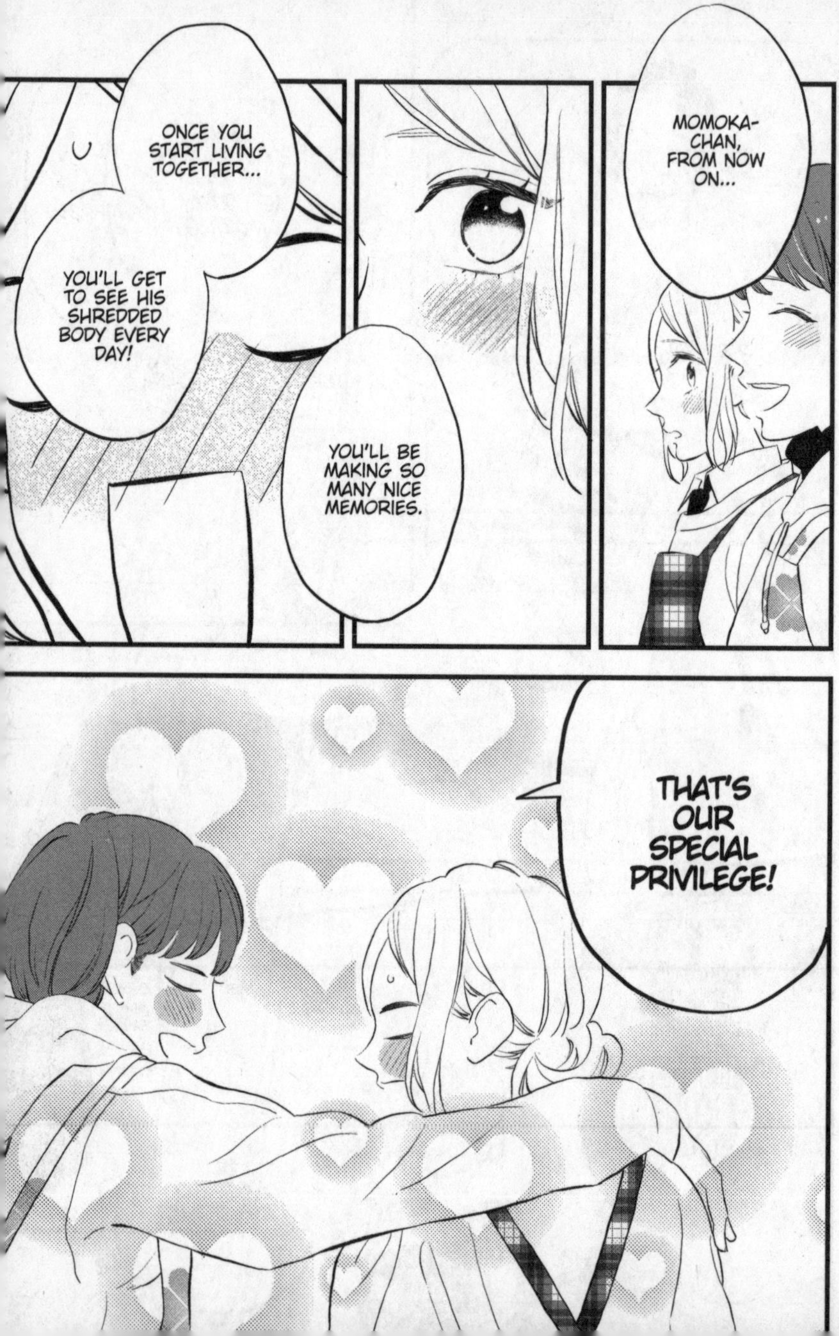
MOMOKA-CHAN, FROM NOW ON...
YOU'LL BE MAKING SO MANY NICE MEMORIES.
ONCE YOU START LIVING TOGETHER...
YOU'LL GET TO SEE HIS SHREDDED BODY EVERY DAY!
THAT'S OUR SPECIAL PRIVILEGE!

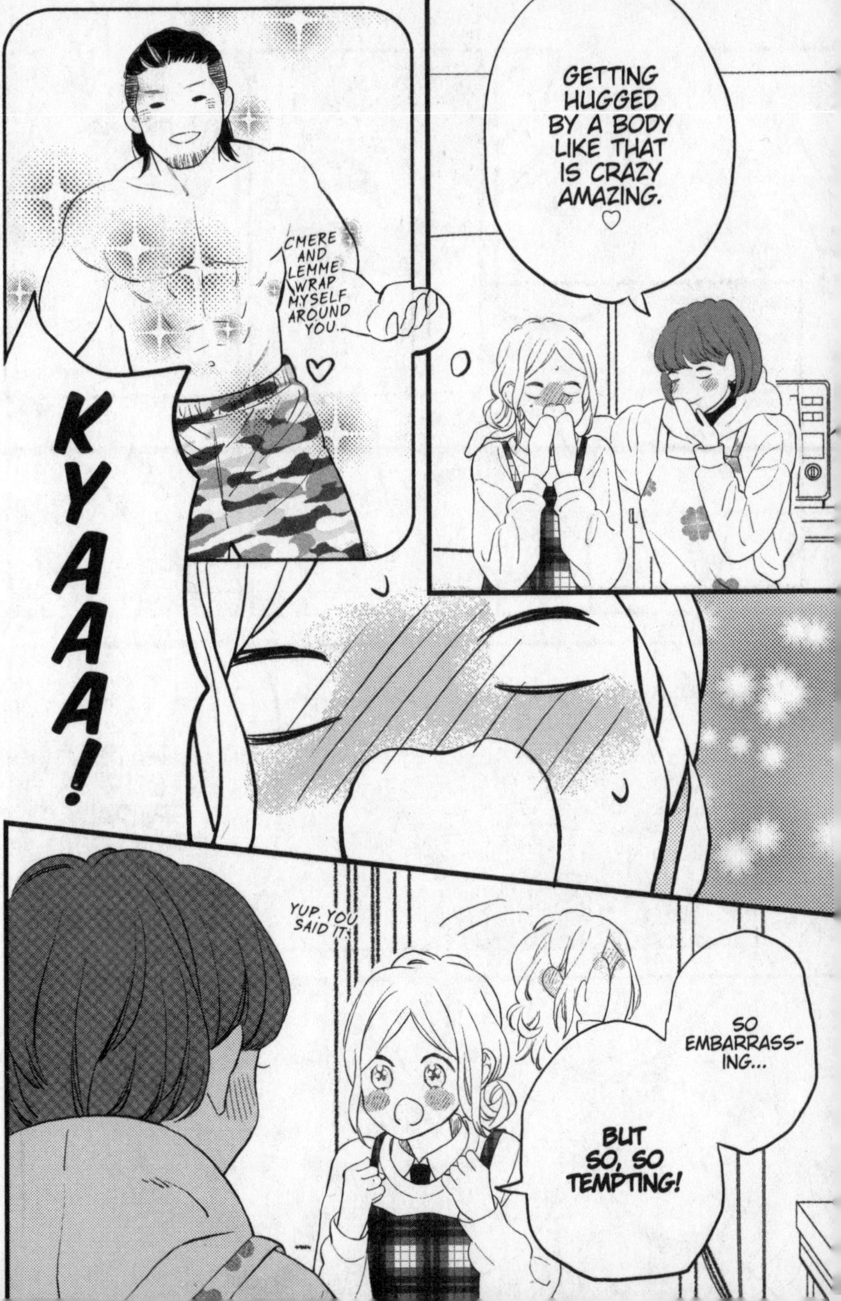
GETTING HUGGED BY A BODY LIKE THAT IS CRAZY AMAZING. ♡
C'MERE AND LEMME WRAP MYSELF AROUND YOU. ♡
KYAAAA!
SO EMBARRASS-ING...
BUT SO, SO TEMPTING!
YUP. YOU SAID IT.

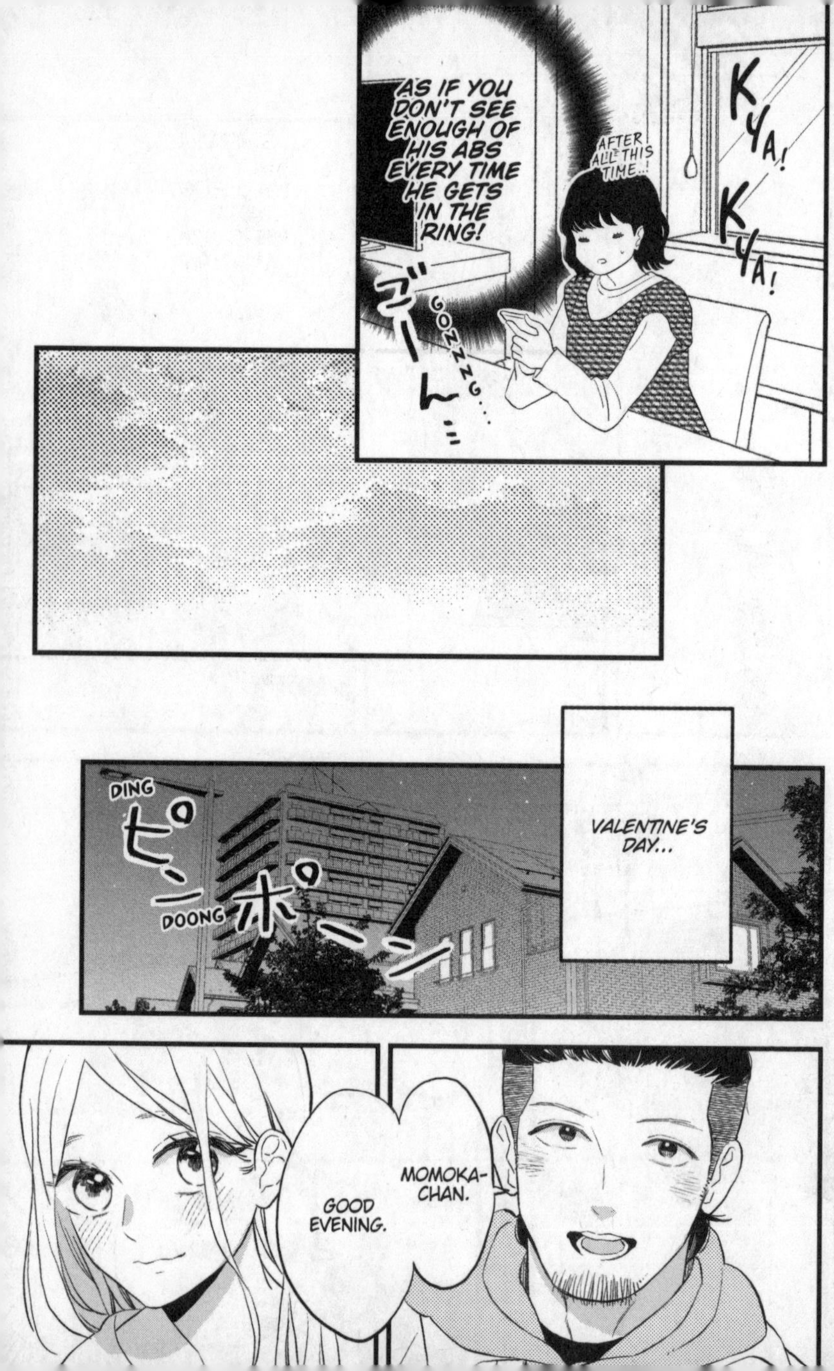
KYA! KYA!
AFTER ALL THIS TIME...!
AS IF YOU DON'T SEE ENOUGH OF HIS ABS EVERY TIME HE GETS IN THE RING!
ゴーん…
GONNNG...
VALENTINE'S DAY...
DING
ピーポーン
DOONG
MOMOKA-CHAN.
GOOD EVENING.

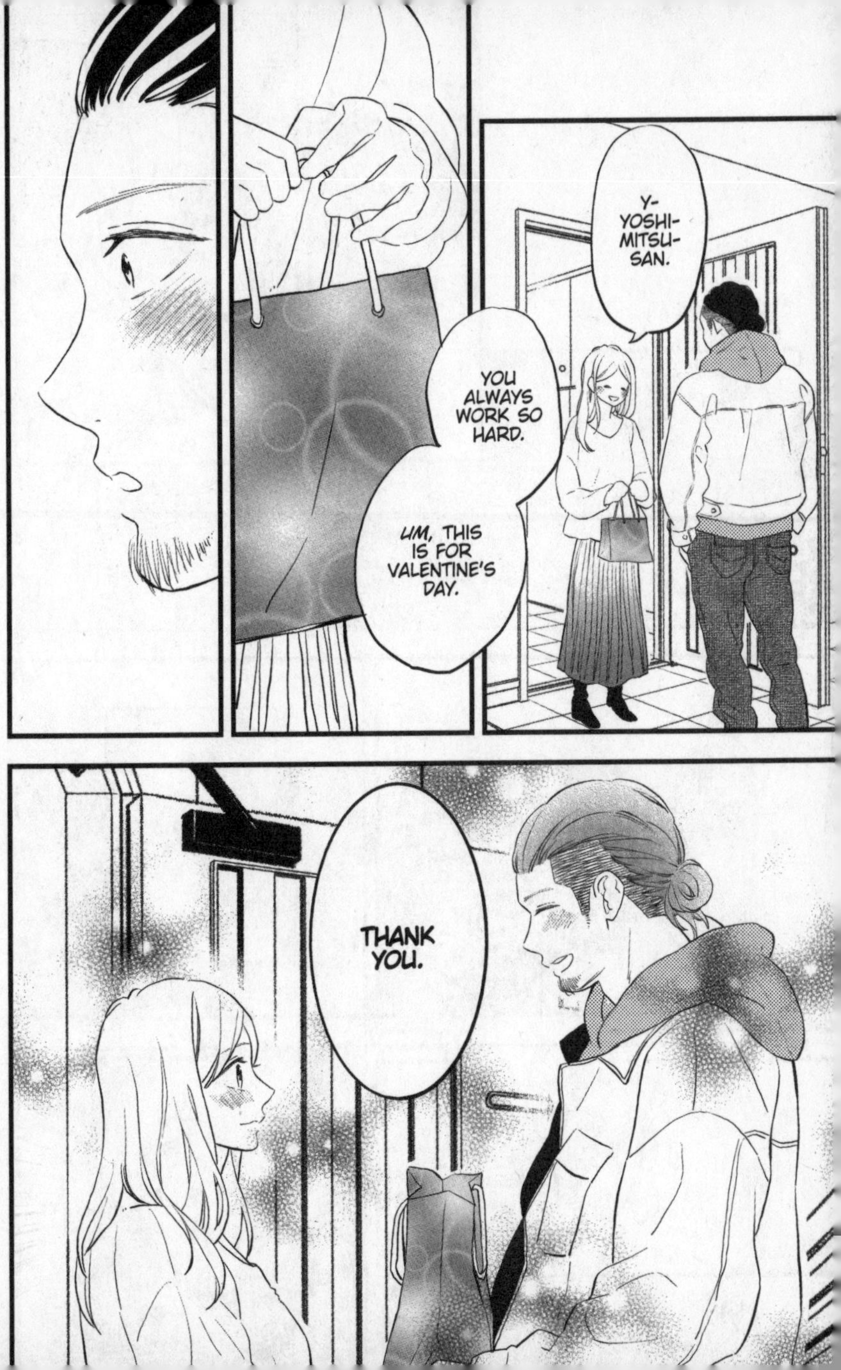
Y-YOSHIMITSU-SAN.
YOU ALWAYS WORK SO HARD.
UM, THIS IS FOR VALENTINE'S DAY.
THANK YOU.

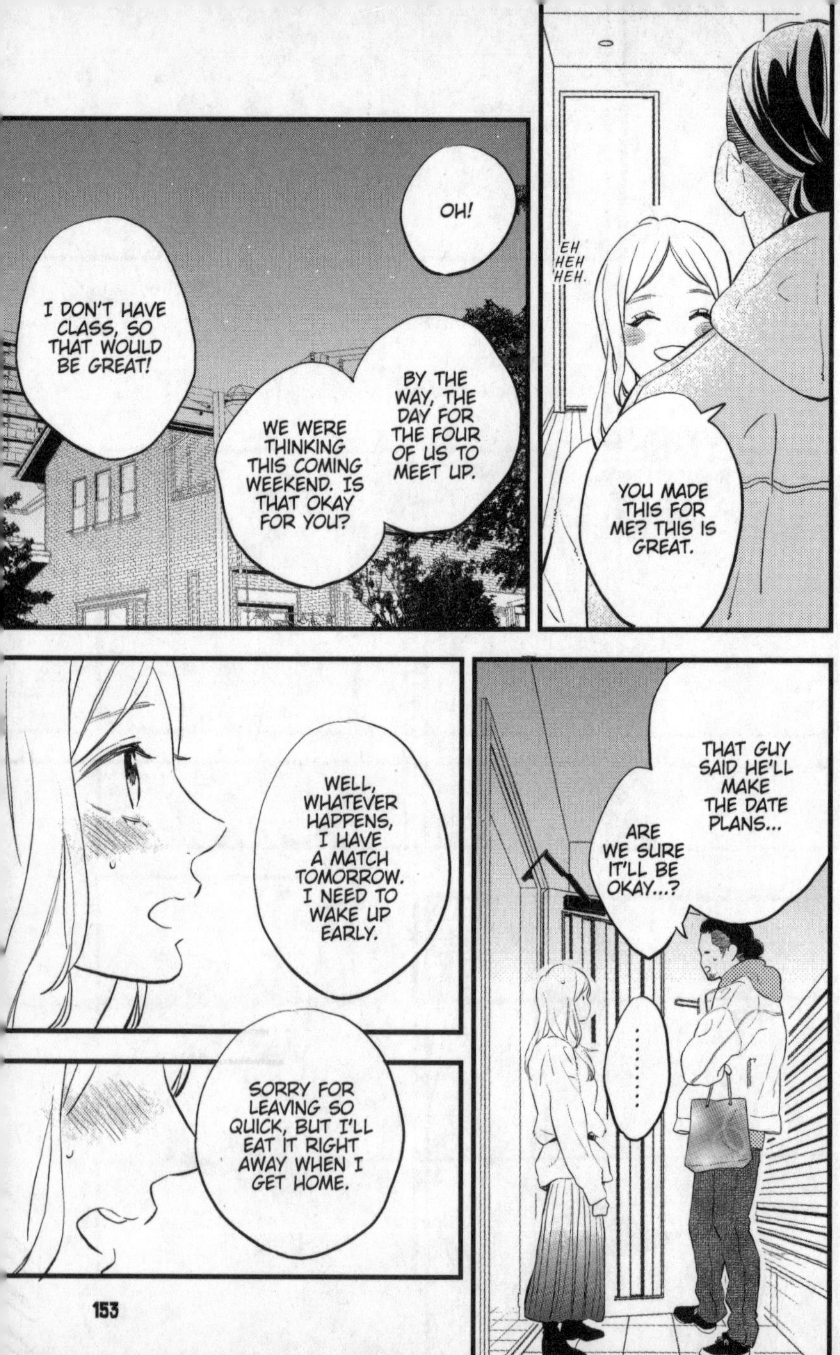
EH HEH HEH.
YOU MADE THIS FOR ME? THIS IS GREAT.
OH!
BY THE WAY, THE DAY FOR THE FOUR OF US TO MEET UP.
WE WERE THINKING THIS COMING WEEKEND. IS THAT OKAY FOR YOU?
I DON'T HAVE CLASS, SO THAT WOULD BE GREAT!
THAT GUY SAID HE'LL MAKE THE DATE PLANS...
ARE WE SURE IT'LL BE OKAY...?
......
WELL, WHATEVER HAPPENS, I HAVE A MATCH TOMORROW. I NEED TO WAKE UP EARLY.
SORRY FOR LEAVING SO QUICK, BUT I'LL EAT IT RIGHT AWAY WHEN I GET HOME.

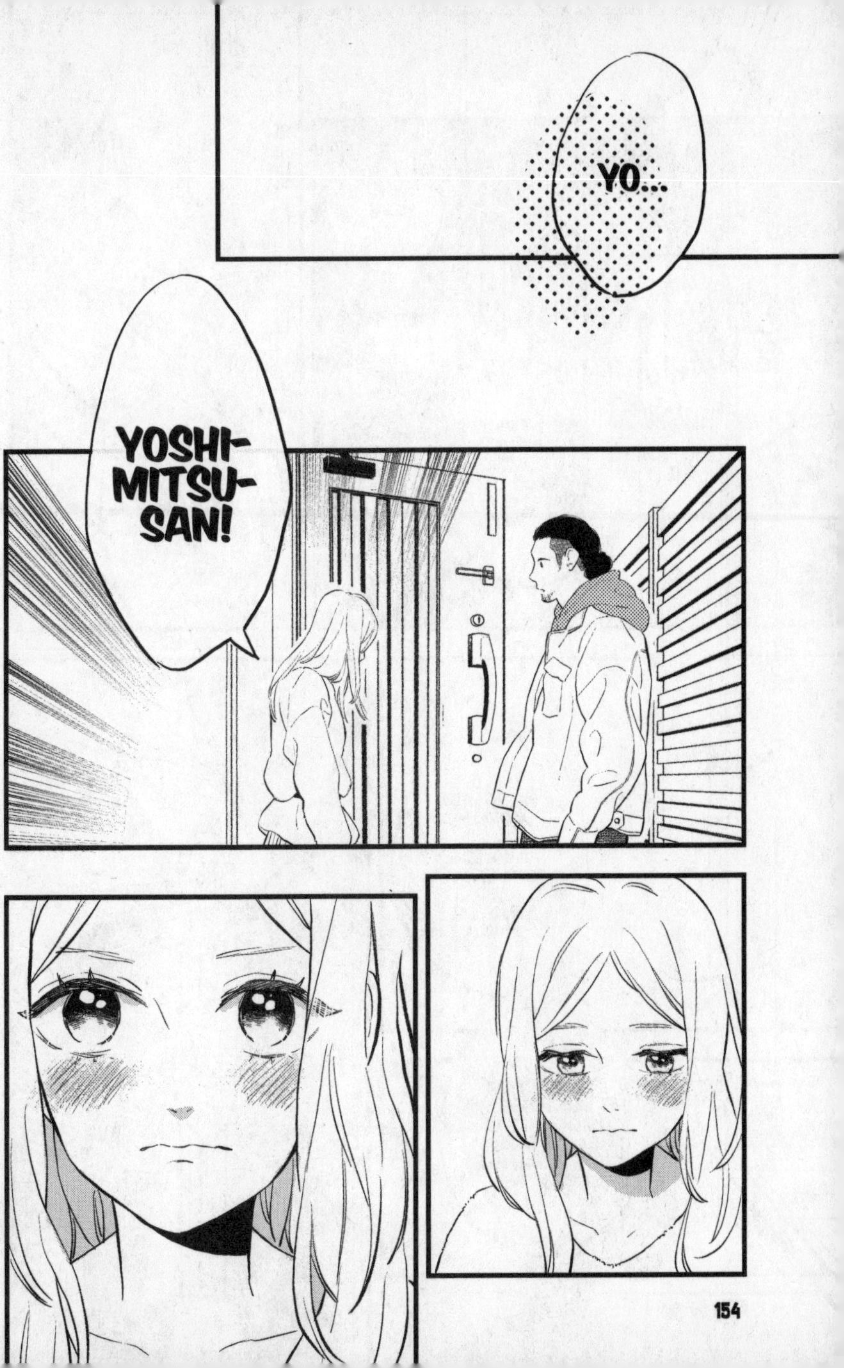
YO...
YOSHI-MITSU-SAN!

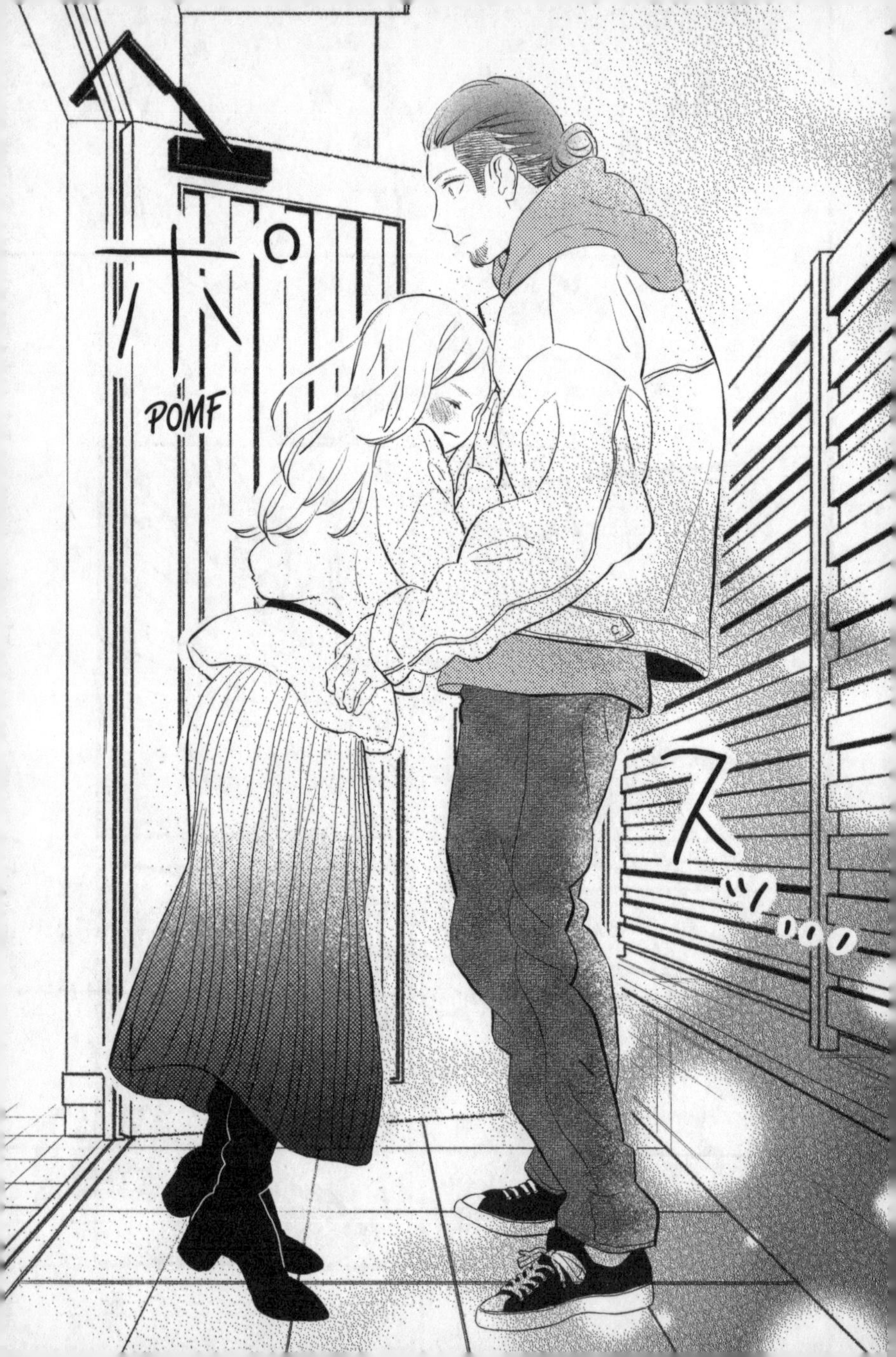
ポ
POMF
スッ…

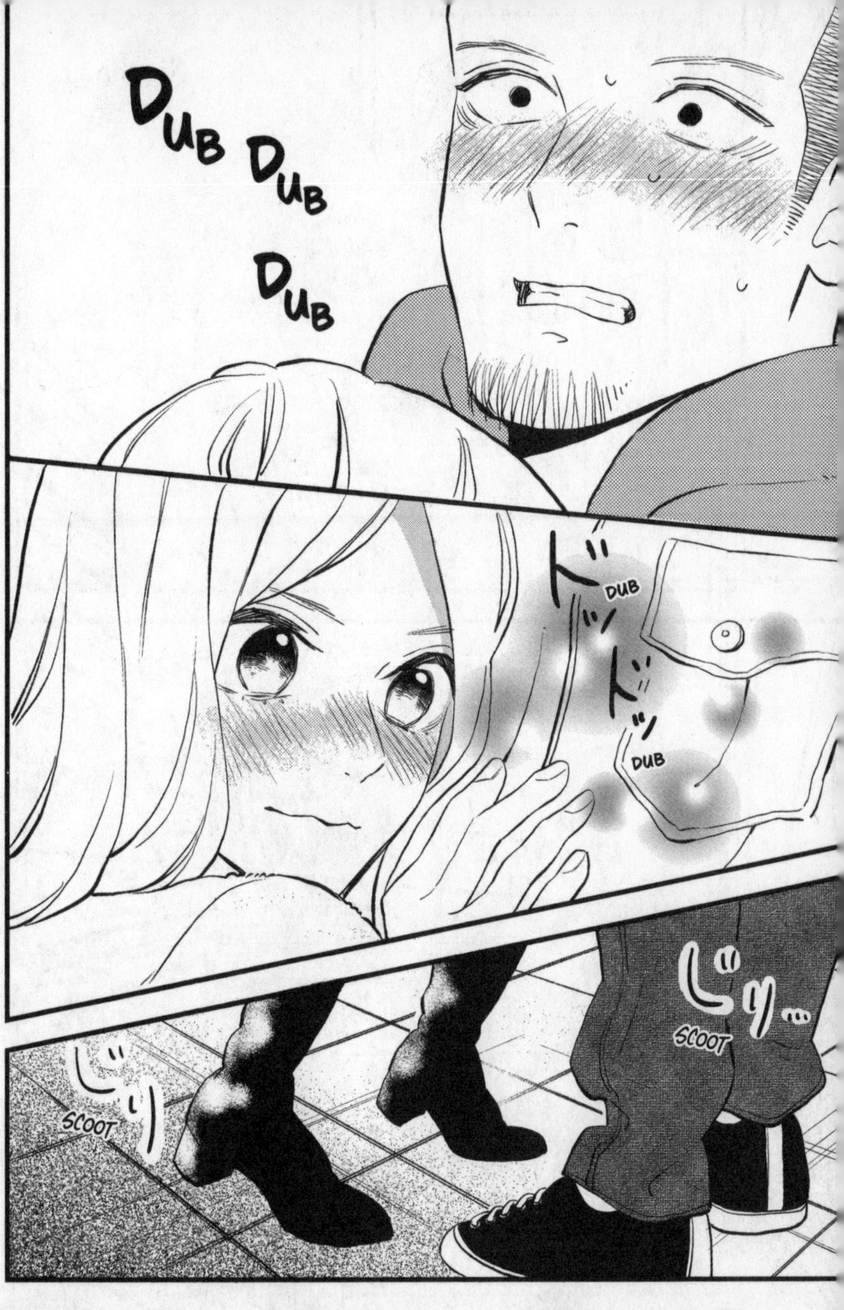
DUB DUB
DUB
ドッ
DUB
ドッ
DUB
じり…
SCOOT
じり
SCOOT

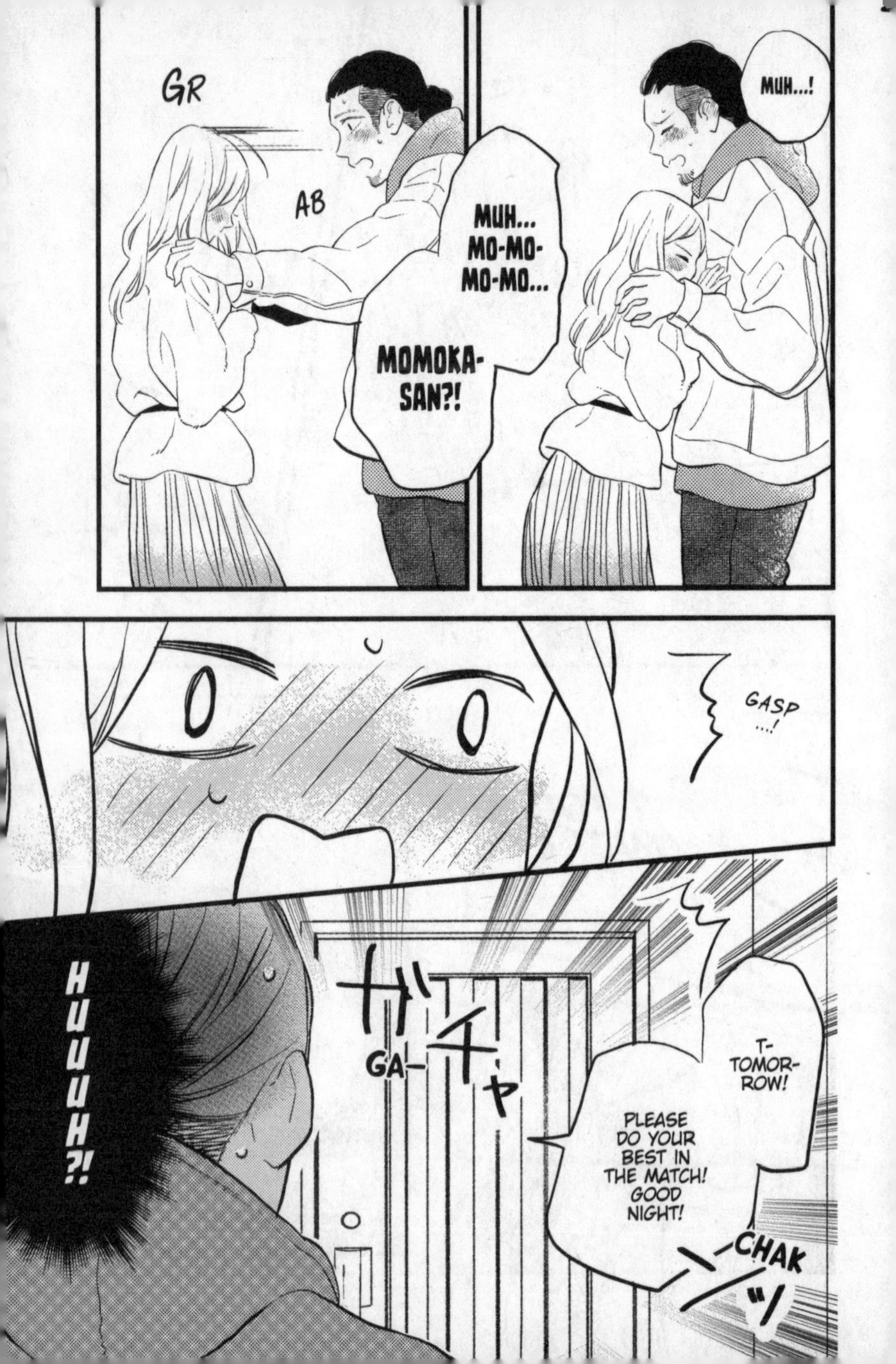
MUH...!
MUH... MO-MO- MO-MO...
MOMOKA-SAN?!
AB
GR
GASP ...!
T-TOMORROW!
PLEASE DO YOUR BEST IN THE MATCH! GOOD NIGHT!
ガチャ
GA-
ッ
-CHAK
HUUUUH?!

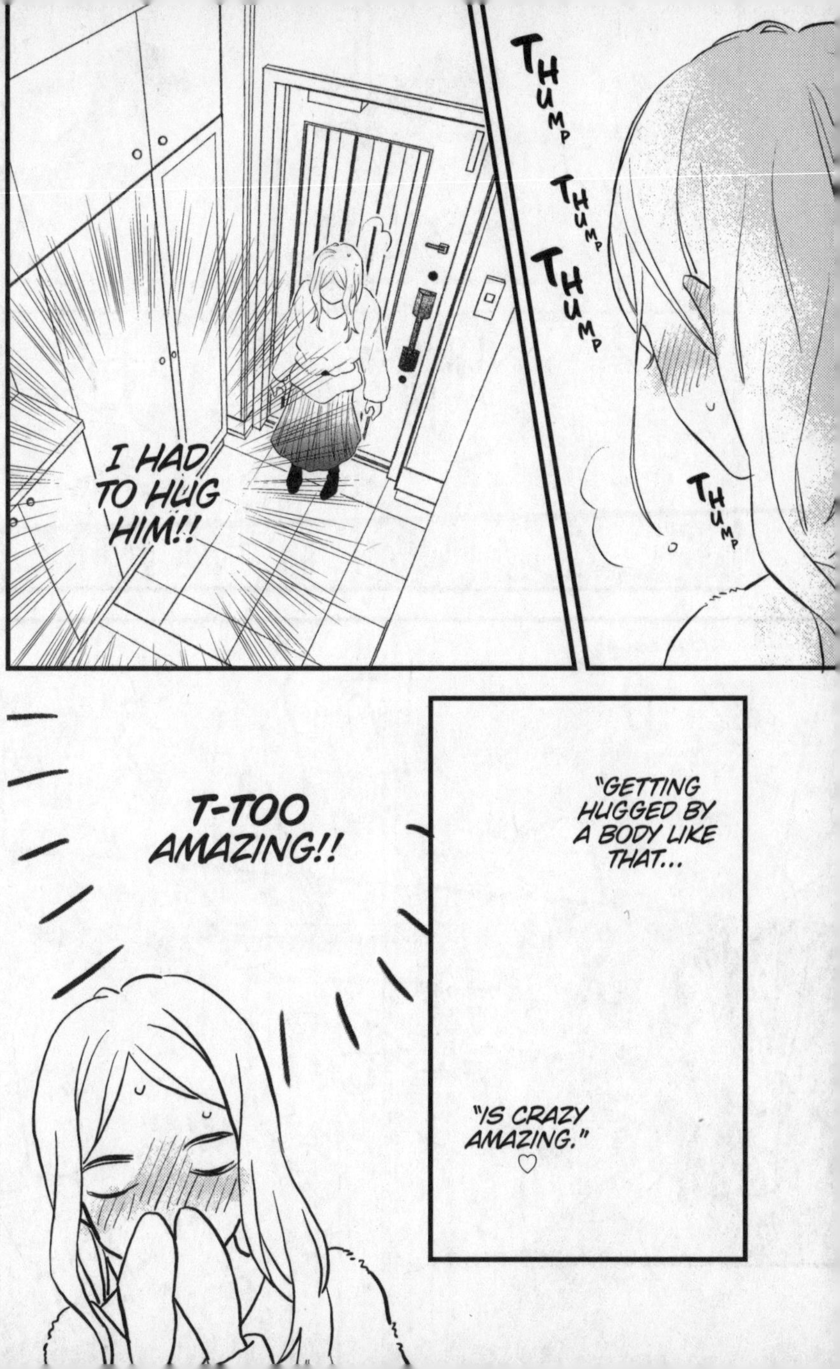
THUMP THUMP THUMP
THUMP
I HAD TO HUG HIM!!
"GETTING HUGGED BY A BODY LIKE THAT...
"IS CRAZY AMAZING." ♡
T-TOO AMAZING!!

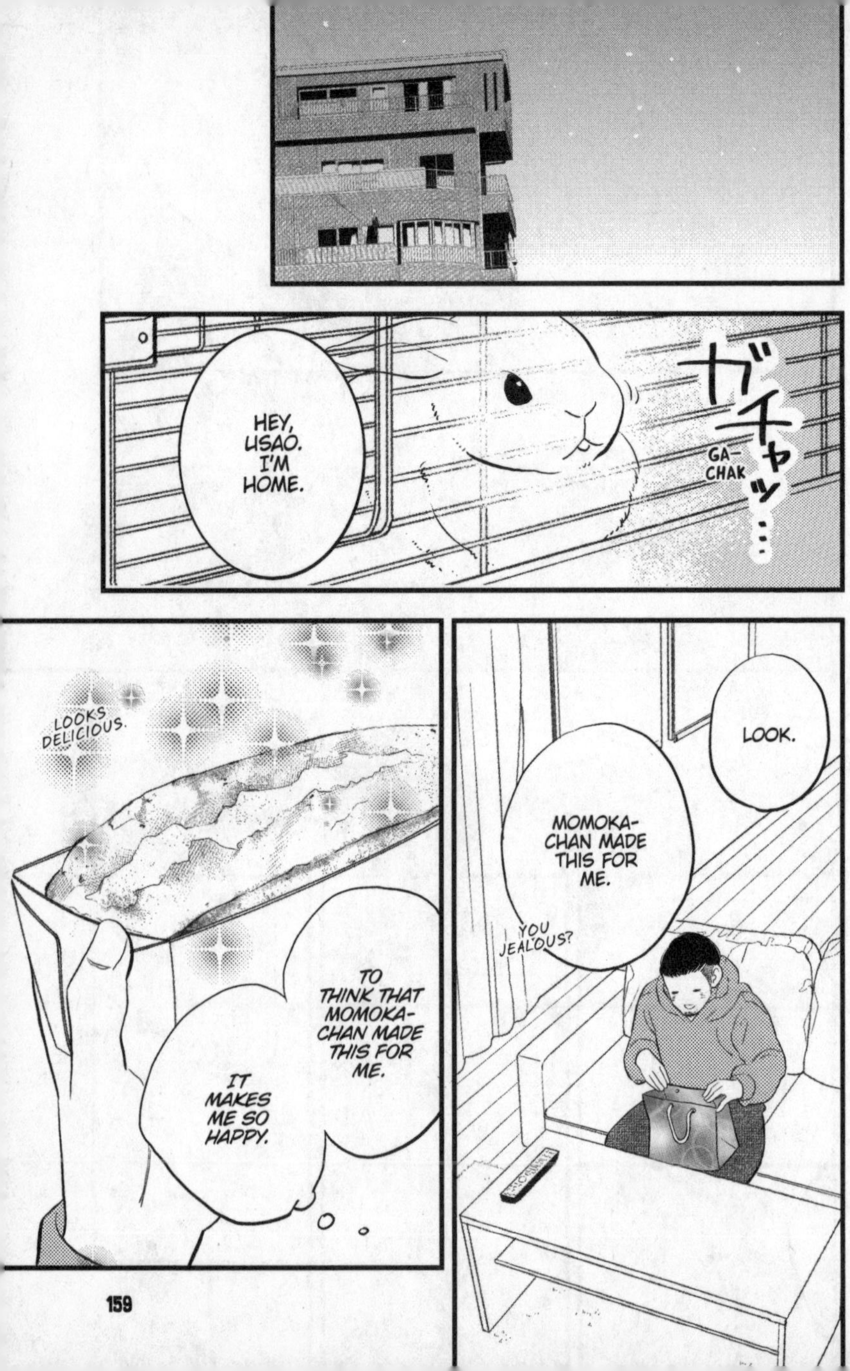
ガチャッ…
GA-CHAK
HEY, USAO. I'M HOME.
LOOK.
MOMOKA-CHAN MADE THIS FOR ME.
YOU JEALOUS?
LOOKS DELICIOUS.
TO THINK THAT MOMOKA-CHAN MADE THIS FOR ME.
IT MAKES ME SO HAPPY.

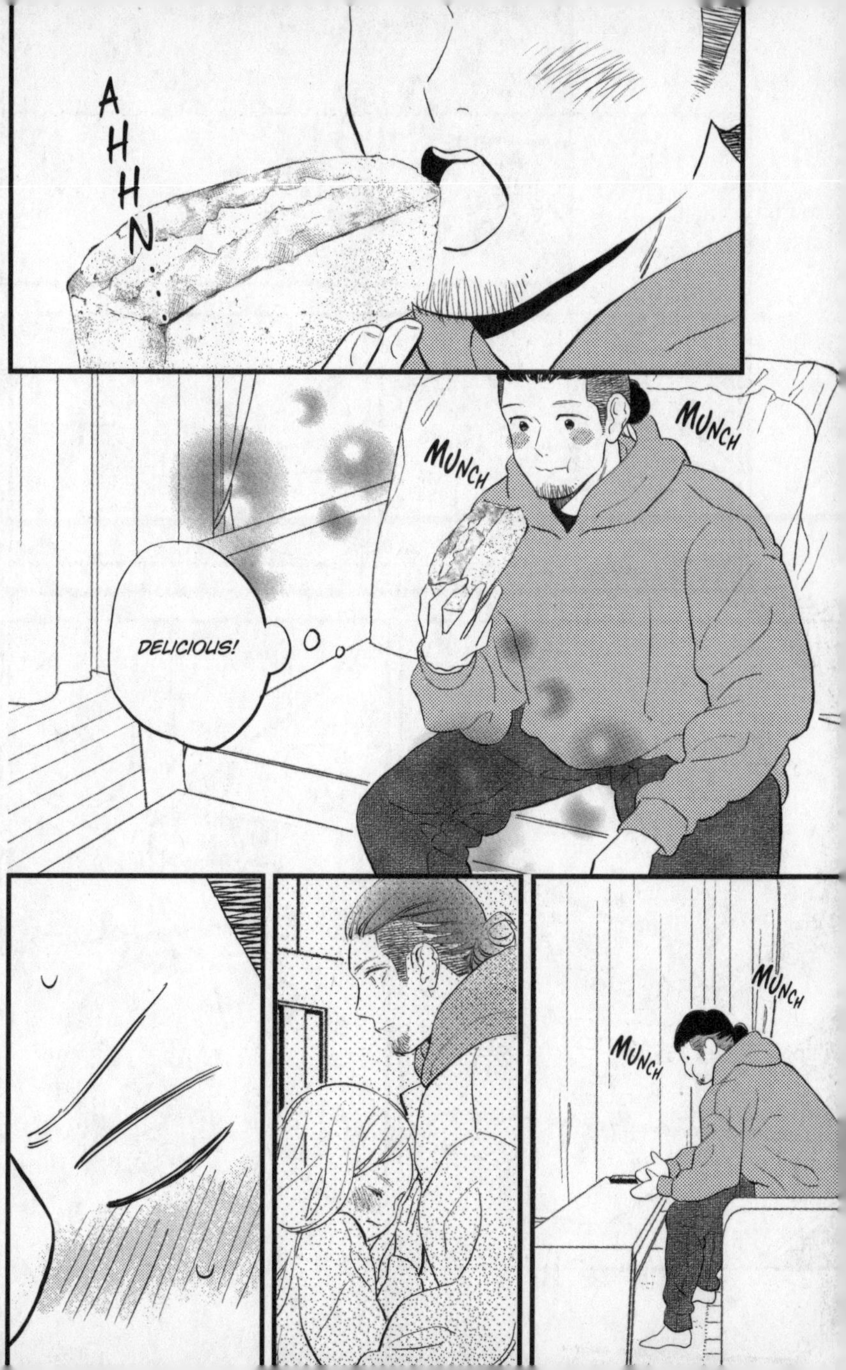
AHHN...
MUNCH
MUNCH
DELICIOUS!
MUNCH
MUNCH

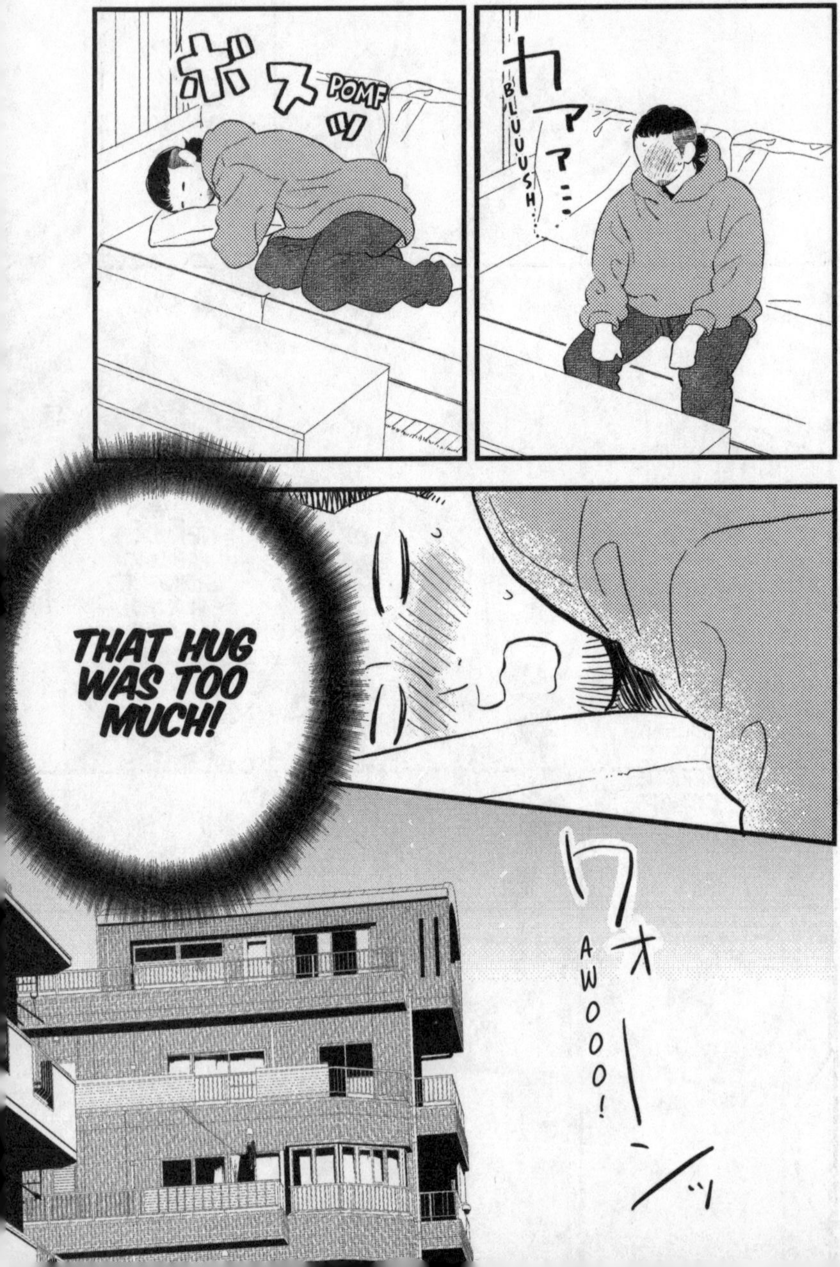
カァァ…
BLUUUSH…
ボスッ
POMF
THAT HUG WAS TOO MUCH!
ワオーーッ
AWOOOO!

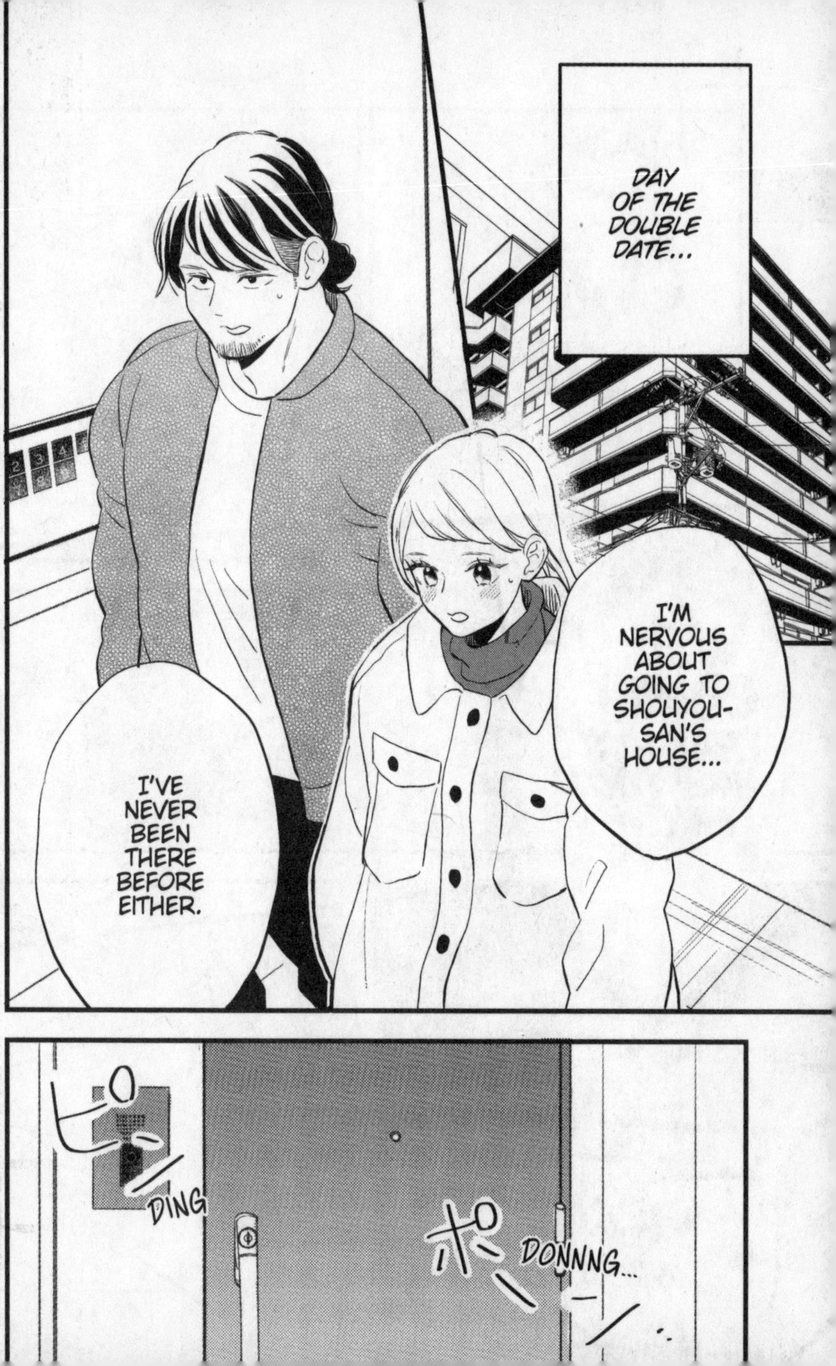
DAY OF THE DOUBLE DATE...
I'M NERVOUS ABOUT GOING TO SHOUYOU-SAN'S HOUSE...
I'VE NEVER BEEN THERE BEFORE EITHER.
DING
DONNNG...

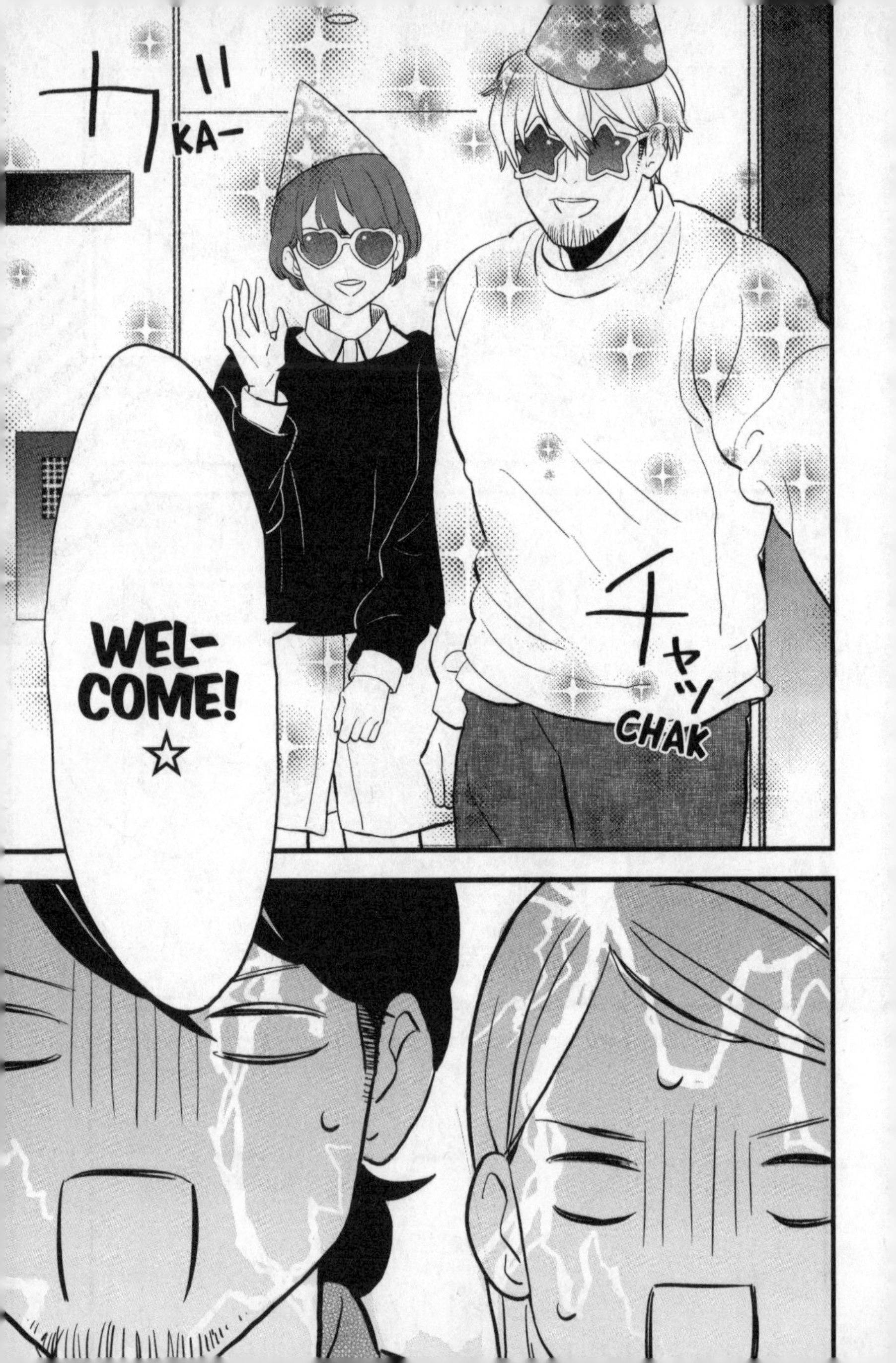
カー
KA—
WEL-
COME!
☆
チャッ
CHAK

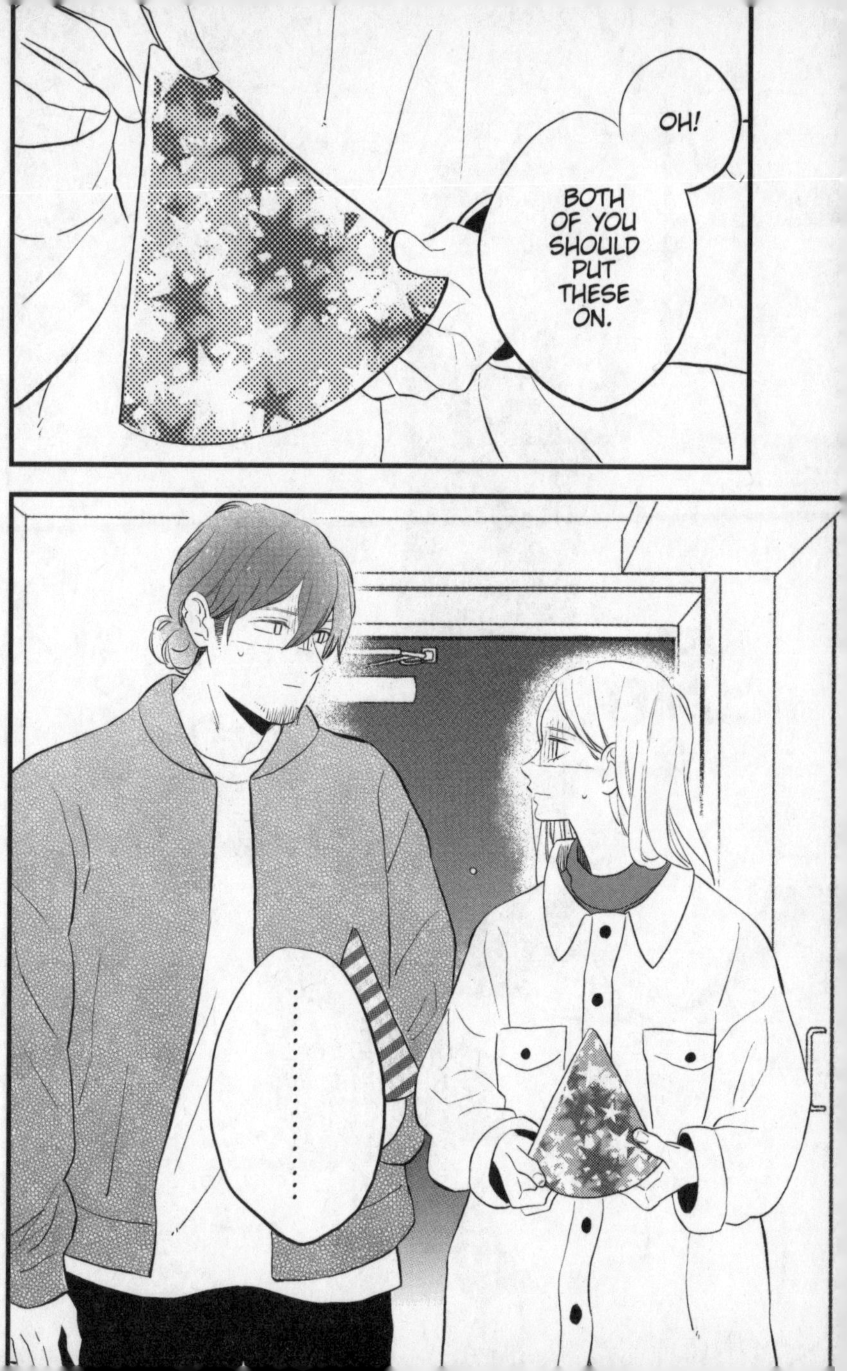
OH!
BOTH OF YOU SHOULD PUT THESE ON.
......

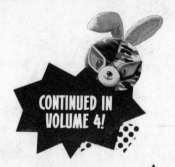

Cutie and the BEAST

CONTINUED IN
VOLUME 4!

AFTERWORD

THANK YOU FOR READING *CUTIE AND THE BEAST*, VOLUME 3. LATELY I HAVE RECEIVED MESSAGES FROM FANS OVERSEAS, AND IT MAKES ME HAPPY TO FEEL THE SPREAD OF JAPANESE PRO WRESTLING. I HOPE THAT A LOT OF PEOPLE CONTINUE READING MY MANGA AND LEARN ABOUT PRO WRESTLING!! I WILL TRY MY BEST TO SEE YOU AGAIN IN VOLUME 4. PLEASE CONTINUE TO TAKE CARE OF ME!!

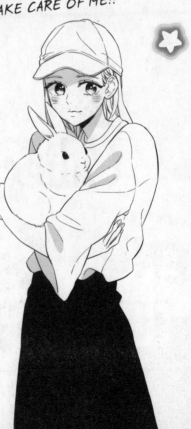

IN THE END, THANKS TO:
* EDITOR-SAMA
* ASSISTANT-SAMA
* MY FAMILY
* EVERYONE WHO PICKED
  UP THIS BOOK

THANK YOU ALL SO
VERY MUCH!!

安曇ゆうひ
YUHI AZUMI
TWITTER @YUUHI_AZUMI

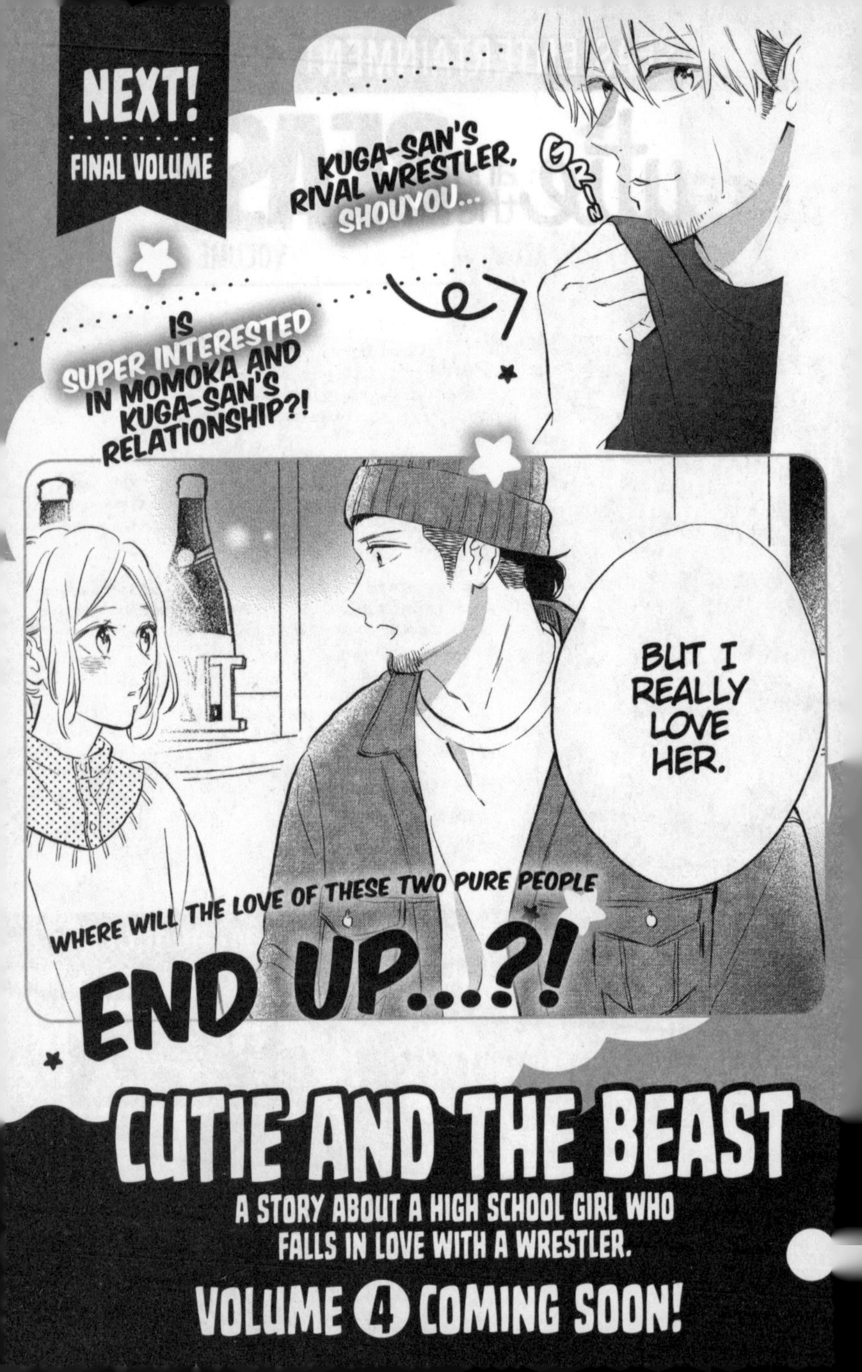
NEXT!
FINAL VOLUME
KUGA-SAN'S RIVAL WRESTLER, SHOUYOU...
GRIN
IS SUPER INTERESTED IN MOMOKA AND KUGA-SAN'S RELATIONSHIP?!
BUT I REALLY LOVE HER.
WHERE WILL THE LOVE OF THESE TWO PURE PEOPLE
END UP...?!
CUTIE AND THE BEAST
A STORY ABOUT A HIGH SCHOOL GIRL WHO FALLS IN LOVE WITH A WRESTLER.
VOLUME 4 COMING SOON!

SEVEN [SEAS] [PRE]SENTS

story and art by **YUHI AZUMI**

TRANSLATION
Angela Liu

ADAPTATION
Andrea Puckett

LETTERING AND RETOUCH
Erika Terriquez

COVER DESIGN
Nicky Lim
(LOGO) **George Panella**

PROOFREADER
Dawn Davis, Brett Hallahan

EDITOR
J.P. Sullivan

PREPRESS TECHNICIAN
Rhiannon Rasmussen-Silverstein

PRODUCTION MANAGER
Lissa Pattillo

MANAGING EDITOR
Julie Davis

ASSOCIATE PUBLISHER
Adam Arnold

PUBLISHER
Jason DeAngelis

PUJO TO YAJU VOL. 3
©2020 Yuhi Azumi. All rights reserved.
First published in Japan in 2020 by Kodansha Ltd., Tokyo.
Publication rights for this English edition arranged through Kodansha Ltd., Tokyo.

Seven Seas press and purchase enquiries can be sent to Marketing Manager Lianne Sentar at press@gomanga.com. Information regarding the distribution and purchase of digital editions is available from Digital Manager CK Russell at digital@gomanga.com.

Seven Seas and the Seven Seas logo are trademarks of Seven Seas Entertainment. All rights reserved.

ISBN: 978-1-64827-254-7

Printed in Canada

First Printing: July 2021

10 9 8 7 6 5 4 3 2 1

FOLLOW US ONLINE: *www.sevenseasentertainment.com*

READING DIRECTIONS

This book reads from *right to left*, Japanese style. If this is your first time reading manga, you start reading from the top right panel on each page and take it from there. If you get lost, just follow the numbered diagram here. It may seem backwards at first, but you'll get the hang of it! Have fun!!

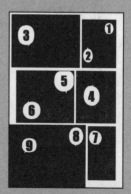